The Reactionary Mind

THE REACTIONARY MIND

Conservatism from Edmund Burke to Sarah Palin

COREY ROBIN

OXFORD
UNIVERSITY PRESS

OXFORD
UNIVERSITY PRESS

Oxford University Press, Inc., publishes works that further
Oxford University's objective of excellence
in research, scholarship, and education.

Oxford   New York
Auckland   Cape Town   Dar es Salaam   Hong Kong   Karachi
Kuala Lumpur   Madrid   Melbourne   Mexico City   Nairobi
New Delhi   Shanghai   Taipei   Toronto

With offices in
Argentina   Austria   Brazil   Chile   Czech Republic   France   Greece
Guatemala   Hungary   Italy   Japan   Poland   Portugal   Singapore
South Korea   Switzerland   Thailand   Turkey   Ukraine   Vietnam

Published by Oxford University Press, Inc.
198 Madison Avenue, New York, NY 10016

www.oup.com

Oxford is a registered trademark of Oxford University Press

Library of Congress Cataloging-in-Publication Data
Robin, Corey, 1967–
The reactionary mind : conservatism from
Edmund Burke to Sarah Palin / Corey Robin.
   p.   cm.
Includes bibliographical references and index.
ISBN 978-0-19-979374-7 (hardcover : alk. paper)
1. Conservatism—History. I. Title.
JC573.R63   2011
320.52—dc22   2011006039

9 8 7 6 5 4

Printed in the United States of America
on acid-free paper

For Laura

CONTENTS

Acknowledgments   ix

Epigraph   xiii

Introduction   3

Part 1 **Profiles in Reaction**

1. Conservatism and Counterrevolution   41
2. The First Counterrevolutionary   61
3. Garbage and Gravitas   76
4. Inside Out   97
5. The Ex-Cons   109
6. Affirmative Action Baby   130

Part 2 **Virtues of Violence**

7. A Color-Coded Genocide   151
8. Remembrance of Empires Past   161
9. Protocols of Machismo   184
10. Potomac Fever   201
11. Easy to Be Hard   217

Conclusion   246

Notes   249

Index   281

ACKNOWLEDGMENTS

Much of this book originated in literary periodicals and maga-
zines. Were it not for editors Alex Star, Paul Laity, Mary-Kay
Wilmers, Paul Meyerscough, Adam Shatz, John Palattella, and
Jackson Lears, I never would have written about the right. It's
often assumed that academics who publish in nonacademic
venues are trotting out their scholarly research for popular consumption, simplifying complex ideas first worked out in the labo-
ratories of academe. For me, the process of writing this book
has been the reverse: conservatism became a scholarly interest of
mine through my nonacademic writing, and most of my ideas
about the right were formulated in conversation with and writing
for these editors, especially Alex and John.

Intellectually, this book owes its inspiration to Arno Mayer and
Karen Orren. No two scholars have done more to advance my understanding of "the persistence of the old regime"—in Europe and the
United States—than Karen and Arno. Against the conventional wisdom
of the left and the right, which assumes that medievalism has been
washed away by modernity, Karen and Arno opened my eyes to the
"belated feudalism" of our post-feudal world. While they undoubtedly
would disagree with my interpretation of conservatism, I could not
have come to it without their enormously generative work.

In the course of writing and revising these essays, I have been
sustained by a broad circle of readers: historians and political

scientists, poets and essayists, theorists and philosophers, literary critics and sociologists, journalists and editors. For their contributions to one or more of these essays, I would like to thank Jed Abrahamian, Bruce Ackerman, Joel Allen, Gaston Alonso, Joyce Appleby, Moustafa Bayoumi, Seyla Benhabib, Marshall Berman, Sara Bershtel, Akeel Bilgrami, Norman Birnbaum, Steve Bronner, Dan Brook, Sebastian Budgen, Josh Cohen, Peter Cole, Paisley Currah, Lizzie Donahue, Jay Driskell, Tom Dumm, John Dunn, Sam Farber, Liza Featherstone, Jason Frank, Steve Fraser, Josh Freeman, Paul Frymer, Sam Goldman, Manu Goswami, Alex Gourevitch, Pete Hallward, Harry Harootunian, Chris Hayes, Doug Henwood, Dick Howard, David Hughes, Judy Hughes, Allen Hunter, Jack Jacobs, Ira Katznelson, Gordon Lafer, Jill Lepore, Penny Lewis, Joe Lowndes, Steven Lukes, Kieko Matteson, Kevin Mattson, John Medeiras, Kathy Newman, Molly Nolan, Anne Norton, Jolie Olcott, Christian Parenti, Di Paton, Rick Perlstein, Ros Petchesky, Kim Phillips-Fein, Katha Pollitt, Aziz Rana, Andy Rich, Andrew Ross, Kristin Ross, Saskia Sassen, Ellen Schrecker, George Scialabba, Richard Seymour, Nikhil Singh, Quentin Skinner, Jim Sleeper, Rogers Smith, Katrina vanden Heuvel, John Wallach, Eve Weinbaum, Keith Whittington, Daniel Wilkinson, Wesley Yang, Brian Young, and Marilyn Young.

A good portion of this material has been presented in workshops and talks at universities across the country. I am grateful for the comments and suggestions I received on those occasions from Arash Abizadeh, Anthony Appiah, Banu Bargu, Seyla Benhabib, Akeel Bilgrami, Elizabeth Cohen, Josh Cohen, Julie Cooper, the late Jack Diggins, Matt Evans, Nancy Fraser, Mark Graber, Nan Keohane, Steve Macedo, Karuna Mantena, Andrew March, Tom Medvetz, Andrew Murphy, Andrew Norris, Anne Norton, Joshua Ober, Philip Pettit, Andy Polsky, Robert Reich, Austin Sarat, Peter

Singer, Rogers Smith, Miranda Spieler, Zofia Stemplowska, Nadia Urbinati, and Leo Zaibert.

I would like to thank the following institutions for providing much needed release time from my teaching: the American Council of Learned Societies; the Princeton University Center for Human Values; the Office of the Provost at Brooklyn College; and the Professional Staff Congress of the City University of New York.

An extra special thanks goes to my kitchen cabinet of first readers: Greg Grandin, Adina Hoffman, Robert Perkinson, and Scott Saul; to Marco Roth, who came up with the book's title; to Charles Petersen, copy editor extraordinaire; to my students at Brooklyn College and the CUNY Graduate Center, who have worked with me through the texts and tomes of the right; to Alexandra Dauler and Marc Schneider at Oxford University Press (OUP); and to David McBride, my editor at OUP, an unfailing source of excellent advice who believed in this project from its inception and shepherded it through with what seems to be effortless wisdom, patience, and grace.

My greatest thanks go to Laura Brahm, who listened to these ideas when they were half-sentences and read them when they were half-baked. She has brought to these essays an eye for what matters and an unerring sense of taste. She is always and inevitably the only reader I want to please.

Dont you know that "No" is the wildest word we consign to Language?

—Emily Dickinson

The Reactionary Mind

Introduction

A political party may find that it has had a history, before it is fully aware of or agreed upon its own permanent tenets; it may have arrived at its actual formation through a succession of metamorphoses and adaptations, during which some issues have been superannuated and new issues have arisen. What its fundamental tenets are, will probably be found only by careful examination of its behaviour throughout its history and by examination of what its more thoughtful and philosophical minds have said on its behalf; and only accurate historical knowledge and judicious analysis will be able to discriminate between the permanent and the transitory; between those doctrines and principles which it must ever, and in all circumstances, maintain, or manifest itself a fraud, and those called forth by special circumstances, which are only intelligible and justifiable in the light of those circumstances.

—**T. S. Eliot,** "The Literature of Politics"

Since the modern era began, men and women in subordinate positions have marched against their superiors in the state, church, workplace, and other hierarchical institutions. They have gathered under different banners—the labor movement, feminism, abolition, socialism—and shouted different slogans: freedom, equality, rights, democracy, revolution. In virtually every instance, their superiors have resisted them, violently and nonviolently, legally and illegally, overtly and covertly. That march and demarche of democracy is the story of modern politics or at least one of its stories.

This book is about the second half of that story, the demarche, and the political ideas—variously called conservative, reactionary, revanchist, counterrevolutionary—that grow out of and give rise to it. These ideas, which occupy the right side of the political spectrum, are forged in battle. They always have been, at least since they first emerged as formal ideologies during the French Revolution, battles between social groups rather than nations; roughly speaking, between those with more power and those with less. To understand these ideas, we have to understand that story. For that is what conservatism is: a meditation on—and theoretical rendition of—the felt experience of having power, seeing it threatened, and trying to win it back.

Despite the very real differences between them, workers in a factory are like secretaries in an office, peasants on a manor, slaves on a plantation—even wives in a marriage—in that they live and labor in conditions of unequal power. They submit and obey, heeding the demands of their managers and masters, husbands and lords. They are disciplined and punished. They do much and receive little. Sometimes their lot is freely chosen—workers contract with their employers, wives with their husbands—but its entailments seldom are. What contract, after all, could ever itemize the ins and outs, the daily pains and ongoing sufferance, of a job or a marriage? Throughout American history, in fact, the contract often has served as a conduit to unforeseen coercion and constraint, particularly in institutions like the workplace and the family where men and women spend so much of their lives. Employment and marriage contracts have been interpreted by judges, themselves friendly to the interests of employers and husbands, to contain all sorts of unwritten and unwanted provisions of servitude to which wives and workers tacitly consent, even when they have no knowledge of such provisions or wish to stipulate otherwise.[1]

Until 1980, for example, it was legal in every state in the union for a husband to rape his wife.[2] The justification for this dates back to a 1736 treatise by English jurist Matthew Hale. When a woman marries, Hale argued, she implicitly agrees to give "up herself in this kind [sexually] unto her husband." Hers is a tacit, if unknowing, consent "which she cannot retract" for the duration of their union. Having once said yes, she can never say no. As late as 1957—during the era of the Warren Court—a standard legal treatise could state, "A man does not commit rape by having sexual intercourse with his lawful wife, even if he does so by force and against her will." If a woman (or man) tried to write into the marriage contract a requirement that express consent had to be given in order for sex to proceed, judges were bound by common law to ignore or override it. Implicit consent was a structural feature of the contract that neither party could alter. With the exit option of divorce not widely available until the second half of the twentieth century, the marriage contract doomed women to be the sexual servants of their husbands.[3] A similar dynamic was at work in the employment contract: workers consented to be hired by their employers, but until the twentieth century that consent was interpreted by judges to contain implicit and irrevocable provisions of servitude; meanwhile, the exit option of quitting was not nearly as available, legally or practically, as many might think.[4]

Every once in a while, however, the subordinates of this world contest their fates. They protest their conditions, write letters and petitions, join movements, and make demands. Their goals may be minimal and discrete—better safety guards on factory machines, an end to marital rape—but in voicing them, they raise the specter of a more fundamental change in power. They cease to be servants or supplicants and become agents, speaking and acting on their own behalf. More than the reforms themselves, it is this assertion of agency by the subject class—the appearance of an insistent and independent voice of demand—that vexes their superiors. Guatemala's Agrarian Reform of 1952 redistributed a million and a half acres of land to 100,000 peasant families. That was nothing, in the minds of the country's ruling classes, compared to the riot of political talk the bill seemed to unleash. Progressive reformers, Guatemala's archbishop complained, sent local peasants "gifted with facility with words" to the capital, where they were given opportunities "to speak in public." That was the great evil of the Agrarian Reform.[5]

In his last major address to the Senate, John C. Calhoun, former vice president and chief spokesman of the Southern cause, identified the decision by Congress in the mid-1830s to receive abolitionist petitions as the moment when the nation set itself on an irreversible course of confrontation over slavery. In a four-decade career that had seen such defeats to the slaveholder position as the Tariff of Abominations, the Nullification Crisis, and the Force Bill, the mere appearance of slave speech in the nation's capital stood out for the dying Calhoun as the sign that the revolution had begun.[6] And when, a half-century later, Calhoun's successors sought to put the abolitionist genie back into the bottle, it was this same assertion of black agency that they targeted. Explaining the proliferation across the South in the 1890s and 1900s of constitutional conventions restricting the franchise, a delegate to one such convention declared, "The great underlying principle of this Convention movement . . . was the elimination of the negro from the politics of this State."[7]

American labor history is filled with similar complaints from the employing classes and their allies in government: not that unionized workers are violent, disruptive, or unprofitable but that they are independent and self-organizing. Indeed, so potent is their self-organization that it threatens—in the eyes of their superiors—to render superfluous the employer and the state. During the Great Upheaval of 1877, striking railroad workers in St. Louis took to running the trains themselves. Fearful the public might conclude the workers were capable of managing the railroad, the owners tried to stop them—in effect, launching a strike of their own in order to prove it was the owners, and only the owners, who could make the trains run on time. During the Seattle general strike of 1919, workers went to great lengths to provide basic government services, including law and order. So successful were they that the mayor concluded it was this, the workers' independent capacity to limit violence and anarchy, that posed the greatest threat.

> The so-called sympathetic Seattle strike was an attempted revolution. That there was no violence does not alter the fact. . . . True, there were no flashing guns, no bombs, no killings. Revolution, I repeat, doesn't need violence. The general strike, as practiced in Seattle, is of itself the weapon of revolution, all the more dangerous because quiet. . . . That is to say, it puts the government out of operation. And that is all there is to revolt— no matter how achieved.[8]

Into the twentieth century, judges regularly denounced unionized workers for formulating their own definitions of rights and compiling their own register of shop-floor rules. Workers like these, claimed one federal court, saw themselves as "exponents of some higher law than that . . . administered by courts." They were exercising "powers belonging only to Government," declared the Supreme Court, constituting themselves as a "self-appointed tribunal" of law and order.[9]

Conservatism is the theoretical voice of this animus against the agency of the subordinate classes. It provides the most consistent and profound argument as to why the lower orders should not be allowed to exercise their independent will, why they should not be allowed to govern themselves or the polity. Submission is their first duty, agency, the prerogative of the elite.

Though it is often claimed that the left stands for equality while the right stands for freedom, this notion misstates the actual disagreement between right and left. Historically, the conservative has favored liberty for the higher orders and constraint for the lower orders. What the conservative sees and dislikes in equality, in other words, is not a threat to freedom but its extension. For in that extension, he sees a loss of his own freedom. "We are all agreed as to our own liberty," declared Samuel Johnson. "But we are not agreed as to the liberty of others: for in proportion as we take, others must lose. I believe we hardly wish that the mob should have liberty to govern us."[10] Such was the threat Edmund Burke saw in the French Revolution: not merely an expropriation of property or explosion of violence but an inversion of the obligations of deference and command. "The levellers," he claimed, "only change and pervert the natural order of things."

> The occupation of an hair-dresser, or of a working tallow-chandler, cannot be a matter of honour to any person—to say nothing of a number of other more servile employments. Such descriptions of men ought not to suffer oppression from the state; but the state suffers oppression, if such as they, either individually or collectively, are permitted to rule.[11]

By virtue of membership in a polity, Burke allowed, men had a great many rights—to the fruits of their labor, their inheritance, education, and more. But the one right he refused to concede to all men was that "share of power, authority, and direction" they might think they ought to have "in the management of the state."[12]

Even when the left's demands shift to the economic realm, the threat of freedom's extension looms large. If women and workers are provided with the economic resources to make independent choices, they will be free not to obey their husbands and employers.

That is why Lawrence Mead, one of the leading intellectual opponents of the welfare state in the 1980s and 1990s, declared that the welfare recipient "must be made *less* free in certain senses rather than more."[13] For the conservative, equality portends more than a redistribution of resources, opportunities, and outcomes—though he certainly dislikes these, too.[14] What equality ultimately means is a rotation in the seat of power.

The conservative is not wrong to construe the threat of the left in these terms. Before he died, G. A. Cohen, one of contemporary Marxism's most acute voices, made the case that much of the left's program of economic redistribution could be understood as entailing not a sacrifice of freedom for the sake of equality, but an extension of freedom from the few to the many.[15] And, indeed, the great modern movements of emancipation—from abolition to feminism to the struggle for workers' rights and civil rights—have always posited a nexus between freedom and equality. Marching out of the family, the factory, and the field, where unfreedom and inequality are the flip sides of the same coin, they have made freedom and equality the irreducible yet mutually reinforcing parts of a single whole. The link between freedom and equality has not made the argument for redistribution any more palatable to the right. As one conservative wag complained of John Dewey's vision of social democracy, "The definitions of liberty and of equality have been so juggled that both refer to approximately the same condition."[16] Far from being a sleight of the progressive hand, however, this synthesis of freedom and equality is a central postulate of the politics of emancipation. Whether the politics conforms to the postulate is, of course, another story. But for the conservative, the concern is less the betrayal of the postulate than its fulfillment.

One of the reasons the subordinate's exercise of agency so agitates the conservative imagination is that it takes place in an intimate setting. Every great political blast—the storming of the Bastille, the taking of the Winter Palace, the March on Washington—is set off by a private fuse: the contest for rights and standing in the family, the factory, and the field. Politicians and parties talk of constitution and amendment, natural rights and inherited privileges. But the real subject of their deliberations is the private life of power. "Here is the secret of the opposition to woman's equality in the state," Elizabeth Cady Stanton wrote. "Men are not ready to recognize it in the home."[17] Behind the riot in the street or debate in Parliament is the maid talking back to her mistress, the worker disobeying her boss. That is why our political arguments—not only about the family but also the welfare state, civil rights, and much else—can be so explosive: they touch upon the most personal relations of power. It is also why it has so often fallen to our novelists to explain to us our politics. At the height of the civil rights movement, James Baldwin traveled to Tallahassee. There, in an imagined handshake, he found the hidden transcript of a constitutional crisis.[18]

I am the only Negro passenger at Tallahassee's shambles of an airport. It is an oppressively sunny day. A black chauffeur, leading a small dog on a leash, is meeting his white employer. He is attentive to the dog, covertly very aware of me and respectful of her in a curiously watchful, waiting way. She is middle-aged, beaming and powdery-faced, delighted to see both the beings who make her life agreeable. I am sure that it has never occurred to her that either of them has the ability to judge her or would judge her harshly. She might almost, as she goes toward her chauffeur, be greeting a friend. No friend could make her face brighter. If she were smiling at me that way I would expect to shake her hand. But if I should put out my hand, panic, bafflement, and horror would then overtake that face, the atmosphere would darken, and danger, even the threat of death, would immediately fill the air.

On such small signs and symbols does the southern cabala depend.[19]

The conflict over American slavery—the looming precedent to this set piece of Baldwin's imagination—offers an instructive example. One of the distinguishing characteristics of slavery in the United States is that unlike slaves in the Caribbean or serfs in Russia, many slaves in the South lived on small holdings with their masters in residence. Masters knew their slaves' names; tracked their births, marriages, and deaths; and held parties to honor these dates. The personal interaction between master and slave was unparalleled, leading a visiting Frederick Law Olmsted to remark upon the "close cohabitation and association of black and white" in Virginia, the "familiarity and closeness of intimacy that would have been noticed with astonishment, if not with manifest displeasure, in almost any chance company at the North."[20] Only the "relations of husband and wife, parent and child, brother and sister," wrote the slavery apologist Thomas Dew, produced "a closer tie" than that of master and slave; the latter relationship, declared William Harper, another defender of slavery, was "one of the most intimate relations of society."[21] Conversely, after slavery was abolished, many whites lamented the chill in relations between the races. "I'm fond of the Negro," said one Mississippian in 1918, "but the bond between us is not as close as it was between my father and his slaves."[22]

Much of this talk was propaganda and self-delusion, of course, but in one respect it was not: the nearness of master to slave did make for an exceptionally personal mode of rule. Masters devised and enforced "unusually detailed" rules for their slaves, dictating when they had to get up, eat, work, sleep, garden, visit, and pray. Masters decided upon their slaves' mates and marriages. They named their children, and when the market dictated, separated those children from their parents. And while masters—as well as their sons and overseers—availed themselves of the bodies of their female slaves whenever they wished, they saw fit to patrol and punish any and all sexual congress between their slaves.[23] Living with their slaves, masters had direct means to control their behavior and a detailed map of all the behavior there was to control.

The consequences of this proximity were felt not just by the slave but by the master as well. Living every day with his mastery, he became entirely identified with it. So complete was this identification that any sign of the slave's disobedience—much less her emancipation—was seen as an intolerable assault upon his person. When Calhoun declared that slavery "has grown up with our society and institutions, and is so interwoven with them, that to destroy it would be to destroy us as a people," he wasn't just referring to society in the aggregate or abstract.[24] He was thinking of individual men absorbed in the day-to-day experience of ruling other men and women. Take that experience away, and you destroyed not only the master but also the man—and the many men who sought to become, or thought they already were like, the master.

Because the master put so little distance between himself and his mastery, he would go to unprecedented lengths to keep his holdings. Throughout the Americas slaveholders defended their privileges, but nowhere with the intensity or violence of the master class in the South. Outside the South, wrote C. Vann Woodward, the end of slavery was "the liquidation of an investment." Inside, it was "the death of a society."[25] And when, after the Civil War, the master class fought with equal ferocity to restore its privileges and power, it was the proximity of command, the nearness of rule, that was uppermost in its mind. As Henry McNeal Turner, a black Republican in Georgia, put it in 1871: "They do not care so much about Congress admitting Negroes to their halls . . . but they do not want the negroes over them at home." One hundred years later, a black sharecropper in Mississippi would still resort to the most domestic of idioms to describe relations between blacks and whites: "We had to mind them as our children mind us."[26]

When the conservative looks upon a democratic movement from below, this (and the exercise of agency) is what he sees: a terrible disturbance in the private life of power. Witnessing the election of Thomas Jefferson in 1800, Theodore Sedgwick lamented, "The aristocracy of virtue is destroyed; personal influence is at an end."[27] Sometimes the conservative is personally implicated in that life, sometimes not. Regardless, it is his apprehension of the private grievance behind the public commotion that lends his theory its tactile ingenuity and moral ferocity. "The real object" of the French Revolution, Burke told Parliament in 1790, is "to break all those connexions, natural and civil, that regulate and hold together the community by a chain of subordination; to raise soldiers against their officers; servants against their masters; tradesmen against their customers; artificers against their employers; tenants against their landlords; curates against their bishops; and children against their parents."[28] Personal insubordination rapidly became a regular and consistent theme of Burke's pronouncements on the unfolding events in France. A year later, he wrote in a letter that because of the Revolution, "no house is safe from its servants, and no Officer from his Soldiers, and no State or constitution from conspiracy and insurrection."[29] In another speech before Parliament in 1791, he declared that "a constitution founded on what was called the rights of man" opened "Pandora's box" throughout the world, including Haiti: "Blacks rose against whites, whites against blacks, and each against one another in murderous hostility; subordination was destroyed."[30] Nothing to the Jacobins, he declared at the end of his life, was worthy "of the name of the publick virtue, unless it indicates violence on the private."[31]

So powerful is that vision of private eruption that it can turn a man of reform into a man of reaction. Schooled in the Enlightenment, John Adams believed that "consent of the people" was "the only moral foundation of government."[32] But when his wife suggested that a muted version of these principles be extended to the family, he was not pleased. "And, by the way," Abigail wrote him, "in the new code of laws which I suppose it will be necessary for you to make, I desire you would remember the ladies and be more generous and favorable to them than your ancestors. Do not put such unlimited power into the hands of the husbands. Remember, all men would be tyrants if they could."[33] Her husband's response:

> We have been told that our struggle has loosened the bands of government everywhere; that children and apprentices were disobedient; that schools and colleges were grown turbulent; that Indians slighted their guardians, and Negroes grew insolent to their masters. But your letter was the first intimation that another tribe, more numerous and powerful than all of the rest, were grown discontented.

Though he leavened his response with playful banter—he prayed that George Washington would shield him from the "despotism of the petticoat"[34]—Adams was clearly rattled by this appearance of democracy in the private sphere. In a letter to James Sullivan, he worried that the Revolution would "confound and destroy all distinctions," unleashing throughout society a spirit of insubordination so intense that all order would be dissolved. "There will be no end of it."[35] No matter how democratic the state, it was imperative that society remain a federation of private dominions, where husbands ruled over wives, masters governed apprentices, and each "should know his place and be made to keep it."[36]

Historically, the conservative has sought to forestall the march of democracy in both the public and the private spheres, on the assumption that advances in the one necessarily spur advances in the other. "In order to keep the state out of the hands of the people," wrote the French monarchist Louis de Bonald, "it is necessary to keep the family out of the hands of women and children."[37] Even in the United States, this effort has periodically yielded fruit. Despite our Whiggish narrative of the steady rise of democracy, historian Alexander Keyssar has demonstrated that the struggle for the vote in the United States has been as much a story of retraction and contraction as one of progress and expansion, "with class tensions and apprehensions" on the part of political and economic elites constituting "the single most important obstacle to universal suffrage . . . from the late eighteenth century to the 1960s."[38]

Still, the more profound and prophetic stance on the right has been Adams's: cede the field of the public, if you must, stand fast in the private. Allow men and women to become democratic citizens of the state; make sure they remain feudal subjects in the family, the factory, and the field. The priority of conservative political argument has been the maintenance of private regimes of power—even at the cost of the strength and integrity of the state. We see this political arithmetic at work in the ruling of a Federalist court in Massachusetts that a Loyalist woman who fled the Revolution was the adjutant of her husband, and thus should not be held responsible for fleeing and should not have her property confiscated by the state; in the refusal of Southern slaveholders to yield their slaves to the Confederate cause; and the more recent insistence of the Supreme Court that women could not be legally obliged to sit on juries because they are "still regarded as the center of home and family life" with their "own special responsibilities."[39]

Conservatism, then, is not a commitment to limited government and liberty—or a wariness of change, a belief in evolutionary reform, or a politics of virtue. These may be the byproducts of conservatism, one or more of its historically specific and ever-changing modes of expression. But they are not its animating purpose. Neither is conservatism a makeshift fusion of capitalists, Christians, and warriors, for that fusion is impelled by a more elemental force—the opposition to the liberation of men and women from the fetters of their superiors, particularly in the private sphere. Such a view might seem miles away from the libertarian defense of the free market, with its celebration of the atomistic and autonomous individual. But it is not. When the libertarian looks out upon society, he does not see isolated individuals; he sees private, often hierarchical, groups, where a father governs his family and an owner his employees.[40]

No simple defense of one's own place and privileges—the conservative, as I've said, may or may not be directly involved in or benefit from the practices of rule he defends; many, as we'll see, are not—the conservative position stems from a genuine conviction that a world thus emancipated will be ugly, brutish, base, and dull. It will lack the excellence of a world where the better man commands the worse. When Burke adds, in the letter quoted above, that the "great Object" of the Revolution is "to root out that thing called an *Aristocrat* or Nobleman and Gentleman," he is not simply referring to the power of the nobility; he is also referring to the distinction that power brings to the world.[41] If the power goes, the distinction goes with it. This vision of the connection between excellence and rule is what brings together in postwar America that unlikely alliance of the libertarian, with his vision of the employer's untrammeled power in the workplace; the traditionalist, with his vision of the father's rule at home; and the statist, with his vision of a heroic leader pressing his hand upon the face of the earth. Each in his own way subscribes to this typical statement, from the nineteenth century, of the conservative creed:

"To obey a real superior . . . is one of the most important of all virtues—a virtue absolutely essential to the attainment of anything great and lasting."[42]

The notion that conservative ideas are a mode of counterrevolutionary practice is likely to raise some eyebrows, even hackles. It has long been an axiom on the left that the defense of power and privilege is an enterprise devoid of ideas. "Intellectual history," a recent study of American conservatism submits, "is never unwelcome," but it "is not the most direct approach to explaining the power of conservatism in America."[43] Liberal writers have always portrayed right-wing politics as an emotional swamp rather than a movement of considered opinion: Thomas Paine claimed counterrevolution entailed "an obliteration of knowledge"; Lionel Trilling described American conservatism as a mélange of "irritable mental gestures which seek to resemble ideas"; Robert Paxton called fascism an "affair of the gut," not "of the brain."[44] Conservatives, for their part, have tended to agree.[45] It was Palmerston, after all, when he was still a Tory, who first attached the epithet "stupid" to the Conservative Party. Playing the part of the dull-witted country squire, conservatives have embraced the position of F. J. C. Hearnshaw that "it is commonly sufficient for practical purposes if conservatives, without saying anything, just sit and think, or even if they merely sit."[46] While the aristocratic overtones of that discourse no longer resonate, the conservative still holds onto the label of the untutored and the unlettered; it's part of his populist charm and demotic appeal. As the conservative *Washington Times* observes, Republicans "often call themselves the 'stupid party.'"[47] Nothing, as we shall see, could be further from the truth. Conservatism is an idea-driven praxis, and no amount of preening from the right or polemic from the left can reduce or efface the catalog of mind one finds there.

Conservatives themselves will likely be put off by this argument for a different reason: it threatens the purity and profundity of conservative ideas. For many, the word "reaction" connotes an unthinking, lowly grab for power.[48] But reaction is not reflex. It begins from a position of principle—that some are fit, and thus ought, to rule others—and then recalibrates that principle in light of a democratic challenge from below. This recalibration is no easy task, for such challenges tend by their very nature to disprove the principle. After all, if a ruling class is truly fit to rule, why and how has it allowed a challenge to its power to emerge? What does the emergence of the one say about the fitness of the other?[49] The conservative faces an additional hurdle: How to defend a principle of rule in a world where nothing is solid, all is in flux? From the moment conservatism came onto the scene, it has had to contend with the decline of ancient and medieval ideas of an orderly universe, in which permanent hierarchies of power reflected the eternal structure of the cosmos. The overthrow of the old regime reveals not only the weakness and incompetence of its leaders but also a larger truth about the lack of design in the world. (The idea that conservatism reflects the revelation that the world has no natural hierarchies might seem odd in our age of Intelligent Design. But as Kevin Mattson and others have pointed out, Intelligent Design is not based on the same kind of medieval assumption of a firm eternal structure to the universe, and there is more than a touch of relativism and skepticism to its arguments. Indeed, one of Intelligent Design's leading proponents has claimed that though he's "no postmodernist," he has "learned a lot" from postmodernism.[50]) Reconstructing the old regime in the face of a declining faith in permanent hierarchies has proven to be a difficult feat. Not surprisingly, it also has produced some of the most remarkable works of modern thought.

But there is another reason we should be wary of the effort to dismiss the reactionary thrust of conservatism, and that is the testimony of the tradition itself. Ever since Burke, it has been a point of pride among conservatives that theirs is a contingent mode of thought. Unlike their opponents on the left, they do not unfurl a blueprint in advance of events. They read situations and circumstances, not texts and tomes; their preferred mode is adaptation and intimation rather than assertion and declamation. There's a certain truth to this claim, as we will see: the conservative mind is extraordinarily supple, alert to changes in context and fortune long before others realize they are occurring. With his deep awareness of the passage of time, the conservative possesses a tactical virtuosity few can match. It seems only logical that conservatism would be intimately bound up with, its antennae ever sensitive to, the movements and countermovements of power sketched above. These are, as I've said, the story of modern politics, and it would seem strange if a mind so attuned to the contingencies around it were not well versed in that story. Not just well versed, but awakened and aroused by it as by no other story.

Indeed, from Burke's claim that he and his ilk had been "alarmed into reflexion" by the French Revolution to Russell Kirk's admission that conservatism is a "system of ideas" that "has sustained men . . . in their resistance against radical theories and social transformation ever since the beginning of the French Revolution," the conservative has consistently affirmed that his is a knowledge produced in reaction to the left.[51] (Burke would go on to lay down as his "foundation" the notion that "never greater" an evil had "existed" than the French Revolution.)[52] Sometimes, that affirmation has been explicit. Three times prime minister, Salisbury wrote in 1859 that "hostility to Radicalism, incessant, implacable hostility, is the essential definition of Conservatism. The fear that the Radicals may triumph is the only final cause that the Conservative Party can plead for its own existence."[53] More than a half-century later, his son Hugh Cecil—among other things, best man at Winston Churchill's wedding and provost of Eton—reaffirmed the father's stance: "I think the government will find in the end that there is only one way of defeating revolutionary tactics and that is by presenting an organized body of thought which is non-revolutionary. That body of thought I call Conservatism."[54] Others, like Peel, have taken a more circuitous route to get to the same place:

> My object for some years past, that which I have most earnestly labored to accomplish, has been to lay the foundation of a great party, which, existing in the House of Commons, and deriving its strength from the popular will, should diminish the risk and deaden the shock of a collision between the two deliberative branches of the legislature—which should enable us to check the too importunate eagerness of well-intending men, for hasty and precipitate changes in the constitution and laws of the country, and by which we should be enabled to say, with a voice of authority, to the restless spirit of revolutionary change, "Here are thy bounds, and here shall thy vibrations cease."[55]

Lest we think such sentiments—and circumlocutions—are peculiarly English, consider how the court historian of the American right approached the matter in 1976. "What is conservatism?" George Nash asked in his now classic *The Conservative Intellectual Movement in America since 1945*. After a page of hesitation—conservatism resists definition, it "varies enormously with time and place" (what political idea doesn't?), it should not be "confused with the Radical Right"—Nash settled upon an answer that could have been given (indeed, was given) by Peel, Salisbury and son, Kirk, and most of the thinkers on the Radical Right. Conservatism, he said, is defined by "resistance to certain forces perceived to be leftist, revolutionary, and profoundly subversive of what conservatives at the time deemed worth cherishing, defending, and perhaps dying for."[56]

These are the explicit professions of the counterrevolutionary creed. More interesting are the implicit statements, where antipathy to radicalism and reform is embedded in the very syntax of the argument. Take Michael Oakeshott's famous definition in his essay "On Being Conservative": "To be conservative, then, is to prefer the familiar to the unknown, to prefer the tried to the untried, fact to mystery, the actual to the possible, the limited to the unbounded, the near to the distant, the sufficient to the superabundant, the convenient to the perfect, present laughter to utopian bliss." One cannot, it seems, enjoy fact *and* mystery, near *and* distant, laughter *and* bliss. One must choose. Far from affirming a simple hierarchy of preferences, Oakeshott's either/or signals that we are on existential ground, where the choice is not between something and its opposite but between something and its negation. The conservative would enjoy familiar things in the absence of forces seeking their destruction, Oakeshott concedes, but his enjoyment "will be strongest when" it "is combined with evident risk of loss." The conservative is a "man who is acutely aware of having something to lose which he has learned to care for." And while Oakeshott suggests that such losses can be engineered by a variety of forces, the engineers invariably seem to work on the left. (Marx and Engels are "the authors of the most stupendous of our political rationalisms," he writes elsewhere. "Nothing . . . can compare with" their abstract utopianism.) For that reason, "it is not at all inconsistent to be conservative in respect of government and radical in respect of almost every other activity."[57] Not at all inconsistent—or altogether necessary? Radicalism is the raison d'être of conservatism; if it goes, conservatism goes too.[58] Even when the conservative seeks to extricate himself from this dialogue with the left, he cannot, for his most lyrical motifs—organic change, tacit knowledge, ordered liberty, prudence, and precedent—are barely audible without the call and response of the left. As Disraeli discovered in his *Vindication of the English Constitution* (1835), it is only by contrast to a putative revolutionary rationalism that the invocation of ancient and tacit wisdom can have any purchase on the modern mind.

> The formation of a free government on an extensive scale, while it is assuredly one of the most interesting problems of humanity, is certainly the greatest achievement of human wit. Perhaps I should rather term it a superhuman achievement; for it requires such refined prudence, such comprehensive knowledge, and such perspicacious sagacity, united with such almost illimitable powers of combination, that it is nearly in vain to hope for qualities so rare to be congregated in a solitary mind. Assuredly this *summum bonum* is not to be found ensconced behind a revolutionary barricade, or floating in the bloody gutters of an incendiary metropolis. It cannot be scribbled down—this great invention—in a morning on the envelope of a letter by some charter-concocting monarch, or sketched with ludicrous facility in the conceited commonplace book of a Utilitarian sage.[59]

There is more to this antagonistic structure of argument than the simple antinomies of partisan politics, the oppositional position-taking that is a requirement of winning elections. As Karl Mannheim argued, what distinguishes conservatism from traditionalism—the universal "vegetative" tendency to remain attached to things as they are, which is manifested in nonpolitical behaviors such as a refusal to buy a new pair of pants until the current pair is shredded beyond repair—is that conservatism is a deliberate, conscious effort to preserve or recall "those forms of experience which can no longer be had in an authentic way." Conservatism "becomes conscious and reflective when other ways of life and thought appear on the scene, against which it is compelled to take up arms in the ideological struggle."[60] Where the traditionalist can take the objects of desire for granted—he can enjoy them as if they are at hand because they are at hand—the conservative cannot. He seeks to enjoy them precisely as they are being—or have been—taken away. If he hopes to enjoy them again, he must contest their divestment in the public realm. He must speak of them in a language that is politically serviceable and intelligible. But as soon as those objects enter the medium of political speech, they cease to be items of lived experience and become incidents of an ideology. They get wrapped in a narrative of loss—in which the revolutionary or reformist plays a necessary part—and presented in a program of recovery. What was tacit becomes articulate, what was fluid becomes formal, what was practice becomes polemic.[61] Even if the theory is a paean to practice—as conservatism often is—it cannot escape becoming a polemic. The fussiest conservative who would deign to enter the street is compelled by the left to pick up a paving stone and toss it at the barricades. As Lord Hailsham put it in his 1947 *Case for Conservatism*:

> Conservatives do not believe that political struggle is the most important thing in life. In this they differ from Communists, Socialists, Nazis, Fascists, Social Creditors and most members of the British Labour Party. The simplest among them prefer fox-hunting—the wisest religion. To the great majority of Conservatives, religion, art, study, family, country, friends, music, fun, duty, all the joy and riches of existence of which the poor no less than the rich are the indefeasible freeholders, all these are higher in the scale than their handmaiden, the political struggle. This makes them easy to defeat—at first. But, once, defeated, they will hold to this belief with the fanaticism of a Crusader and the doggedness of an Englishman.[62]

Because there is so much confusion about conservatism's opposition to the left, it is important that we be clear about what the conservative is and is not opposing in the left. It is not change in the abstract. No conservative opposes change as such or defends order as such. The conservative defends particular orders—hierarchical, often private regimes of rule—on the assumption, in part, that hierarchy is order. "Order cannot be had," declared Johnson, "but by subordination."[63] For Burke, it was axiomatic that "when the multitude are not under this discipline" of "the wiser, the more expert, and the more opulent," "they can scarcely be said to be in civil society."[64] In defending such orders, moreover, the conservative invariably launches himself on a program of reaction and counterrevolution, often requiring an overhaul of the very regime he is defending. "If we want things to stay as they are," in Lampedusa's classic formulation, "things will have to change."[65] To preserve the regime, as I show in part 1, the conservative must reconstruct the regime. This program entails far more than clichés about "preservation through renovation" would suggest: often, it can require the conservative to take the most radical measures on the regime's behalf.

Some of the stuffiest partisans of order on the right have been more than happy, when it has suited their purposes, to indulge in a little bit of mayhem and madness. Kirk, the self-styled Burkean, wished to "espouse conservatism with the vehemence of a radical. The thinking conservative, in truth, must take on some of the outward characteristics of the radical, today: he must poke about the roots of society, in the hope of restoring vigor to an old tree strangled in the rank undergrowth of modern passions." That was in 1954. Fifteen years later, at the height of the student movement, he wrote, "Having been for two decades a mordant critic of what is foolishly called the higher learning in America, I confess to relishing somewhat . . . the fulfillment of my predictions and the present plight of the educationist Establishment. I even own to a sneaking sympathy, after a fashion, with the campus revolutionaries." In *God and Man at Yale*, William F. Buckley declared conservatives "the new radicals." Upon reading the first few issues of *National Review*, Dwight Macdonald was inclined to agree: "Had [Buckley] been born a generation earlier, he would have been making the cafeterias of 14th Street ring with Marxian dialectics."[66] Even Burke himself wrote that "the madness of the wise" is "better than the sobriety of fools."[67]

There's a fairly simple reason for the embrace of radicalism on the right, and it has to do with the reactionary imperative that lies at the core of conservative doctrine. The conservative not only opposes the left; he also believes that the left has been in the driver's seat since, depending on who's counting, the French Revolution or the Reformation.[68] If he is to preserve what he values, the conservative must declare war against the culture as it is. Though the spirit of militant opposition pervades the entirety of conservative discourse, Dinesh D'Souza has put the case most clearly.

> Typically, the conservative attempts to conserve, to hold on to the values of the existing society. But . . . what if the existing society is inherently hostile to conservative beliefs? It is foolish for a conservative to attempt to conserve that culture. Rather, he must seek to undermine it, to thwart it, to destroy it at the root level. This means that the conservative must . . . be philosophically conservative but temperamentally radical.[69]

By now, it should also be clear that it is not the style or pace of change that the conservative opposes. The conservative theorist likes to draw a "manifest marked distinction" between evolutionary reform and radical change.[70] The first is slow, incremental, and adaptive; the second is fast, comprehensive, and by design. But that distinction, so dear to Burke and his followers, is often less clear in practice than the theorist allows.[71] Political theory is designed to be abstract, but what abstraction has impelled such diametrically opposed political programs as the preference for reform over radicalism, evolution over revolution? In the name of slow, organic, adaptive change, self-declared conservatives opposed the New Deal (Robert Nisbet, Kirk, and Whittaker Chambers) and endorsed the New Deal (Peter Viereck, Clinton Rossiter, and Whittaker Chambers).[72] A belief in evolutionary reform could lead one to adopt a Hayekian defense of the free market or the democratic socialism of Edward Bernstein. "Even Fabian Socialists," Nash tartly observes, "who believed in 'the inevitability of gradualness' might be labeled conservatives."[73] Conversely, as Abraham Lincoln pointed out, it's just as easy for the left to claim the mantle of preservation as it is for the right. "You say you are conservative," he declared to the slaveholders.

> Eminently conservative—while we are revolutionary, destructive, or something of the sort. What is conservatism? Is it not adherence to the old and tried, against the new and untried? We stick to, contend for, the identical old policy on the point in controversy which was adopted by "our fathers who framed the Government under which we live"; while you with one accord reject, and scout, and spit upon that old policy, and insist upon substituting something new. . . . Not one of all your various plans can show a precedent or an advocate in the century within which our Government originated. Consider, then, whether your claim of conservatism for yourself, and your charge of destructiveness against us, are based on the most clear and stable foundations.[74]

More often, however, the blurriness of the distinction has allowed the conservative to oppose reform on the grounds either that it will lead to revolution or that it is revolution. (Indeed, with the exception of Peel and Baldwin, no Tory leader has ever pursued a consistent program of preservation through reform, and even Peel could not persuade his party to follow him.[75]) Burke himself was not immune to the argument that reform leads to revolution. Even though he spent the better part of the decade preceding the American Revolution contesting that argument, he still wondered, "When you open" a constitution "to enquiry in one part," which would seem to be the definition of slow reform, "where will the enquiry stop?"[76] Other conservatives have argued that any demand from or on behalf of the lower orders, no matter how tepid or tardy, is too much, too soon, too fast. Reform is revolution, improvement is insurrection. "It may be good or bad," a gloomy Lord Carnarvon wrote of the Second Reform Act of 1867—a bill twenty years in the making that tripled the size of the British electorate—"but it is a revolution." Minus the opening qualification, this was a repeat of what Wellington had said about the first Reform Act.[77] Across the Atlantic, Wellington's contemporary Nicholas Biddle was denouncing Andrew Jackson's veto of the Second Bank (that most constitutionally exercised of constitutional powers) in similar terms: "It has all the fury of a chained panther biting at the bars of his cage. It really is a manifesto of anarchy—such as Marat or Robespierre might have issued to the mob."[78]

Today's conservative may have made his peace with some emancipations past; others, like labor unions and reproductive freedom, he still contests. But that does not alter the fact that when those emancipations first arose as a question, whether in the context of revolution or reform, his predecessor was in all likelihood against them. Michael Gerson, former speechwriter for George W. Bush, is one of the few contemporary conservatives who acknowledge the history of conservative opposition to emancipation. Where other conservatives like to lay claim to the abolitionist or civil rights mantle, Gerson admits that "honesty requires the recognition that many conservatives, in other times, have been hostile to religiously motivated reform" and that "the conservative habit of mind once opposed most of these changes."[79] Indeed, as Samuel Huntington suggested a half-century ago, saying no to such movements in real time may be what makes someone a conservative throughout time.[80]

Forged in response to challenges from below, conservatism has none of the calm or composure that attends an enduring inheritance of power. One will look in vain throughout the canon of the right for steady assurances of a Great Chain of Being. Conservative statements of organic unity, such as they are, either have an air of quiet—and not so quiet—desperation about them or, as in the case of Kirk, lack the texture, the knowing feel, of a longstanding witness to power. Even Maistre's professions of divine providence cannot conceal or contain the turbulent democracy that generated them. Made and mobilized to counter the claims of emancipation, such statements do not disclose a dense ecology of deference; they reveal instead a rapidly thinning forest. Conservatism is about power besieged and power protected. It is an activist doctrine for an activist time. It waxes in response to movements from below and wanes in response to their disappearance, as Hayek and other conservatives admit.[81]

Far from compromising the vision of excellence set out above—in which the prerogatives of rule are supposed to bring an element of grandeur to an otherwise drab and desultory world—the activist imperative only strengthens it. "Light and perfection," Matthew Arnold wrote, "consist, not in resting and being, but in growing and becoming, in a perpetual advance in beauty and wisdom."[82] To the conservative, power in repose is power in decline. The "mere husbanding of already existing resources," wrote Joseph Schumpeter about industrial dynasties, "no matter how painstaking, is always characteristic of a declining position."[83] If power is to achieve the distinction the conservative associates with it, it must be exercised.[84] And there is no better way to exercise power than to defend it against an enemy from below. Counterrevolution, in other words, is one of the ways in which the conservative makes feudalism seem fresh and medievalism modern.

But it is not the only way. Conservatism also offers a defense of rule, independent of its counterrevolutionary imperative, that is agonistic and dynamic and dispenses with the staid traditionalism and harmonic registers of hierarchies past. And here we come to the conservative's deepest intimations of the good life, of that reactionary utopia he hopes one day to bring into being. Unlike the feudal past, where power was presumed and privilege inherited, the conservative future envisions a world where power is demonstrated and privilege earned: not in the antiseptic and anodyne halls of the meritocracy, where admission is readily secured—"the road to eminence and power, from obscure condition, ought not to be made too easy, nor a thing too much of course"[85]—but in the arduous struggle for supremacy. In that struggle, nothing matters, not inheritance, social connections, or economic resources, but one's native intelligence and innate strength. Genuine excellence is revealed and rewarded, true nobility is secured. "'Nitor in adversum' [I strive against adversity] is the motto for a man like me," declares Burke, after dismissing a to-the-manor-born politician who was "swaddled, and rocked, and dandled into a legislator."[86] Even the most biologically inclined and deterministic racist believes that the members of the superior race must personally wrest their entitlement to rule through the subjugation or elimination of the inferior races.

The recognition that race is the substratum of all civilization must not, however, lead any one to feel that membership in a superior race is a sort of comfortable couch on which he can go to sleep. . . . the biological heritage of the mind is no more imperishable than the biological heritage of the body. If we continue to squander that biological mental heritage as we have been squandering it during the last few decades, it will not be many generations before we cease to be the superiors of the Mongols. Our ethnological studies must lead us, not to arrogance, but to action.[87]

The battlefield, as we shall see in part 2, is the natural proving ground of superiority; there, it is only the soldier, with his wits and weapon, who determines his standing in the world. With time, however, the conservative will find another proving ground in the marketplace. Though most early conservatives were ambivalent about capitalism,[88] their successors will come to believe that warriors of a different kind can prove their mettle in the manufacture and trade of commodities. Such men wrestle the earth's resources to and from the ground, taking for themselves what they want and thereby establishing their superiority over others. The great men of money are not born with privilege or right; they seize it for themselves, without let or permission.[89] "Liberty is a conquest," wrote William Graham Sumner.[90] The primal act of transgression—requiring daring, vision, and an aptitude for violence and violation[91]—is what makes the capitalist a warrior, entitling him not only to great wealth but also, ultimately, to command. For that is what the capitalist is: not a Midas of riches but a ruler of men. A title to property is a license to dispose, and if a man has the title to another's labor, he has a license to dispose of it—to dispose, that is, of the body in motion—as he sees fit.

Such have been called "captains of industry." The analogy with military leaders suggested by this name is not misleading. The great leaders in the development of the industrial organization need those talents of executive and administrative skill, power to command, courage, and fortitude, which were formerly called for in military affairs and scarcely anywhere else. The industrial army is also as dependent on its captains as a military body is on its generals. . . . Under the circumstances there has been a great demand for men having the requisite ability for this function. . . . The possession of the requisite ability is a natural monopoly.[92]

The warrior and the businessman will become twin icons of an age in which, as Burke foresaw, membership in the ruling classes must be earned, often through the most painful and humiliating of struggles. "At every step of my progress in life (for in every step was I traversed and opposed), and at every turnpike I met, I was obliged to shew my passport, and again and again to prove my sole title to the honour of being useful to my Country. . . . Otherwise, no rank, no toleration even, for me."[93]

Even though war and the market are the modern agones of power—with Nietzsche the theoretician of the first and Hayek of the second—the embrace of capitalism on the right has never been unqualified. To this day, as I show in part 2, conservatives remain leery of the shabbiness and shallowness of making money, of the political autism the market seems to induce in the governing classes, and of the foolishness and frivolity of consumer culture. For this wing of the movement war will always remain the only activity where the best man can truly prove his right to rule. It's a bloody business, to be sure, but how else to be an aristocrat when all that's solid melts into air?

In the last two decades, there has been a flurry of interest in the American right, resulting in a body of scholarship—much of it by younger historians, many of them on the left—that has dramatically transformed our understanding of conservatism in the United

States.[94] Much of my own reading of conservative thought has been informed by this literature—its emphasis on the lived realities of race, class, and gender as they have manifested themselves in the partisan struggles of the last half-century; the syncretism between high politics and mass culture; and the creative tension between elites and activists, businessmen and intellectuals, suburbs and Southerners, movement and media. Believing with T. S. Eliot that conservatism is best understood by "careful examination of its behavior throughout its history and by examination of what its more thoughtful and philosophical minds have said on its behalf,"[95] I have read the theory in light of the practice (and the practice in light of the theory). With the help of this scholarship, I have listened for the "metaphysical pathos" of conservative thought—the hum and buzz of its implications, the assumptions it invokes and associations it evokes, the inner life of the movement it describes.[96] The felt presence of this scholarship is what distinguishes, I hope, my interpretation of conservative thought from other interpretations, which tend to read the theory in seclusion from the practice or in relation to a highly stylized account of that practice.[97]

As sophisticated as the recent literature about conservatism is, however, it suffers from three weaknesses. The first is a lack of comparative perspective. Scholars of the American right rarely examine the movement in relation to its European counterpart. Indeed, among many writers, it seems to be an article of faith that, like all things American, conservatism in the United States is exceptional. "There is a distinctly *American* feel to Bush and his intellectual defenders," writes Mattson. "A conservatism that draws on Edmund Burke, a conservatism of wisdom and tradition deeply rooted in a European context" is "the sort of conservatism that has never taken hold in America."[98] The commitment to laissez-faire capitalism on this side of the Atlantic is supposed to differentiate American conservatism from the traditionalism of a Burke or Disraeli; a native pragmatism renders American conservatism inhospitable to the pessimism and fanaticism of a Bonald; democracy and populism make untenable the aristocratic biases of a Tocqueville. But this assumption is premised, I will show, on misapprehensions about the European right: not even Burke was as traditional as writers have made him out to be, while Maistre held views on the economy that were—like so much else in his revanchist writings—surprisingly modern.[99] Indeed, there are deep points of contact—particularly over questions of race and violence—between the radical right in Europe and figures like Calhoun, Teddy Roosevelt, Barry Goldwater, and the neoconservatives. In the postwar era, many of conservatism's leading lights self-consciously turned to Europe in search of guidance and instruction, a service European émigrés—most notably, Hayek, Ludwig von Mises, and Leo Strauss—were only too happy to provide.[100] Indeed, for all the focus on the Frankfurt School and Hannah Arendt, it seems that the only political movements in postwar America that truly felt the impress of the European mind were on the right.

The second weakness is a lack of historical perspective. No matter how far back writers and scholars push the origins of contemporary conservatism (the latest move argues for a long conservative movement that connects the Tea Party to the 1920s),[101] there is a notion in the recent literature that contemporary conservatism is fundamentally different from earlier iterations. At some point, the argument goes, American conservatism broke with its predecessors—it became populist, ideological, and so on—and it is this break, depending upon one's perspective, that either saved or doomed it.[102] But this argument ignores the continuities between figures like Adams and Calhoun and more recent voices on the American right. Far from an innovation of the last decades, the populism of the Tea Party and the futurism of a Reagan or Gingrich can be found in the earliest voices of conservatism, on both sides of the Atlantic. Likewise the adventurism, racism, and penchant for ideological thinking.

The third weakness derives from the second. The further back analysts trace the origins of contemporary conservatism, the less inclined they are to believe that it is a politics of reaction or backlash. If the commitments of the contemporary conservative can be situated in the writings of Albert Jay Nock or John Adams, these scholars argue, conservatism must reflect ideas and commitments more transcendent than mere opposition to the Great Society would suggest.[103] But a recognition of the long history of the right need not undermine the claim that contemporary conservatism is a backlash politics. Instead the long view should help us to understand better the nature and dynamics, as well as the idiosyncrasies and contingencies, of that backlash. Indeed, only by setting the contemporary right against the backdrop of its predecessors can we understand its specificity and particularity.

Against these three assumptions, which dwell on difference and distinction, I treat the right as a unity, as a coherent body of theory and practice that transcends the divisions so often emphasized by scholars and pundits.[104] I use the words conservative, reactionary, and counterrevolutionary interchangeably: not all counterrevolutionaries are conservative—Walt Rostow immediately comes to mind—but all conservatives are, in one way or another, counterrevolutionary. I seat philosophers, statesmen, slaveholders, scribblers, Catholics, fascists, evangelicals, businessmen, racists, and hacks at the same table: Hobbes next to Hayek, Burke across from Palin, Nietzsche in between Ayn Rand and Antonin Scalia, with Adams, Calhoun, Oakeshott, Ronald Reagan, Tocqueville, Theodore Roosevelt, Margaret Thatcher, Ernst Jünger, Carl Schmitt, Winston Churchill, Phyllis Schlafly, Richard Nixon, Irving Kristol, Francis Fukuyama, and George W. Bush interspersed throughout.

This is not to say that there is no change in conservatism across time or space. If conservatism is a specific reaction to a specific movement of emancipation, it stands to reason that each reaction will bear the traces of the movement it opposes. As I argue in chapter 1, not only has the right reacted against the left, but in the course of conducting its reaction, it also has consistently borrowed from the left. As the movements of the left change—from the French Revolution to abolition to the right to vote to the right to organize to the Bolshevik Revolution to the struggles for black freedom and women's liberation—so do the reactions of the right.

Beyond these contingent changes, we can also trace a longer structural change in the imagination of the right: namely, the gradual acceptance of the entrance of the masses onto the political stage. From Hobbes to the slaveholders to the neoconservatives, the right has grown increasingly aware that any successful defense of the old regime must incorporate the lower orders in some capacity other than underlings or starstruck fans. The masses must either be able to locate themselves symbolically in the ruling class or be provided with real opportunities to become faux aristocrats themselves in the family, the factory, and the field. The former path makes for an upside-down populism, in which the lowest of the low see themselves projected in the highest of the high; the latter makes for a democratic feudalism, in which the husband or supervisor plays the part of a lord. The former path was pioneered by Hobbes, Maistre, and various prophets of racism and nationalism, the latter by Southern slaveholders, European imperialists, and Gilded Age apologists. (And neo–Gilded Age apologists: "There is no single elite in America," writes David Brooks. "Everyone can be an aristocrat within his own Olympus."[105]) Occasionally, as in the writing of Werner Sombart, the two paths converge: ordinary people get to see themselves in the ruling class by virtue of belonging to a great nation among nations, and they also get to govern lesser beings through the exercise of imperial rule.

We Germans, too, should go through the world of our time in the same way, proud heads held high, in the secure feeling of being God's people. Just as the German bird, the eagle, soars high over all animals on this earth, so the German must feel himself above all other peoples that surround him and that he sees in boundless depth below him.

But aristocracy has its obligations, and this is true here, too. The idea that we are chosen people places formidable duties—and only duties—on us. We must above all maintain ourselves as a strong nation in the world.[106]

While these historical differences on the right are real, there is an underlying affinity that draws these differences together. One cannot perceive this affinity by focusing on disagreements of policy or contingent statements of practice (states' rights, federalism, and so on); one must look to the underlying arguments, the idioms and metaphors, the deep visions and metaphysical pathos evoked in each disagreement and statement. Some conservatives criticize the free market, others defend it; some oppose the state, others embrace it; some believe in God, others are atheists. Some are localists, others nationalists, and still others internationalists. Some, like Burke, are all three at the same time. But these are historical improvisations—tactical and substantive—on a theme. Only by juxtaposing these voices—across time and space—can we make out the theme amid the improvisation.

For many, the notion of a unity on the right will be the most contentious claim of this book. Even though we continue to use the term "conservative" in our everyday discourse (indeed, political discussion would be inconceivable without it); even though conservatism in both Europe and the United States has managed, for more than a century, to attract and hold together a coalition of traditionalists, warriors, and capitalists; even though the opposition between left and right has proven to be an enduring "political distinction" of the modern era (despite the attempts, every generation or so, to deny or overcome this opposition via a "third way")[107]—many continue to believe the differences on the right are so great it would be impossible to say anything about the right.[108] But if it is impossible to say anything about the right—to define, describe, explain, analyze, and interpret the right as a distinctive formation—how can we say that it even exists?

Hoping to avoid that radical skepticism, which would render unintelligible much of what goes on in our politics, some scholars have retreated to a nominalist position: conservatives are people who call themselves conservative or, more elaborately, conservatives are people who people who call themselves conservative call conservative.[109] This only begs the question: What do these people who call themselves conservative—or who others who call themselves conservative call conservative—mean by "conservative"? Why do they opt for that self-description as opposed to liberal, socialist, or aardvark? Unless these people think they are referring to idiosyncratic identities—in which case we're back to the skeptical position—we need to understand what the term means, independent of its use. How else can we understand why individuals from different times and places, adopting different positions on different issues, would call themselves and their kindred spirits conservative? While not every reader need accept my claim about what unites the right, it seems a necessary condition of intelligent discussion that we agree that there is something called the right and that it has some set of common features that make it right.

The eleven chapters of this book have been culled from a decade's worth of writing about the right. Some chapters originally appeared as lengthy review essays for periodicals like *The Nation* and the *London*

Review of Books; others are academic research articles, reported pieces, or stand-alone essays. I have made some alterations to these pieces to account for new developments or changes in my views. Occasionally, I have eliminated entire sections because they no longer seemed relevant. But on the whole I have tried to leave the pieces intact in the hope that their varied approaches capture this notion of the right as a set of historical improvisations on a continuous theme.

The book is divided into two parts. Part 1 opens with a general statement about the counterrevolutionary thrust of conservative politics, from the French Revolution through today. This chapter focuses less on the aims and intentions of the counterrevolution and more on its moves and maneuvers: how it breaks with the very regime it is defending and looks to the left in its efforts to reconstruct the right. I then move chronologically, from an examination of Thomas Hobbes and the English Civil War to a concluding analysis of Justice Scalia and his originalist jurisprudence. Along the way, I discuss Rand, Goldwater, the New Right, and conservatives after the Cold War. Part 2 looks at the fraught topic of violence in conservatism. Though I open with a brief look back at the Latin American Cold War and conclude with a more general reflection on how the right has approached violence since Burke, most of the discussion in these chapters is drawn from the past decade: 9/11, the war on terror, the war in Iraq. These events, and the giddiness they inspired among conservatives, more than anything drove me to think and write about the right. As I came to realize, and as chapter 11 argues, the infatuation with violence on today's right is not an aberration; it is constitutive of the tradition itself.

**PART 1** Profiles in Reaction

1

Conservatism and Counterrevolution

Whoever fights monsters should see to it that in the process
he does not become a monster.

—Friedrich Nietzsche, *Beyond Good and Evil*

When John McCain announced Sarah Palin as his running mate
during the 2008 presidential campaign, voices in the conservative
movement expressed surprise, even shock. It wasn't just that
McCain had chosen a political novice, an ingénue and outsider to
the ways and means of governance in the lower forty-eight states.
It was how he had chosen her: with little to no vetting and a great
deal of faith in the superiority of intuition and impulse (his and
hers) over reason and reflection. It was, it seemed, a most unconservative decision: impetuous, ill-considered, imprudent.

This was hardly the first time that a standard-bearer of conservatism failed to live up to the self-image of the conservative. In the
spring of 2003, several conservatives voiced concern over the audacity of George W. Bush's decision to fight what was essentially a
war of choice. They also noted the liberal pedigree of one of the
Iraq War's justifications: spreading democracy and human rights.
Here was a conservative leader, again it seemed, acting in the most

This chapter originally appeared in *Raritan* 30, no. 1 (Summer 2010): 1–17.

unconservative of ways: jettisoning the realism of his father and his party for an internationalism long considered the exclusive property of the left, pressing the forward march of history against the status quo of the Middle East.

Ever since Edmund Burke invented conservatism as an idea, the conservative has styled himself a man of prudence and moderation, his cause a sober—and sobering—recognition of limits. "To be conservative," we heard Michael Oakeshott declare in the introduction, "is to prefer the familiar to the unknown . . . the tried to the untried, fact to mystery, the actual to the possible, the limited to the unbounded, the near to the distant."[1] Yet the political efforts that have roused the conservative to his most profound reflections—the reactions against the French and Bolshevik revolutions; the defense of slavery and Jim Crow; the attack on social democracy and the welfare state; and the serial backlashes against the New Deal, the Great Society, civil rights, feminism, and gay rights—have been anything but that. Whether in Europe or the United States, in this century or previous ones, conservatism has been a forward movement of restless and relentless change, partial to risk taking and ideological adventurism, militant in its posture and populist in its bearings, friendly to upstarts and insurgents, outsiders and newcomers alike. While the conservative theorist claims for his tradition the mantle of prudence and moderation, there is a not-so-subterranean strain of imprudence and immoderation running through that tradition—a strain that, however counterintuitive it seems, connects Sarah Palin to Edmund Burke.

A consideration of this deeper strain of conservatism gives us a clearer sense of what conservatism is about. While conservatism is an ideology of reaction—originally against the French Revolution, more recently against the liberation movements of the sixties and seventies—that reaction has not been well understood. Far from yielding a knee-jerk defense of an unchanging old regime or a thoughtful traditionalism, the reactionary imperative presses conservatism in two rather different directions: first, to a critique and reconfiguration of the old regime; and second, to an absorption of the ideas and tactics of the very revolution or reform it opposes. What conservatism seeks to accomplish through that reconfiguration of the old and absorption of the new is to make privilege popular, to transform a tottering old regime into a dynamic, ideologically coherent movement of the masses. A new old regime, one could say, which brings the energy and dynamism of the street to the antique inequalities of a dilapidated estate.

As the forty-year dominion of the right begins to fade, however fitfully, writers like Sam Tanenhaus, Andrew Sullivan, Jeffrey Hart, Sidney Blumenthal, and John Dean claim that conservatism went into decline when Palin, or Bush, or Reagan, or Goldwater, or Buckley, or someone took it off the rails. Originally, the argument goes, conservatism was a responsible discipline of the governing classes, but somewhere between Joseph de Maistre and Joe the Plumber, it got carried away with itself. It became adventurous, fanatical, populist, ideological. What this story of decline overlooks—whether it emanates from the right or the left—is that all of these supposed vices of contemporary conservatism were present at the beginning, in the writings of Burke and Maistre, only they weren't viewed as vices. They were seen as virtues. Conservatism has always been a wilder and more extravagant movement than many realize—and it is precisely this wildness and extravagance that has been one of the sources of its continuing appeal.

It is hardly provocative to say that conservatism arose in reaction to the French Revolution. Most historically minded conservatives would agree.[2] But if we look more carefully at two emblematic voices of that reaction—Burke and Maistre—we find several surprising and seldom-noticed elements. The first is an antipathy, bordering on contempt, for the old regime they claim as their cause. The opening chapters of Maistre's *Considerations on France* are an unrelenting assault on the three pillars of the ancien régime: the aristocracy, the church, and the monarchy. Maistre divides the nobility into two categories: the treasonous and the clueless. The clergy is corrupt, weakened by its wealth and lax morals. The monarchy is soft and lacks the will to punish. Maistre dismisses all three with a line from Racine: "Now see the sad fruits your faults produced, / Feel the blows you have yourselves induced."[3]

In Burke's case, the criticism is subtler but runs deeper. (Though by the end of his life, he was speaking in the same unmodulated tones as Maistre.)[4] It comes during his account in *Reflections on the Revolution in France* of the storming of the palace at Versailles and the capture of the royal family. There, Burke describes Marie Antoinette as a "delightful vision . . . glittering like the morning star, full of life, and splendor, and joy." Burke takes her beauty as a symbol of the loveliness of the old regime, where feudal manners and mores "made power gentle" and "by a bland assimilation, incorporated into politics the sentiments which beautify and soften private society."[5]

Ever since he wrote those lines, Burke has been mocked for his sentimentality. But readers of Burke's earlier work on aesthetics, *A Philosophical Enquiry into the Origins of Our Ideas of the Sublime and the Beautiful*, will know that beauty, for Burke, is never a sign of power's vitality; it is always a sign of decadence. Beauty arouses pleasure, which gives way to indifference or leads to a total dissolution of the self. "Beauty acts," Burke writes, "by relaxing the solids of the whole system."[6] It is this relaxation and dissolution of bodies—physical, social, political bodies—that makes beauty such a potent symbol and agent of degeneration and death. "Our most salutary and most beautiful institutions yield nothing but dust and smut."[7]

What these two opening statements of the conservative persuasion suggest is that the greatest enemy of the old regime is neither the revolutionary nor the reformer; it is the old regime itself or, to be more precise, the defenders of the old regime.[8] They simply lack the ideological wherewithal to press the cause of the old regime with the requisite vigor, clarity, and purpose. As Burke declared of George Grenville, in the very different context of Britain's relationship with its American colonies:

> But it may be truly said, that men too much conversant in office, are rarely minds of remarkable enlargement. . . . persons who are nurtured in office do admirably well as long as things go on in their common order; but when the high roads are broken up, and the waters out, when a new and troubled scene is opened, and the file affords no precedent, then it is that a greater knowledge of mankind, and a far more extensive comprehension of things, is requisite, than ever office gave, or than office can ever give.[9]

Later conservatives will make this claim in various ways. Sometimes they'll accuse the defenders of the old regime of having been cowed by the revolutionary or reformist challenge. According to Thomas Dew, one of the earliest and most aggressive apologists for American slavery, the Nat Turner rebellion destroyed "all feeling of security and confidence" among the master class. So frightened were they that "reason was almost banished from the mind." It wasn't just the slaves' violence that frightened them. It was the moral indictment leveled by the slaves and the abolitionists, which had somehow insinuated itself into the slaveholders' minds and made them unsure of their own position. "We ourselves," wrote William Harper, another defender of slavery, "have in some measure pleaded guilty to the impeachment."[10]

More than a century later, Barry Goldwater would take up the same theme. The very first paragraph of *The Conscience of a Conservative* directs its fire not at liberals or Democrats or even the welfare state; it is aimed at the moral timidity of what will later be called the "Republican Establishment."

> I have been much concerned that so many people today with Conservative instincts feel compelled to apologize for them. Or if not to apologize directly, to qualify their commitment in a way that amounts to breast beating. "Republican candidates," Vice President Nixon has said, "should be economic conservatives, but conservatives with a heart." President Eisenhower announced during his first term, "I am conservative when it comes to economic problems but liberal when it comes to human problems." . . . These formulations are tantamount to an admission that Conservatism is a narrow, mechanistic economic theory that may work very well as a bookkeeper's guide, but cannot be relied upon as a comprehensive political philosophy.[11]

More often, conservatives have argued that the defender of the old regime is simply obtuse. He has grown lazy, fat, and complacent, so roundly enjoying the privileges of his position that he cannot see the coming catastrophe. Or, if he can see it, he can't do anything to fend it off, his political muscles having atrophied long ago. John C. Calhoun was one such conservative, and throughout the 1830s, when the abolitionists began pressing their cause, he drove himself into a rage over the easy living and willful cluelessness of his comrades on the plantation. His fury reached a peak in 1837, when, in a speech on the Senate floor, he urged Congress not to receive an abolitionist petition—a moment, as we saw in the introduction, that he would remember to his dying day. "All we want is concert," he pleaded with his fellow Southerners, to "unite with zeal and energy in repelling approaching dangers." But, he went on, "I dare not hope that any thing I can say will arouse the South to a due sense of danger. I fear it is beyond the power of the mortal voice to awaken it in time from the fatal security into which it has fallen."[12]

In his influential essay, Oakeshott argued that conservatism "is not a creed or a doctrine, but a disposition." Specifically, he thought, it is a disposition to enjoy the present. Not because the present is better than the alternatives or even because it is good on its own terms. That would imply a level of conscious reflection and ideological choice that Oakeshott believes is alien to the conservative. No, the reason the conservative enjoys the present is simply and merely because it is familiar, because it is there, because it is at hand.[13]

Oakeshott's view of the conservative—and this view is widely shared on both the left and the right—is not an insight; it is a conceit. It overlooks the fact that conservatism invariably arises in response to a threat to the old regime or after the old regime has been destroyed. (Oakeshott openly admits that loss or threatened loss makes us value the present, as I argued in the introduction, but he does not allow that insight to penetrate or dislodge his overall understanding of conservatism.) Oakeshott is describing the old regime in an easy chair, when its mortality is a distant notion and time is a warming medium rather than an acrid solvent. This is the old regime of Charles Loyseau, who wrote nearly two centuries before the French Revolution that the nobility has no "beginning" and thus no end. It "exists time out of mind," without consciousness or awareness of the passage of history.[14]

Conservatism appears on the scene precisely when—and precisely because—such statements can no longer be made. Walter Berns, one of the many future neoconservatives at Cornell who were traumatized in 1969 by the black students, takeover of Willard Straight Hall, stated in his farewell speech when he resigned from the university: "We had too good a world; it couldn't last."[15] Nothing so disturbs the idyll of inheritance as the sudden and often brutal replacement of one world with another. Having witnessed the death of what was supposed to live forever, the conservative can no longer look upon time as the natural ally or habitat of power. Time is now the enemy. Change, not permanence, is the universal governor, with change signifying neither progress nor improvement but death, and an early, unnatural death at that. "The decree of violent death," says Maistre, is "written on the very frontiers of life."[16] The problem with the defender of the old regime, says the conservative, is that he doesn't know this truth or, if he does, he lacks the will to do anything about it.

The second element we find in these early voices of reaction is a surprising admiration for the very revolution they are writing against. Maistre's most rapturous comments are reserved for the Jacobins, whose brutal will and penchant for violence—their "black magic"—he plainly envies. The revolutionaries have faith, in their cause and themselves, which transforms a movement of mediocrities into the most implacable force Europe has ever seen. Thanks to their efforts, France has been purified and restored to its rightful pride of place among the family of nations. "The revolutionary government," Maistre concludes, "hardened the soul of France by tempering it in blood."[17]

Burke, again, is more subtle but cuts more deeply. Great power, he suggests in *The Sublime and the Beautiful,* should never aspire to be—and can never actually be—beautiful. What great power needs is sublimity. The sublime is the sensation we experience in the face of extreme pain, danger, or terror. It is something like awe but tinged with fear and dread. Burke calls it "delightful horror." Great power should aspire to sublimity rather than beauty because sublimity produces "the strongest emotion which the mind is capable of feeling." It is an arresting yet invigorating emotion, which has the simultaneous but contradictory effect of diminishing and magnifying us. We feel annihilated by great power; at the same time, our sense of self "swell[s]" when "we are conversant with terrible objects." Great power achieves sublimity when it is, among other things, obscure and mysterious, and when it is extreme. "In all things," writes Burke, the sublime "abhors mediocrity."[18]

In the *Reflections*, Burke suggests that the problem in France is that the old regime is beautiful while the revolution is sublime. The landed interest, the cornerstone of the old regime, is "sluggish, inert, and timid." It cannot defend itself "from the invasions of ability," with ability standing in here for the new men of power that the revolution brings forth. Elsewhere in the *Reflections*, Burke says that the moneyed interest, which is allied with the revolution, is stronger than the aristocratic interest because it is "more ready for any adventure" and "more disposed to new enterprises of any kind." The old regime, in other words, is beautiful, static, and weak; the revolution is ugly, dynamic, and strong. And in the horrors that the revolution perpetrates—the rabble rushing into the bedchamber of the queen, dragging her half-naked into the street, and marching her and her family to Paris—the revolution achieves a kind of sublimity: "We are alarmed into reflexion," writes Burke of the revolutionaries' actions. "Our minds . . . are purified by terror and pity; our weak unthinking pride is humbled, under the dispensations of a mysterious wisdom."[19]

Beyond these simple professions of envy or admiration, the conservative actually copies and learns from the revolution he opposes. "To destroy that enemy," Burke wrote of the Jacobins, "by some means or other, the force opposed to it should be made to bear some analogy and resemblance to the force and spirit which that system exerts."[20] This is one of the most interesting and least understood aspects of conservative ideology. While conservatives are hostile to the goals of the left, particularly the empowerment of society's lower castes and classes, they often are the left's best students. Sometimes, their studies are self-conscious and strategic, as they look to the left for ways to bend new vernaculars, or new media, to their suddenly delegitimated aims. Fearful that the philosophes had taken control of popular opinion in France, reactionary theologians in the middle of the eighteenth century looked to the example of their enemies. They stopped writing abstruse disquisitions for each other and began to produce Catholic agitprop, which would be distributed through the very networks that brought enlightenment to the French people. They spent vast sums funding essay contests, like those in which Rousseau made his name, to reward writers who wrote accessible and popular defenses of religion. Previous treatises of faith, declared Charles-Louis Richard, were "useless to the multitude who, without arms and without defenses, succumbs rapidly to *Philosophie*." His work, by contrast, was written "with the design of putting in the hands of all those who know how to read a victorious weapon against the assaults of this turbulent *Philosophie*."[21]

Pioneers of the Southern Strategy in the Nixon administration, to cite a more recent example, understood that after the rights revolutions of the sixties they could no longer make simple appeals to white racism. From now on, they would have to speak in code, preferably one palatable to the new dispensation of color blindness. As White House chief of staff H. R. Haldeman noted in his diary, Nixon "emphasized that you have to face the fact that the whole problem is really the blacks. The key is to devise a system that recognized this while not appearing to."[22] Looking back on this strategy in 1981, Republican strategist Lee Atwater spelled out its elements more clearly:

You start out in 1954 by saying, "Nigger, nigger, nigger." By 1968 you can't say "nigger"—that hurts you. Backfires. So you say stuff like forced busing, states' rights and all that stuff. You're getting so abstract now you're talking about cutting taxes, and all these things you're talking about are totally economic things and a by-product of them is blacks get hurt worse than whites. And subconsciously maybe that is part of it.[23]

More recently still, David Horowitz has encouraged conservative students "to use the language that the left has deployed so effectively in behalf of its own agendas. Radical professors have created a 'hostile learning environment' for conservative students. There is a lack of 'intellectual diversity' on college faculties and in academic classrooms. The conservative viewpoint is 'underrepresented' in the curriculum and on its reading lists. The university should be an 'inclusive' and intellectually 'diverse' community."[24]

At other times, the education of the conservative is unknowing, happening, as it were, behind his back. By resisting and thus engaging with the progressive argument day after day, he comes to be influenced, often in spite of himself, by the very movement he opposes. Setting out to bend a vernacular to his will, he finds his will bent by the vernacular. Atwater claims this is precisely what occurred within the Republican Party; after suggesting "subconsciously maybe that is part of it." He adds:

> I'm not saying that. But I'm saying that if it is getting that abstract, and that coded, that we are doing away with the racial problem one way or the other. You follow me—because obviously sitting around saying, "We want to cut this," is much more abstract than even the busing thing, and a hell of a lot more abstract than "Nigger, nigger."[25]

Republicans have learned to disguise their intentions so well, Atwater argues, that the disguise has seeped into and transformed the intention. Assuming such a transformation has indeed occurred, we might well ask whether the conservative has ceased to be what he set out to be. But that is a question for another day.

Even without directly engaging the progressive argument, conservatives may absorb, by some elusive osmosis, the deeper categories and idioms of the left, even when those idioms run directly counter to their official stance. After years of opposing the women's movement, for example, Phyllis Schlafly seemed genuinely incapable of conjuring the prefeminist view of women as deferential wives and mothers. Instead, she celebrated the activist "power of the positive woman." And then, as if borrowing a page from *The Feminine Mystique*, she railed against the meaninglessness and lack of fulfillment among American women; only she blamed these ills on feminism rather than on sexism.[26] When she spoke out against the Equal Rights Amendment (ERA), she didn't claim that it introduced a radical new language of rights. Her argument was the opposite. The ERA, she told the *Washington Star*, "is a takeaway of women's rights." It will "take away the right of the wife in an ongoing marriage, the wife in the home."[27] Schlafly was obviously using the language of rights in a way that was opposed to the aims of the feminist movement; she was using rights talk to put women back into the home, to keep them as wives and mothers. But that is the point: conservatism adapts and adopts, often unconsciously, the language of democratic reform to the cause of hierarchy.

One also can detect a certain sexual frankness—even feminist concern—in the early conversations of the Christian Right that would have been unthinkable prior to the women's movement. In 1976, Beverly and Tim LaHaye wrote a book, *The Act of Marriage,* which Susan Faludi has rightly called "the evangelical equivalent of *The Joy of Sex*." There, the LaHayes claimed that "women are much too passive in lovemaking." God, the LaHayes told their female readers, "placed [your clitoris] there for your enjoyment." They also complained that "some husbands are carryovers from the

Dark Ages, like the one who told his frustrated wife, 'Nice girls aren't supposed to climax.' Today's wife knows better."[28]

What the conservative ultimately learns from his opponents, wittingly or unwittingly, is the power of political agency and the potency of the mass. From the trauma of revolution, conservatives learn that men and women, whether through willed acts of force or some other exercise of human agency, can order social relationships and political time. In every social movement or revolutionary moment, reformers and radicals have to invent—or rediscover—the idea that inequality and social hierarchy are not natural phenomena but human creations. If hierarchy can be created by men and women, it can be uncreated by men and women, and that is what a social movement or revolution sets out to do. From these efforts, conservatives learn a version of the same lesson. Where their predecessors in the old regime thought of inequality as a naturally occurring phenomenon, an inheritance passed on from generation to generation, the conservatives' encounter with revolution teaches them that the revolutionaries were right after all: inequality is a human creation. And if it can be uncreated by men and women, it can be recreated by men and women.

"Citizens!" exclaims Maistre at the end of *Considerations on France*. "This is how counterrevolutions are made."[29] Under the old regime, monarchy—like patriarchy or Jim Crow—isn't made. It just is. It would be difficult to imagine a Loyseau or Bossuet declaring, "Men"—much less citizens—"this is how a monarchy is made." But once the old regime is threatened or toppled, the conservative is forced to realize that it is human agency, the willed imposition of intellect and imagination upon the world, that generates and maintains inequality across time. Coming out of his confrontation with the revolution, the conservative voices the kind of affirmation of political agency one finds in this 1957 editorial from William F. Buckley's *National Review*: "The central question that emerges" from the civil rights movement "is whether the White community in the South is entitled to take such measures as are necessary to prevail, politically and culturally, in areas in which it does not predominate numerically? The sobering answer is Yes— the White community is so entitled because, for the time being, it is the advanced race."[30]

The revolutionary declares the Year I, and in response the conservative declares the Year Negative I. From the revolution, the conservative develops a particular attitude toward political time, a belief in the power of men and women to shape history, to propel it forward or backward; and by virtue of that belief, he comes to adopt the future as his preferred tense. Ronald Reagan offered the perfect distillation of this phenomenon when he invoked, repeatedly, Thomas Paine's dictum that "we have it in our power to begin the world over again."[31] Even when the conservative claims to be preserving a present that's threatened or recovering a past that's lost, he is impelled by his own activism and agency to confess that he's making a new beginning and creating the future.

Burke was especially attuned to this problem and so was often at pains to remind his comrades in the battle against the Revolution that whatever was rebuilt in France after the restoration would inevitably, as he put it in a letter to an émigré, "be in some measure a new thing."[32] Other conservatives have been less ambivalent, happily affirming the virtues of political creativity and moral originality. Alexander Stephens, vice president of the U.S. Confederacy, proudly declared that "our new government is the first, in the history of the world" to be founded upon the "great physical, philosophical, and moral truth" that "the negro is not equal to the white man; that slavery—subordination to the superior race—is his natural and normal condition."[33] Barry Goldwater said simply, "Our future, like our past, will be what we make it."[34]

From revolutions, conservatives also develop a taste and talent for the masses, mobilizing the street for spectacular displays of power while making certain power is never truly shared or redistributed. That is the task of right-wing populism: to appeal to the mass without disrupting the power of elites or, more precisely, to harness the energy of the mass in order to reinforce or restore the power of elites. Far from being a recent innovation of the Christian Right or the Tea Party movement, reactionary populism runs like a red thread throughout conservative discourse from the very beginning.

Maistre was a pioneer in the theater of mass power, imagining scenes and staging dramas in which the lowest of the low could see themselves reflected in the highest of the high. "Monarchy," he writes, "is without contradiction, the form of government that gives the most distinction to the greatest number of persons." Ordinary people "share" in its "brilliance" and glow, though not, Maistre is careful to add, in its decisions and deliberations: "man is honored not as an agent but as a portion of sovereignty."[35] Archmonarchist that he was, Maistre understood that the king could never return to power if he did not have a touch of the plebeian about him. So when Maistre imagines the triumph of the counterrevolution, he takes care to emphasize the populist credentials of the returning monarch. The people should identify with this new king, says Maistre, because like them he has attended the "terrible school of misfortune" and suffered in the "hard school of adversity." He is "human," with humanness here connoting an almost pedestrian, and reassuring, capacity for error. He will be like them. Unlike his predecessors, he will know it, which "is a great deal."[36]

But to appreciate fully the inventiveness of right-wing populism, we have to turn to the master class of the Old South. The slaveholder created a quintessential form of democratic feudalism, turning the white majority into a lordly class, sharing in the privileges and prerogatives of governing the slave class. Though the members of this ruling class knew that they were not equal to each other, they were compensated by the illusion of superiority—and the reality of rule—over the black population beneath them.

One school of thought—call it the equal opportunity school—located the democratic promise of slavery in the fact that it put the possibility of personal mastery within the reach of every white man. The genius of the slaveholders, wrote Daniel Hundley in his *Social Relations in Our Southern States*, is that they are "not an exclusive aristocracy. Every free white man in the whole Union has just as much right to become an Oligarch." This was not just propaganda: by 1860, there were 400,000 slaveholders in the South, making the American master class one of the most democratic in the world. The slaveholders repeatedly attempted to pass laws encouraging whites to own at least one slave and even considered granting tax breaks to facilitate such ownership. Their thinking, in the words of one Tennessee farmer, was that "the minute you put it out of the power of common farmers to purchase a Negro man or woman . . . you make him an abolitionist at once."[37]

That school of thought contended with a second, arguably more influential, school. American slavery was not democratic, according to this line of thinking, because it offered the opportunity for personal mastery to white men: American slavery was democratic because it made every white man, slaveholder or not, a member of the ruling class by virtue of the color of his skin. In the words of Calhoun: "With us the two great divisions of society are not the rich and poor, but white and black; and all the former, the poor as well as the rich, belong to the upper class, and are respected and treated as equals."[38] Or as his junior colleague James Henry Hammond put it, "In a slave country every freeman is an aristocrat."[39] Even without slaves or the material prerequisites for freedom, a poor white man could style himself a member of the nobility and thus be relied upon to take the necessary measures in its defense.

Whether one subscribed to the first or second school of thought, the master class believed that democratic feudalism was a potent counter to the egalitarian movements then roiling Europe and Jacksonian America. European radicals, declared Dew, "wish all mankind to be brought to one common level. We believe slavery, in the United States, has accomplished this." By freeing whites from "menial and low offices," slavery had eliminated "the greatest cause of distinction and separation of the ranks of society."[40] As the nineteenth-century ruling classes contended with challenge after challenge to their power, the master class offered up racial domination as a way of harnessing the energy of the white masses, in support of, rather than in opposition to, the privileges and powers of established elites. This program would find its ultimate fulfillment a century later and a continent away.

These populist currents can help us make sense of a final element of conservatism. From the beginning, conservatism has appealed to and relied upon outsiders. Maistre was from Savoy, Burke from Ireland. Alexander Hamilton was born out of wedlock in Nevis and rumored to be part black. Disraeli was a Jew, as are many of the neoconservatives who helped transform the Republican Party from a cocktail party in Darien into the party of Scalia, d'Souza, Gonzalez, and Yoo. (It was Irving Kristol who first identified "the historical task and political purpose of neoconservatism" as the conversion of "the Republican Party, and American conservatism in general, against their respective wills, into a new kind of conservative politics suitable to governing a modern democracy.")[41] Allan Bloom was a Jew and a homosexual. And as she never tired of reminding us during the 2008 campaign, Sarah Palin is a woman in a world of men, an Alaskan who said no to Washington (though she really didn't), a maverick who rode shotgun to another maverick.

Conservatism has not only depended upon outsiders; it also has seen itself as the voice of the outsider. From Burke's cry that "the gallery is in the place of the house" to Buckley's complaint that the modern conservative is "out of place," the conservative has served as a tribune for the displaced, his movement a conveyance of their grievances.[42] Far from being an invention of the politically correct, victimhood has been a talking point of the right ever since Burke decried the mob's treatment of Marie Antoinette. The conservative, to be sure, speaks for a special type of victim: one who has lost something of value, as opposed to the wretched of the earth, whose chief complaint is that they never had anything to lose. His constituency is the contingently dispossessed—William Graham Sumner's "forgotten man"—rather than the preternaturally oppressed. Far from diminishing his appeal, this brand of victimhood endows the conservative complaint with a more universal significance. It connects his disinheritance to an experience we all share—namely, loss—and threads the strands of that experience into an ideology promising that that loss, or at least some portion of it, can be made whole.

People on the left often fail to realize this, but conservatism really does speak to and for people who have lost something. It may be a landed estate or the privileges of white skin, the unquestioned authority of a husband or the untrammeled rights of a factory owner. The loss may be as material as money or as ethereal as a sense of standing. It may be a loss of something that was never legitimately owned in the first place; it may, when compared with what the conservative retains, be small. Even so, it is a loss, and nothing is ever so cherished as that which we no longer possess. It used to be one of the great virtues of the left that it alone understood the often zero-sum nature of politics, where the gains of one class necessarily entail the losses of another. But as that sense of conflict diminishes on the left, it has fallen to the right to remind voters that there really are losers in politics and that it is they—and only they—who speak for them. "All conservatism begins with loss," Andrew Sullivan rightly notes, which makes conservatism not the Party of Order, as Mill and others have claimed, but the party of the loser.[43]

The chief aim of the loser is not—and indeed cannot be—preservation or protection. It is recovery and restoration. That, I believe, is one of the secrets of conservatism's success. For all of its demotic frisson and ideological grandiosity, for all of its insistence upon triumph and will, movement and mobilization, conservatism can be an ultimately pedestrian affair. Because his losses are recent—the right agitates against reform in real time, not millennia after the fact—the conservative can credibly claim to his constituency, indeed to the polity at large, that his goals are practical and achievable. He merely seeks to regain what is his, and the fact that he once had it—indeed, probably had it for some time—suggests that he is capable of possessing it again. "It is not an old structure," Burke declared of Jacobin France, but "a recent wrong."[44] Where the left's program of redistribution raises the question of whether its beneficiaries are truly prepared to wield the powers they seek, the conservative project of restoration suffers from no such challenge. Unlike the reformer or the revolutionary, moreover, who faces the nearly impossible task of empowering the powerless—that is, of turning people from what they are into what they are not—the conservative merely asks his followers to do more of what they always have done (albeit, better and differently). As a result, his counterrevolution will not require the same disruption that the revolution has visited upon the country. "Four or five persons, perhaps," writes Maistre, "will give France a king."[45]

For some, perhaps many, in the conservative movement, this knowledge comes as a source of relief: their sacrifice will be small, their reward great. For others, it is a source of bitter disappointment. To this subset of activists and militants, the battle is all. To learn that it soon will be over and will not require so much from them is enough to prompt a complex of despair: disgust over the shabbiness of their effort, grief over the disappearance of their foe, anxiety over the early retirement into which they have been forced. As Irving Kristol complained after the end of the Cold War, the defeat of the Soviet Union and the left more generally "deprived" conservatives like himself "of an enemy," and "in politics, being deprived of an enemy is a very serious matter. You tend to get relaxed and dispirited. Turn inward."[46] Depression haunts conservatism as surely as does great wealth. But again, far from diminishing the appeal of conservatism, this darker dimension only enhances it. Onstage, the conservative waxes Byronic, moodily surveying the sum of his losses before an audience of the lovelorn and the starstruck. Offstage, and out of sight, his managers quietly compile the sum of their gains.

2

The First Counterrevolutionary

Revolution sent Thomas Hobbes into exile; counterrevolution sent him back. In 1640, parliamentary opponents of Charles I, such as John Pym, were denouncing anyone "preaching for absolute monarchy that the king may do what he list." Hobbes had recently finished writing *The Elements of Law*, which did just that. After the king's top adviser and a theologian arguing for unlimited royal power were both arrested, Hobbes decided it was time to go. Not waiting for his bags to be packed, he fled England for France.[1]

Eleven years and a civil war later, Hobbes fled France for England. This time, he was running from the royalists. As before, Hobbes had just finished a book. *Leviathan,* he would later explain, "fights on behalf of all kings and all those who under whatever name bear the rights of kings."[2] It was the second half of that claim, with its seeming indifference about the identity of the sovereign, that was now getting him into trouble. *Leviathan* justified, no, demanded, that men submit to any person or persons capable of protecting them from foreign attack and civil unrest. With the monarchy abolished and Oliver Cromwell's forces in control of

This chapter originally appeared as a review of Quentin Skinner's *Hobbes and Republican Liberty* (New York: Cambridge University Press, 2008) in *The Nation* (October 19, 2009): 25–32.

England and providing for the people's safety, *Leviathan* seemed to suggest that everyone, including the defeated royalists, profess their allegiance to the Commonwealth. Versions of that argument had already gotten Anthony Ascham, ambassador for the Commonwealth, assassinated by royalist exiles in Spain. So when Hobbes learned that clergymen in France were trying to arrest him—*Leviathan* was also vehemently anti-Catholic, which offended the Queen Mother—he slipped out of Paris and made his way back to London.[3]

It's no accident that Hobbes fled his enemies and then his friends, for he was fashioning a political theory that shredded long-standing alliances. Rather than reject the revolutionary argument, he absorbed and transformed it. From its deepest categories and idioms he derived an uncompromising defense of the most hide-bound form of rule. He sensed the centrifugal forces of early modern Europe—the priesthood of all believers; the democratic armies massing under the banner of ancient republican ideals; science and skepticism—and sought to channel them to a single center: a sovereign so terrible and benign as to make any challenge to such authority seem immoral and irrational. Not unlike the Italian Futurists, Hobbes put dissolution in the service of resolution. He was the first and, along with Nietzsche, the greatest philosopher of counterrevolution, a blender avant la lettre of cultural modernism and political reaction who understood that to defeat a revolution, you must become the revolution.

And how has he been treated by the right? Not well. T. S. Eliot (an adroit blender himself) called Hobbes "one of those extraordinary little upstarts whom the chaotic motions of the Renaissance tossed into an eminence which they hardly deserved."[4] Of the four twentieth-century political theorists identified by Perry Anderson as "The Intransigent Right"[5]—Leo Strauss, Carl Schmitt, Michael Oakeshott, and Friedrich Hayek—only Oakeshott saw in Hobbes a kindred spirit.[6] The rest viewed him as the source of a malignant liberalism, Jacobinism, or even Bolshevism.[7]

Orthodox custodians of the old regime often mistake the counterrevolutionary for the opposition because they can't follow the alchemy of his argument. All they sense is what's there—a newfangled way of thinking that sounds dangerously like the revolutionary's—and what's not there: the traditional justification for authority. To the orthodox, the counterrevolutionary looks like a revolutionary. That makes the counterrevolutionary a suspect, in their eyes, not a comrade. In this they are not entirely wrong. Neither left nor, conventionally speaking, right—one of Hayek's most famous pieces of writing is called "Why I Am Not a Conservative"[8]—the counterrevolutionary is a pastiche of incongruities, high and low, old and new, irony and faith. The counterrevolutionary attempts nothing less than to square the circle, making prerogative popular and remaking a regime that claims never to have been made in the first place (the old regime was, is, and will be; it is not made). These are tasks no other political movement must undertake. The counterrevolutionary is not disposed to paradox; he's simply forced to straddle historical contradictions, for power's sake.

But why even bring Hobbes before the bar of conservatism, the right, and counterrevolution? After all, none of these terms came into circulation until the French Revolution or later, and most historians no longer believe the English Civil War was a revolution. The forces that overthrew the monarchy may have been looking for the Roman Republic or the ancient constitution. They may have wanted a reformation of religious manners or limitations on royal power. But a revolution lay nowhere in their sights. How could Hobbes have been a counterrevolutionary if there was no revolution for him to oppose?

Hobbes, for one, thought otherwise. In *Behemoth*, his most considered treatment of the issue, he firmly declared the English Civil

War a revolution.[9] And though he meant by that term something like what the ancients meant—a cyclical process of regime change, more akin to the orbit of the planets than a great leap forward— Hobbes saw in the overthrow of the monarchy a zealous (and, to his mind, toxic) yearning for democracy, a firm desire to redistribute power to a greater number of men. That, for Hobbes, was the essence of the revolutionary challenge; and so it has remained ever since—whether in Russia in 1917, Flint in 1937, or Selma in 1965. That this democratic expansion was inspired by visions of the past rather than the future need not detain us any more than it did Hobbes—or Benjamin Constant or Karl Marx, for that matter, both of whom saw how easy it was for the French to make their revolution while (or even by) looking backward.[10]

Hobbes clearly opposed the "democraticals," as he called the parliamentary forces and their followers.[11] A considerable sum of his philosophical energy was expended in this opposition, and his greatest innovations derived from it.[12] His specific target was the republicans' conception of liberty, their notion that individual freedom entailed men collectively governing themselves. Hobbes unfastened the republican links between personal freedom and the possession of political power. He thus was able to argue that men could be free in an absolute monarchy—or at least no less free than they were in a republic or a democracy. It was "an epoch-making moment in the history of Anglophone political thought," says Quentin Skinner. The result was a novel account of liberty to which we remain indebted to this day.[13]

Every counterrevolutionary faces the same question: how to defend an old regime that has been or is being destroyed? The first impulse—to reiterate the regime's ancient truths—is usually the worst, for it is often those truths that got the regime into trouble in the first place. Either the world has so changed that they no longer command assent, or they have grown so pliable that they mutate into arguments for revolution. Either way, the counterrevolutionary must look elsewhere for materials from which to fashion his defense of the old regime. This need can put him at odds, as Hobbes came to realize, not only with the revolution, but also with the very regime he claims as his cause.

The monarchy's defenders in the first half of the seventeenth century offered two types of arguments, neither of which Hobbes could endorse. The first was the divine right of kings. Itself a recent innovation—James I, Charles's father, was the major exponent in Britain—it held that the king was God's agent on earth (indeed, was rather like God on earth), that he was accountable only to God, and that he alone was authorized to govern and should not be restrained by the law, institutions, or the people. As Charles's adviser allegedly put it, "the king's little finger should be thicker than the loins of the law."[14]

While such absolutism appealed to Hobbes, the foundation of the theory was shaky. Most divine right theorists presumed what Hobbes and his contemporaries, particularly on the continent, believed no longer to exist: a teleology of human ends that mirrored the natural hierarchy of the universe and produced unassailable definitions of good and evil, just and unjust. After a century of bloodshed over the meaning of those terms and skepticism about the existence of a natural order or our ability to know it, defenses of divine right seemed neither credible nor reliable. With their dubious premises, they were just as likely to spark conflict as to settle it.

Arguably more troubling was that the theory depicted a political theater in which there were only two actors of any consequence: God and king, each performing for the other. Though Hobbes believed the sovereign should never share the stage with anyone, he was too attuned to the democratic distemper of his times not to notice that the theory neglected a third actor: the people. That was all well and good when the people were quiet and deferential, but during the 1640s a closet drama between God and the king was no longer viable. The people were onstage, demanding a leading role; they could not be ignored or given a bit part.

Changes in England, in short, had rendered divine right untenable. The challenge Hobbes faced was intricate: how to preserve the thrust of the theory (unquestioning submission to absolute, undivided power) while ditching its anachronistic premises. With his theory of consent, in which individuals contract with one another to create a sovereign with absolute power over them, and his theory of representation, in which the people are impersonated by the sovereign without his being obliged to them, Hobbes found his solution.

The theory of consent made no assumptions about the definition of good and evil, nor did it rely upon a natural hierarchy inherent in the universe, whose meaning must be apparent to all. To the contrary, the theory of consent presumed that men disagreed about such things; indeed, that they disagreed so violently that the only way they could pursue their conflicting goals and survive was to cede all of their power to the state and submit to it without protest or challenge. Protecting men from one another, the state guaranteed them the space and security to get on with their lives. When combined with Hobbes's account of representation, the theory of consent had an added advantage: though it gave all power to the sovereign, the people could still imagine themselves in his body, in every swing of his sword. The people created him; he represented them; to all intents and purposes, they were him. Except that they weren't: the people may have been the authors of Leviathan—Hobbes's infamous name for the sovereign, derived from the Book of Job—but like any author they had no control over their creation. It was an inspired move, characteristic of all great counterrevolutionary theories, in which the people become actors without roles, an audience that believes it is onstage.

The second argument offered in favor of the monarchy, the constitutional royalist position, had deeper roots in English thought and was therefore more difficult to counter. It held that England was a free society because royal power was limited by the common law or shared with Parliament. That combination of the rule of law and shared sovereignty, claimed Sir Walter Raleigh, was what distinguished the free subjects of the king from the benighted slaves of despots in the East.[15] It was this argument and its radical offshoots that quickened Hobbes's most profound and daring reflections about liberty.[16]

Beneath the constitutionalist conception of political liberty lay a distinction between acting for the sake of reason and acting at the behest of passion. The first is a free act; the second is not. "To act out of passion," writes Skinner in his account of the argument Hobbes arrayed himself against, "is not to act as a free man, or even distinctively as a man at all; such actions are not an expression of true liberty but of mere licence or animal brutishness." Freedom entails acting upon what we have willed; but will should not be confused with appetite or aversion. As Bishop Bramhall, Hobbes's great antagonist, put it: "A free act is only that which proceeds from the free election of the rational will." And "where there is no consideration nor use of reason, there is no liberty at all."[17] Being free entails acting in accordance with reason or, in political terms, living under laws as opposed to arbitrary power.

Like the divine right of kings, the constitutional argument had been rendered anachronistic by recent developments, most notably the fact that no English monarch in the first half of the seventeenth century claimed to believe it. Intent on turning England into a modern state, James and Charles were compelled to advance far more absolutist claims about the nature of their power than the constitutional argument allowed.

More troubling for the regime, however, was how easily the constitutional argument could be turned into a republican one and used against the king. Common lawyers and parliamentary supplicants argued that by flouting the common law and Parliament, Charles was threatening to turn England into a tyranny; radicals insisted that anything short of a republic or democracy, where men lived under laws to which they had consented, constituted a tyranny. All monarchy, in the eyes of the radicals, was despotism.

Hobbes thought that the latter argument derived from the "Histories, and Philosophy of the Antient Greeks, and Romans," which were so influential among educated opponents of the king.[18] That ancient heritage was given new life by Machiavelli's *Discorsi*, translated into English in 1636, which may have been Hobbes's ultimate target in his admonition against popular government. But the underlying premise of the republican argument—that what distinguishes a free man from a slave is that the former is subject to his own will while the latter is subject to the will of another—could also be found in English common law, as Skinner points out, in a "word-for-word" reproduction of "the *Digest* of Roman law," as early as the thirteenth century. Likewise, the distinction between will and appetite, liberty and license, was "deeply embedded" in both the scholastic traditions of the Middle Ages and the humanist culture of the Renaissance. This philosophy of will thus found expression not only in the royalist positions of Bramhall and his ilk, but also among the radicals and regicides who overthrew the king. Beneath the chasm separating royalist and republican lay a deep and volatile bedrock of shared assumption about the nature of liberty.[19] Hobbes's genius was to recognize that assumption; his ambition was to crush it.

While the notion that freedom entails living under laws lent support to the constitutional royalists (who made much of the distinction between lawful monarchs and despotic tyrants) it did not necessarily lead to the conclusion that a free regime had to be a republic or a democracy. To advance that argument, the radicals had to make two additional claims: first, to equate arbitrariness or lawlessness with a will that is not one's own, a will that is external or alien, like the passions; and second, to equate the decisions of a popular government with a will that is one's own, like reason. To be subject to a will that is mine—the laws of a republic or democracy—is to be free; to be subject to a will that is not mine—the edicts of a king or foreign country—is to be a slave.

In making these claims, Skinner argues, the radicals were aided by a peculiar, though popular, understanding of slavery. What made someone a slave, in the eyes of many, was not that he was in chains or that his owner impeded or compelled his movements. It was that he lived and moved under a net, the ever-changing, arbitrary will of his master, that might fall upon him at any moment. Even if that net never fell—the master never told him what to do or never punished him for not doing it, or he never desired to do something different from what the master told him—the slave was still enslaved. The fact that he "lived in total dependence" on the will of another, that he was under the master's jurisdiction, "was sufficient in itself to guarantee the servility" that the master "expected and despised."[20]

> The mere presence of relations of domination and dependence . . . is held to reduce us from the status of . . . "free-men" to that of slaves. It is not sufficient, in other words, to enjoy our civic rights and liberties as a matter of fact; if we are to count as free-men, it is necessary to enjoy them in a particular way. We must never hold them merely by the grace or goodwill of

anyone else; we must always hold them independently of anyone's arbitrary power to take them away from us.[21]

At the individual level, freedom means being one's own master; at the political level, it requires a republic or democracy. Only a full share in public power will ensure we enjoy our freedom in the "particular way" freedom requires; without full political participation, freedom will be fatally abridged. It is this double movement between the personal and the political that is arguably the most radical element of the theory of popular government and, from Hobbes's view, the most dangerous.

Hobbes sets about destroying the argument from the ground up. Breaking with traditional understandings, he argues for a materialist account of the will. The will, he says, is not a decision resulting from our reasoned deliberation about our desires and aversions; it is simply the last appetite or aversion we feel before we act, which then prompts the act. Deliberation is like the oscillating rod of a metronome—back and forth our inclinations go, alternating between appetite and aversion—but less steady. Wherever the rod comes to rest, and produces an action or, conversely, no action at all, turns out to be our will. If this conception seems arbitrary and mechanistic, it should: the will does not stand above our appetites and aversions, judging and choosing between them; the will is our appetites and aversions. There is no such thing as a free or autonomous will; there is only "the last Appetite, or Aversion, immediately adhaering to the action, or to the omission thereof."[22]

Imagine a man with the keenest appetite for wine, racing into a building on fire in order to rescue a case of it; now imagine a man with the fiercest aversion to dogs, racing into that same building to escape a pack of them. Hobbes's opponents would see in these examples the force of irrational compulsion; Hobbes sees the will in action. These may not be the wisest or sanest acts, Hobbes allows, but wisdom and sanity need not play any part in volition. Both acts may be compelled, but so are the actions of a man on a listing vessel who throws his bags overboard in order to lighten the load and save himself. Hard choices, actions taken under duress— these are as much expressions of my will as the decisions I make in the calm of my study. Extending the analogy, Hobbes would argue that the surrender of my wallet to someone holding a gun to my head is also a willed act: I have chosen my life over my wallet.

Against his opponents, Hobbes suggests that there can be no such thing as voluntarily acting against one's will; all voluntary action is an expression of the will. External constraints like being locked in a room can prevent me from acting upon my will; being on a chain gang can force me to act in ways I have not willed (when my neighbor takes a step forward or lifts his tool, I must follow him, unless I have sufficient physical force to resist him and the fellow behind me). But I cannot act voluntarily against my will. In the case of the mugger, Hobbes would say that his gun changed my will: I went from wanting to safeguard the money in my wallet to wanting to protect my life.

If I can't act voluntarily against my will, I can't act voluntarily in accordance with a will that is not my own. If I obey a king because I fear that he will kill or imprison me, that does not signify the absence, forfeiture, betrayal, or subjection of my will; it is my will. I could have willed otherwise—hundreds of thousands during Hobbes's lifetime did—but my survival or liberty was more important to me than whatever it was that may have called for my disobedience.

Hobbes's definition of freedom follows from his understanding of the will. Liberty, he says, is "the absence of . . . externall Impediments of motion," and a free man *"is he, that in those things, which by his strength and wit he is able to do, is not hindred to doe what he has a will to."*[23] I can be rendered un-free, Hobbes insists, only by external obstacles to my movement. Chains and walls are such obstacles; laws and obligations are another, albeit a more metaphorical, sort. If the obstacle lies within me—I don't have the ability to do something; I am too afraid to do it—I lack power or will, not freedom. Hobbes, in a letter to the earl of Newcastle, attributes these deficiencies to "the nature and intrinsical quality of the agent," not the conditions of the agent's political environment.[24]

And that is the purpose of Hobbes's effort: to separate the status of our personal liberty from the state of public affairs. Freedom is dependent on the presence of government but not on the form government takes; whether we live under a king, a republic, or a democracy does not change the quantity or quality of the freedom we enjoy. The separation between personal and political liberty had the dramatic effect of making freedom seem both less present and more present under a king than Hobbes's republican and royalist antagonists had allowed.

On the one hand, Hobbes insists that there is no way to be free and subject at the same time. Submission to government entails an absolute loss of liberty: wherever I am bound by law, I am not free to move. When republicans argue that citizens are free because they make the laws, Hobbes claims, they are confusing sovereignty with liberty: what the citizen has is political power, not freedom. He is just as obliged (perhaps more obliged, Rousseau will later suggest) to submit to the law, and thus just as un-free, as he would be under a monarchy. And when the constitutional royalists argue that the king's subjects are free because the king's power is limited by the law, Hobbes claims that they are just confused.

On the other hand, Hobbes thinks that if freedom is unimpeded motion, it stands to reason that we are a lot freer under a monarch, even an absolute monarch, than the royalist and the republican realize (or care to admit).[25] First and most simply, even when we act out of fear, we are acting freely. "Feare, and Liberty are consistent," says Hobbes, because fear expresses our negative inclinations; these inclinations may be negative, but that doesn't negate the fact that they are *our* inclinations. So long as we are not impeded from acting upon them, we are free. Even when we are most terrified of the King's punishments, we are free: "all actions which men doe in Common-wealths, for *feare* of the law, are actions, which the doers had *liberty* to omit."[26]

More important, wherever the law is silent, neither commanding nor prohibiting, we are free. One need only contemplate all the "ways a man may move himself," Hobbes says in *De Cive*, to see all the ways he can be free in a monarchy. These freedoms, Hobbes explains in *Leviathan*, include "the Liberty to buy, and sell, and otherwise contract with one another; to choose their own aboad, their own diet, their own trade of life, and institute their children as they themselves think fit; & the like."[27] To whatever degree the sovereign can guarantee the freedom of movement, the ability to go about our business without the hindrance of other men, we are free. Submission to his power, in other words, augments our freedom. The more absolute our submission, the more powerful he is and the freer we are. Subjugation is emancipation.

Despite the disclaimers of the "Intransigent Right," the Hobbesian argument continues to haunt modern conservatism. Hobbes's idea of private liberty pervades libertarian discourse, while *Leviathan* casts a long shadow over the conservative ideal of a night watchman state—where the government's primary purpose is to protect the citizenry from foreign attack and criminal trespass; where people are free to go about their business so long as they do not interfere with the movements of others; and where contracts are enforced and security is ensured.

Libertarians will blanch at that association: whatever resonance Hobbesian ideas may find in their writings, the Hobbesian state is a good deal more repressive than any government a libertarian would ever countenance. Except for the fact that it's not. Milton Friedman famously met with the Chilean dictator Augusto Pinochet in 1975 to advise him on economic matters; Friedman's Chicago Boys worked even more closely with Pinochet's junta. Sergio de Castro, Pinochet's finance minister, made the observation, reminiscent of Hobbes, that "a person's actual freedom can only be ensured through an authoritarian regime that exercises power by implementing equal rules for everyone." Hayek admired Pinochet's Chile so much that he decided to hold a meeting of his Mont Pelerin Society in Viña del Mar, the seaside resort where the coup against Allende was planned. In 1978 he wrote to the *London Times* that he had "not been able to find a single person even in much maligned Chile who did not agree that personal freedom was much greater under Pinochet than it had been under Allende."[28]

"Despite my sharp disagreement with the authoritarian political system of Chile," Friedman would later claim, "I do not regard it as evil for an economist to render technical economic advice to the Chilean Government."[29] The marriage between free markets and state terror cannot be annulled so easily. As Hobbes understood, it takes an enormous amount of repression to create the type of men who can exercise their "Liberty to buy, and sell, and otherwise contract with one another" without getting stroppy.[30] They must be free to move—or choose—but not so free as to think about redesigning the highway. Assuming an all-too-easy congruence between capitalism and democracy, the libertarian overlooks just how much coercion is required to make citizens who will use their freedom responsibly and accept distress without turning to the state for relief.

It took Margaret Thatcher, of all people, to explain this fact to the libertarian right. When pressed by Hayek to impose Pinochet's brand of shock therapy in Britain, Thatcher responded, "I am sure you will agree that, in Britain with our democratic institutions and the need for a high degree of consent, some of the measures adopted in Chile are quite unacceptable." It was 1982, and British democracy being what it was, Thatcher had to go slow. But then came the Falklands War and the miners' strike. Once Thatcher realized that she could do to the miners and the trade unions what she had done to President Galtieri and his Argentine generals—"We had to fight the enemy without in the Falklands and now we have to fight the enemy within, which is much more difficult but just as dangerous to liberty"—the stage was set for the full Hayekian monty.[31]

3

Garbage and Gravitas

Saint Petersburg in revolt gave us Vladimir Nabokov, Isaiah Berlin, and Ayn Rand. The first was a novelist, the second a philosopher. The third was neither but thought she was both. Many other people have thought so too. In 1998 readers responding to a Modern Library poll identified *Atlas Shrugged* and *The Fountainhead* as the two greatest novels in English of the twentieth century—surpassing *Ulysses*, *To the Lighthouse*, and *Invisible Man*. In 1991 a survey by the Library of Congress and the Book-of-the-Month Club found that with the exception of the Bible, no book has influenced more American readers than *Atlas Shrugged*.[1]

One of those readers might well have been Farrah Fawcett. Not long before she died, the actress called Rand a "literary genius" whose refusal to make her art "like everyone else's" inspired Fawcett's own experiments in painting and sculpture. The admiration, it seems, was mutual. Rand watched *Charlie's Angels* each week and, according to Fawcett, "saw something" in the show "that the critics didn't."

This chapter originally appeared as a review of Anne C. Heller's *Ayn Rand and the World She Made* (New York: Knopf, 2009) and Jennifer Burns's *Goddess of the Market: Ayn Rand and the American Right* (New York: Oxford University Press, 2009) in *The Nation* (June 7, 2010): 21–27.

She described the show as a "triumph of concept and casting." Ayn said that while *Angels* was uniquely American, it was also the exception to American television in that it was the only show to capture true "romanticism"—it intentionally depicted the world not as it was, but as it should be. Aaron Spelling was probably the only other person to see *Angels* that way, although he referred to it as "comfort television."

So taken was Rand with Fawcett that she hoped the actress (or if not her, Raquel Welch) would play the part of Dagny Taggart in a TV version of *Atlas Shrugged* on NBC. Unfortunately, network head Fred Silverman killed the project in 1978. "I'll always think of 'Dagny Taggart' as the best role I was supposed to play but never did," Fawcett said.[2]

Rand's following in Hollywood has always been strong. Barbara Stanwyck and Veronica Lake fought to play the part of Dominique Francon in the movie version of *The Fountainhead*. Never to be out-done in that department, Joan Crawford threw a dinner party for Rand in which she dressed as Francon, wearing a streaming white gown dotted with aquamarine gemstones.[3] More recently, the author of *The Virtue of Selfishness* and the statement "if civilization is to sur-vive, it is the altruist morality that men have to reject" has found an unlikely pair of fans in the Hollywood humanitarian set.[4] Rand "has a very interesting philosophy," says Angelina Jolie. "You re-evaluate your own life and what's important to you." *The Fountainhead* "is so dense and complex," marvels Brad Pitt, "it would have to be a six-hour movie." (The 1949 film version has a running time of 113 mi-nutes, and it feels long.) Christina Ricci claims that *The Fountainhead* is her favorite book because it taught her that "you're not a bad per-son if you don't love everyone." Rob Lowe boasts that *Atlas Shrugged* is "a stupendous achievement, and I just adore it." And any boyfriend of Eva Mendes, the actress says, "has to be an Ayn Rand fan."[5]

But Rand, at least according to her fiction, shouldn't have attracted any fans at all. The central plot device of her novels is the conflict between the creative individual and the hostile mass. The greater the individual's achievement, the greater the mass's resistance. As Howard Roark, architect hero of *The Fountainhead*, puts it:

> The great creators—the thinkers, the artists, the scientists, the inventors—stood alone against the men of their time. Every great new thought was opposed. Every great new invention was denounced. The first motor was considered foolish. The airplane was considered impossible. The power loom was considered vicious. Anesthesia was considered sinful. But the men of unborrowed vision went ahead. They fought, they suffered and they paid.[6]

Rand clearly thought of herself as one of these creators. In an interview with Mike Wallace she declared herself "the most creative thinker alive." That was in 1957, when Arendt, Quine, Sartre, Camus, Lukács, Adorno, Murdoch, Heidegger, Beauvoir, Rawls, Anscombe, and Popper were all at work. It was also the year of the first performance of *Endgame* and the publication of *Pnin*, *Doctor Zhivago*, and *The Cat in the Hat*. Two years later, Rand told Wallace that "the only philosopher who ever influenced me" was Aristotle. Otherwise, everything came "out of my own mind." She boasted to her friends and to her publisher at Random House, Bennett Cerf, that she was "challenging the cultural tradition of two and a half thousand years." She saw herself as she saw Roark, who said, "I inherit nothing. I stand at the end of no tradition. I may, perhaps, stand at the beginning of one." Yet tens of thousands of fans were already standing with her. In 1945, just two years after its publication, *The Fountainhead* sold 100,000 copies. In 1957, the year *Atlas Shrugged* was published, it sat on the *New York Times* bestseller list for twenty-one weeks.[7]

Rand may have been uneasy about the challenge her popularity posed to her worldview, for she spent much of her later life spinning tales about the chilly response she and her work had received. She falsely claimed that twelve publishers rejected *The Fountainhead* before it found a home. She styled herself the victim of a terrible but necessary isolation, claiming that "all achievement and progress has been accomplished, not just by men of ability and certainly not by groups of men, but by a struggle between man and mob." But how many lonely writers emerge from their study, having just written "The End" on the last page of their novel, to be greeted by a chorus of congratulations from a waiting circle of fans?[8]

Had she been a more careful reader of her work, Rand might have seen this irony coming. However much she liked to pit the genius against the mass, her fiction always betrayed a secret communion between the two. Each of her two most famous novels gives its estranged hero an opportunity to defend himself in a lengthy speech before the untutored and the unlettered. Roark declaims before a jury of "the hardest faces" that includes "a truck driver, a bricklayer, an electrician, a gardener and three factory workers." John Galt takes to the airwaves in *Atlas Shrugged*, addressing millions of listeners for hours on end. In each instance, the hero is understood, his genius acclaimed, his alienation resolved. And that's because, as Galt explains, there are "no conflicts of interest among rational men"—which is just a Randian way of saying that every story has a happy ending.[9]

The chief conflict in Rand's novels, then, is not between the individual and the masses. It is between the demigod-creator and all those unproductive elements of society—the intellectuals, bureaucrats, and middlemen—that stand between him and the masses. Aesthetically, this makes for kitsch; politically, it bends toward fascism. Admittedly, the argument that there is a connection between fascism and kitsch has taken a beating over the years.

Yet surely the example of Rand is suggestive enough to put the question of that connection back on the table.

She was born on February 2, three weeks after the failed revolution of 1905. Her parents were Jewish. They lived in Saint Petersburg, a city long governed by hatred of the Jews. By 1914, its register of antisemitic restrictions ran to nearly 1,000 pages, including one statute limiting Jews to no more than 2 percent of the population. They named her Alissa Zinovievna Rosenbaum.[10]

When she was four or five years old she asked her mother if she could have a blouse like the one her cousins wore. Her mother said no. She asked for a cup of tea like the one being served to the grown-ups. Again her mother said no. She wondered why she couldn't have what she wanted. Someday, she vowed, she would. In later life, Rand would make much of this experience. Her biographer does too: "The elaborate and controversial philosophical system she went on to create in her forties and fifties was, at its heart, an answer to this question."[11]

The story, as told, is pure Rand. There's the focus on a single incident as portent or precipitant of dramatic fate. There's the elevation of a childhood commonplace to grand philosophy. What child, after all, hasn't bridled at being denied what she wants? Though Rand seems to have taken youthful selfishness to its outermost limits—as a child she disliked Robin Hood; as a teenager she watched her family nearly starve while she treated herself to the theater—her solipsism was neither so rare nor so precious as to warrant more than the usual amount of adolescent self-absorption.[12] There is, finally, the inadvertent revelation that one's worldview constitutes little more than a case of arrested development. "It is not that chewing gum undermines metaphysics," Max Horkheimer once wrote about mass culture, "but that it is metaphysics—this is what must be made clear."[13] Rand made it very, very clear.

But the anecdote suggests something additionally distinctive about Rand. Not her opinions or tastes, which were middlebrow and conventional. Rand claimed Victor Hugo as her primary inspiration in matters of fiction; Edmond Rostand's *Cyrano de Bergerac* was another touchstone. She deemed Rachmaninoff superior to Bach, Mozart, and Beethoven. She was offended by a reviewer's admittedly foolish comparison of *The Fountainhead* to *The Magic Mountain*. Mann, Rand thought, was the inferior author, as was Solzhenitsyn.[14]

Nor was it her sense of self that set Rand apart from others. True, she tended toward the cartoonish and the grandiose. She told Nathaniel Branden, her much younger lover and disciple of many years, that he should desire her even if she were eighty and in a wheelchair. Her essays often quote Galt's speeches as if the character were a real person, a philosopher on the order of Plato or Kant. She claimed to have created herself with the help of no one, even though she was the lifelong beneficiary of social democratic largesse. She got a college education thanks to the Russian Revolution, which opened universities to women and Jews and, once the Bolsheviks had seized power, made tuition free. Subsidizing theater for the masses, the Bolsheviks also made it possible for Rand to see cheesy operettas on a weekly basis. After Rand's first play closed in New York City in April 1936, the Works Progress Administration took it on the road to theaters across the country, giving Rand a handsome income of $10 a performance throughout the late 1930s. Librarians at the New York Public Library assisted her with the research for *The Fountainhead*.[15] Still, her narcissism was probably no greater—and certainly no less sustaining—than that of your run-of-the-mill struggling author.

No, what truly distinguished Rand was her ability to translate her sense of self into reality, to will her imagined identity into material fact. Not by being great, but by persuading others, even shrewd biographers, that she was great. Anne Heller, for example, author of *Ayn*

Rand and the World She Made, repeatedly praises Rand's "original, razor sharp mind" and "lightning-quick logic," making one wonder if she's read any of Rand's work. She claims that Rand was able "to write more persuasively from a male point of view than any female writer since George Eliot."[16] Does Heller really believe that Roark or Galt is more credible or persuasive than Lawrence Selden or Newland Archer? Or little James Ramsay, who seems to have acquired more psychic depth in his six years than any of Rand's protagonists, male or female, demonstrate throughout their entire lives? Jennifer Burns, an intellectual historian and author of *Goddess of the Market: Ayn Rand and the American Right*, writes that Rand was "among the first to identify the modern state's often terrifying power and to make it an issue of popular concern," which is true only if one sets aside Montesquieu, Godwin, Constant, Tocqueville, Proudhon, Bakunin, Spencer, Kropotkin, Malatesta, and Emma Goldman. She claims that Rand disliked the "messiness of the bohemian student protestors" of the sixties because she was "raised in the high European tradition." But what kind of high European tradition includes operettas and Rachmaninoff, melodrama and movies? She concludes that "what remains" of enduring value in Rand is her injunction to "be true to yourself." Yet it hardly took Rand to teach us that; indeed, the very same notion figures in a play about a Danish prince written roughly five centuries before Rand's birth.[17]

To understand how Alissa Rosenbaum created Ayn Rand, we need to trace her itinerary not to prerevolutionary Russia, which is the mistaken conceit of her biographers, but to her destination upon leaving Soviet Russia in 1926: Hollywood. For where else but in the dream factory could Rand have learned how to make dreams—about America, capitalism, and herself?

Even before she was in Hollywood, Rand was of Hollywood. In 1925 alone, she saw 117 movies. It was in movies, Burns says, that Rand "glimpsed America"—and, we might add, developed her enduring sense of narrative form. Once there, she became the subject of her very own Hollywood story. She was discovered by Cecil B. DeMille, who saw her mooning about his studio looking for work. Intrigued by her intense gaze, he gave her a ride in his car and a job as an extra, which she quickly turned into a screenwriting gig. Within a few years her scripts were attracting attention from major players, prompting one newspaper to run a story with the headline "RUSSIAN GIRL FINDS END OF RAINBOW IN HOLLYWOOD."[18]

Rand, of course, was not the only European who came to Hollywood during the interwar years. But unlike Fritz Lang, Hanns Eisler, and all the other exiles in paradise, Rand did not escape to Hollywood; she went there willingly, eagerly. Billy Wilder arrived and shrugged his shoulders; Rand came on bended knee. Her mission was to learn, not refine or improve, the art of the dream factory: how to turn a good yarn into a suspenseful plot, an ordinary person into an outsize hero (or villain)—all the tricks of melodramatic narrative designed to persuade millions of viewers that life is really lived at a fever pitch. Most important, she learned how to perform that alchemy upon herself. Ayan Rand was Norma Desmond in reverse: she was small; it was the pictures that got big.

When playing the part of the Philosopher, Rand liked to claim Aristotle as her tutor. "Never have so many"—uncharacteristically, she included herself here—"owed so much to one man."[19] It's not clear how much of Aristotle's work Rand actually read: when she wasn't quoting Galt, she had a habit of attributing to the Greek philosopher statements and ideas that don't appear in any of his writings. One alleged Aristotelianism Rand was fond of citing did appear, complete with false attribution, in the autobiography of Albert Jay Nock, an influential libertarian from the New Deal era. In Rand's copy of Nock's memoir, Burns observes in an endnote, the passage is marked "with six vertical lines."[20]

Rand also liked to cite Aristotle's law of identity or noncontradiction—the notion that everything is identical to itself, captured by the shorthand "A is A"—as the basis of her defense of selfishness, the free market, and the limited state. That particular transport sent Rand's admirers into rapture and drove her critics, even the friendliest, to distraction. Several months before his death in 2002, Harvard philosopher Robert Nozick, the most analytically sophisticated of twentieth-century libertarians, said that "the use that's made by people in the Randian tradition of this principle of logic . . . is completely unjustified so far as I can see; it's illegitimate."[21] In 1961 Sidney Hook wrote in the *New York Times*:

> Since his baptism in medieval times, Aristotle has served many strange purposes. None have been odder than this sacramental alliance, so to speak, of Aristotle with Adam Smith. The extraordinary virtues Miss Rand finds in the law that A is A suggests that she is unaware that logical principles by themselves can test only consistency. They cannot establish truth. . . . Swearing fidelity to Aristotle, Miss Rand claims to deduce not only matters of fact from logic but, with as little warrant, ethical rules and economic truths as well. As she understands them, the laws of logic license her in proclaiming that "existence exists," which is very much like saying that the law of gravitation is heavy and the formula of sugar sweet.[22]

Whether or not Rand read Aristotle, it's clear that he made little impression upon her, particularly when it came to ethics. Aristotle had a distinctive approach to morality, quite out of keeping with modern sensibilities; and while Rand had some awareness of its distinctiveness, its substance seems to have been lost on her. Like a set of faux-leather classics on the living room shelf, Aristotle was there to impress the company—and, in Rand's case, distract from the real business at hand.

Unlike Kant, the emblematic modern who claimed that the rightness of our deeds is determined solely by reason, unsullied by need, desire, or interest, Aristotle rooted his ethics in human nature, in the habits and practices, the dispositions and tendencies, that make us happy and enable our flourishing. And where Kant believed that morality consists of austere rules, imposing unconditional duties upon us and requiring our most strenuous sacrifice, Aristotle located the ethical life in the virtues. These are qualities or states, somewhere between reason and emotion but combining elements of both, that carry and convey us, by the gentlest and subtlest of means, to the outer hills of good conduct. Once there, we are inspired and equipped to scale these lower heights, whence we move onto the higher reaches. A person who acts virtuously develops a nature that wants and is able to act virtuously and that finds happiness in virtue. That coincidence of thought and feeling, reason and desire, is achieved over a lifetime of virtuous deeds. Virtue, in other words, is less a codex of rules, which must be observed in the face of the self's most violent opposition, than it is the food and fiber, the grease and gasoline, of a properly functioning soul.

If Kant is an athlete of the moral life, Aristotle is its virtuoso. Rand, by contrast, is a melodramatist of the moral life. Apprenticed in Hollywood rather than Athens, she has little patience for the quiet habituation in the virtues that Aristotelian ethics entails. She returns instead to her favored image of a heroic individual confronting a difficult path. Difficulty is never the result of confusion or ambiguity; Rand loathed "the cult of moral grayness," insisting that morality is first and always "a code of black and white."[23] What makes the path treacherous—not for the hero, who seems to have been born fully outfitted for it, but for the rest of us—are the obstacles along the way. Doing the right thing brings hardship, penury, and exile, while doing the wrong thing brings wealth, status, and acclaim. Because he refuses to submit to architectural conventions, Roark winds up splitting rocks in a quarry. Peter Keating, Roark's doppelgänger, betrays everyone, including himself, and is the toast of the town. Ultimately, of course, the distribution of rewards and punishments will reverse: Roark is happy, Keating miserable. But ultimately is always and inevitably a long way off.

In her essays, Rand seeks to apply to this imagery a superficial Aristotelian gloss. She, too, roots her ethics in human nature and refuses to draw a distinction between self-interest and the good, between ethical conduct and desire or need. But Rand's metric of good and evil, virtue and vice, is not happiness or flourishing. It is the stern and stark exigencies of life and death. As she writes in "The Objectivist Ethics":

> I quote from Galt's speech: "There is only one fundamental alternative in the universe: existence or nonexistence—and it pertains to a single class of entities: to living organisms. The existence of inanimate matter is unconditional, the existence of life is not: it depends on a specific course of action. Matter is indestructible, it changes its forms, but it cannot cease to exist. It is only a living organism that faces a constant alternative: the issue of life or death. Life is a process of self-sustaining and self-generated action. If an organism fails in that action, it dies; its chemical elements remain, but its life goes out of existence. It is only the concept of 'Life' that makes the concept of 'Value' possible. It is only to a living entity that things can be good or evil."[24]

Rand's defenders like to claim that what Rand has in mind by "life" is not simply biological preservation but the good life of Aristotle's great-souled man, what Rand characterizes as "the survival of man *qua* man."[25] And it's true that Rand isn't much taken with mere life or life for life's sake. That would be too pedestrian. But Rand's naturalism is far removed from Aristotle's. For him life is a fact for her it is a question, and that very question is what makes life, on its own, such an object and source of reflection.

What gives life value is the ever-present possibility that it might (and one day will) end. Rand never speaks of life as a given or ground. It is a conditional, a choice we must make, not once but again and again. Death casts a pall, lending our days an urgency and weight they otherwise would lack. It demands wakefulness, an alertness to the fatefulness of each and every moment. "One must never act like a zombie," Rand enjoins.[26] Death, in short, makes life dramatic. It makes our choices—not just the big ones but the little ones we make every day, every second—matter. In the Randian universe, it's high noon all the time. Far from being exhausting or enervating, such an existence, at least to Rand and her characters, is enlivening and exciting.

If this idea has any moral resonance, it will be heard not in the writings of Aristotle nor in the superficially similar existentialism of Sartre, but in the drill march of fascism. The notion of life as a struggle against and unto death, of every moment laden with destruction, every choice pregnant with destiny, every action weighed upon by annihilation, its lethal pressure generating moral meaning—these are the watchwords of the European night. In his Berlin Sportpalast speech of February 1943, Goebbels declared, "Whatever serves it and its struggle for existence is good and must be sustained and nurtured. Whatever is injurious to it and its struggle for existence is evil and must be removed and eliminated."[27] The "it" in question is the German nation, not the Randian individual. But if we strip the pronoun of its antecedent—and listen for the background hum of *Sein oder Nichtsein*, preservation versus elimination—the similarities between the moral syntax of Randianism and of fascism become clear. Goodness is measured by life, life is a struggle against death, and only our daily vigilance ensures that one does not prevail over the other.

Rand, no doubt, would object to the comparison. There is, after all, a difference between the individual and the collective. Rand thought the former an existential fundament, the latter—whether it took the form of a class, race, or nation—a moral monstrosity. And where Goebbels talked of violence and war, Rand spoke of commerce and trade, production and economy. But fascism is hardly hostile to the heroic individual. That individual, moreover, often finds his deepest calling in economic activity. Far from demonstrating a divergence from fascism, Rand's economic writings register its presence indelibly.

Here is Hitler speaking to a group of industrialists in Düsseldorf in 1932:

> You maintain, gentlemen, that the German economy must be constructed on the basis of private property. Now such a conception of private property can only be maintained in practice if it in some way appears to have a logical foundation. This conception must derive its ethical justification from the insight that this is what nature dictates.[28]

Rand, too, believes that capitalism is vulnerable to attack because it lacks "a philosophical base." If it is to survive, it must be rationally justified. We must "begin at the beginning," with nature itself. "In order to sustain its life, every living species has to follow a certain course of action required by its nature." Because reason is man's "means of survival," nature dictates that "men prosper or fail, survive or perish in proportion to the degree of their rationality." (Notice the slippage between success and failure and life and death.) Capitalism is the one system that acknowledges and incorporates this dictate of nature. "It is the basic, metaphysical fact of man's nature—the connection between his survival and his use of reason—that capitalism recognizes and protects."[29] Like Hitler, Rand finds in nature, in man's struggle for survival, a "logical foundation" for capitalism.

Far from privileging the collective over the individual or subsuming the latter under the former, Hitler believed that it was the "strength and power of individual personality" that determined the economic (and cultural) fate of the race and nation.[30] Here he is in 1933 addressing another group of industrialists:

> Everything positive, good and valuable that has been achieved in the world in the field of economics or culture is solely attributable to the importance of personality. . . . All the worldly goods we possess we owe to the struggle of the select few.[31]

And here is Rand in *Capitalism: The Unknown Ideal* (1967):

> The exceptional men, the innovators, the intellectual giants. . . . It is the members of this exceptional minority who lift the whole of a free society to the level of their own achievements, while rising further and ever further.[32]

If the first half of Hitler's economic views celebrates the romantic genius of the individual industrialist, the second spells out the inegalitarian implications of the first. Once we recognize "the outstanding achievements of individuals," Hitler says in Düsseldorf, we must conclude that "people are not of equal value or of equal importance." Private property "can be morally and ethically justified only if [we] admit that men's achievements are different." An understanding of nature fosters a respect for the heroic individual, which fosters an appreciation of inequality in its most vicious guise. "The creative and decomposing forces in a people always fight against one another."[33]

Rand's appreciation of inequality is equally pungent. I quote from Galt's speech:

> The man at the top of the intellectual pyramid contributes the most to all those below him, but gets nothing except his material payment, receiving no intellectual bonus from others to add to the value of his time. The man at the bottom who, left to himself, would starve in his hopeless ineptitude, contributes nothing to those above him, but receives the bonus of all their brains. Such is the nature of the "competition" between the strong and the weak of the intellect. Such is the pattern of "exploitation" for which you have damned the strong.[34]

Rand's path from nature to individualism to inequality also ends in a world divided between "the creative and decomposing forces." In every society, says Roark, there is a "creator" and a parasitic "second-hander," each with its own nature and code. The first "allows man to survive." The second is "incapable of survival."[35] One produces life, the other induces death. In *Atlas Shrugged* the battle is between the producer and the "looters" and "moochers." It too must end in life or death.

To find Rand in such company should come as no surprise, for she and the Nazis share a patrimony in the vulgar Nietzscheanism that has stalked the radical right, whether in its libertarian or fascist variants, since the early part of the twentieth century. As both of her biographers show, Nietzsche exerted an early grip on Rand that never really loosened. Her cousin teased Rand that Nietzsche "beat you to all your ideas." When Rand arrived in the United States, *Thus Spake Zarathustra* was the first book in English she bought. With Nietzsche on her mind, she was inspired to write in her journals that "the secret of life" is "you must be nothing but will. Know what you want and do it. Know what you are doing and why you are doing it, every minute of the day. All will and all control. Send everything else to hell!" Her entries frequently include phrases like "Nietzsche and I think" and "as Nietzsche said."[36]

Rand was much taken with the idea of the violent criminal as moral hero, a Nietzschean transvaluator of all values; according to Burns, she "found criminality an irresistible metaphor for individualism." A literary Leopold and Loeb, she plotted out a novella based on the actual case of a murderer who strangled a twelve-year-old girl. The murderer, said Rand, "is born with a wonderful, free, light consciousness—resulting from the absolute lack of social instinct or herd feeling. He does not understand, because he has no organ for understanding, the necessity, meaning or importance of other people."[37] That is not a bad description of Nietzsche's master class in *The Genealogy of Morals*.

Though Rand's defenders claim she later abandoned her infatuation with Nietzsche, there is too much evidence of its persistence. There's the figure of Roark himself: "As she jotted down notes on Roark's personality," writes Burns, "she told herself, 'See Nietzsche about laughter.' The book's famous first line indicates the centrality of this connection: 'Howard Roark laughed.'"[38] And then there's *Atlas Shrugged*, which Ludwig von Mises, one of the presiding eminences of neoclassical economics, praised thus:

> You have the courage to tell the masses what no politician told them: you are inferior and all the improvements in your conditions which you simply take for granted you owe to the effort of men who are better than you.[39]

But Nietzsche's influence saturated Rand's writing in a deeper way, one emblematic of the overall trajectory of the right since its birth in the crucible of the French Revolution. Rand was a lifelong atheist with a special animus for Christianity, which she called the "best kindergarten of communism possible."[40] Far from representing a heretical tendency within conservatism, Rand's statement channels a tradition of right-wing suspicion about the insidious effects of religion, particularly Christianity, on the modern world. Where many conservatives since 1789 have rallied to Christianity and religion as an antidote to the democratic revolutions of the eighteenth and nineteenth centuries, a not insignificant subset among them have seen religion, or at least some aspect of religion, as the adjutant of revolution.

Joseph de Maistre was one of the first. An arch-Catholic, he traced the French Revolution to the acrid solvents of the Reformation. With its celebration of "private interpretation" of the Scriptures, Protestantism paved the way for century upon century of regicide and revolt originating in the lower classes.[41]

> It is from the shadow of a cloister that there emerges one of mankind's very greatest scourges. Luther appears; Calvin follows him. The Peasants' Revolt; the Thirty Years' War; the civil war in France . . . the murders of Henry II, Henry IV, Mary Stuart, and Charles I; and finally, in our day, from the same source, the French Revolution.[42]

Nietzsche, the child of a Lutheran pastor, radicalized this argument, painting all of Christianity—indeed all of Western religion, going back to Judaism—as a slave morality, the psychic revolt of the lower orders against their betters. Before there was religion or even morality, there was the sense and sensibility of the master class. The master looked upon his body—its strength and beauty, its demonstrated excellence and reserves of power—and saw and said that it was good. As an afterthought he looked upon the slave, and saw and said that it was bad. The slave never looked upon himself: he was consumed by envy of and resentment toward his master. Too weak to act upon his rage and take revenge, he launched a quiet but lethal revolt of the mind. He called all the master's attributes—power, indifference to suffering, thoughtless cruelty—evil. He spoke of his own attributes—meekness, humility, forbearance—as good. He devised a religion that made selfishness and self-concern a sin, and compassion and concern for others the path to salvation. He envisioned a universal brotherhood of believers, equal before God, and damned the master's order of unevenly distributed excellence.[43] The modern residue of that slave revolt, Nietzsche makes clear, is found not in Christianity, or even in religion, but in the nineteenth-century movements for democracy and socialism:

> Another Christian concept, no less crazy, has passed even more deeply into the tissue of modernity: the concept of the "equality of souls before God." This concept furnishes the prototype of all theories of equal rights: mankind was first taught to stammer the proposition of equality in a religious context, and only later was it made into morality: no wonder that man ended by taking it seriously, taking it practically!—that is to say, politically, democratically, socialistically.[44]

When Rand inveighs against Christianity as the forebear of socialism, when she rails against altruism and sacrifice as inversions of the true hierarchy of values, she is cultivating the strain within conservatism that sees religion as not a remedy to, but a helpmate of, the left. And when she looks, however ineptly, to Aristotle for an alternative morality, she is recapitulating Nietzsche's journey back to antiquity, where he hoped to find a master-class morality untainted by the egalitarian values of the lower orders.

Though Rand's antireligious defense of capitalism might seem out of place in today's political firmament, we would do well to recall the recent revival of interest in her books. More than 800,000 copies of her novels were sold in 2008 alone; as Burns rightly notes, "Rand is a more active presence in American culture now than she was during her lifetime." Indeed, Rand is regularly cited as a formative influence upon an entire new generation of Republican leaders; Burns calls her "the ultimate gateway drug to life on the right."[45] Whether or not she is invoked by name, Rand's presence is palpable in the concern, heard increasingly on the right, that there is something sinister afoot in the institutions and teachings of Christianity.

> I beg you, look for the words "social justice" or "economic justice" on your church website. If you find it, run as fast as you can. Social justice and economic justice, they are code words. Now, am I advising people to leave their church? Yes.

That was Glenn Beck on his March 2, 2010 radio show, taking a stand against, well, pretty much every church in the Christian faith: Catholic, Episcopalian, Methodist, Baptist—even his very own Church of Jesus Christ of Latter-day Saints.[46]

On her own, Rand is of little significance. It is only her resonance in American culture—and the unsavory associations her resonance evokes—that makes her of any interest. She's not unlike the "second-hander" described by Roark: "Their reality is not within them, but somewhere in that space which divides one human body from another. Not an entity, but a relation. . . . The second-hander acts, but the source of his actions is scattered in every other living person."[47] For once, it seems, he knew whence he spoke.

But after all the Nietzsche is said and Aristotle is done, we're still left with a puzzle about Rand: How could such a mediocrity, not just a second-hander but a second-rater, exert such a continuing influence on the culture at large?

We possess an entire literature, from Melville to Mamet, devoted to the con man and the hustler, and it's tempting to see Rand as one of the many fakes and frauds who periodically light up the American landscape. But that temptation should be resisted. Rand represents something different, more unsettling. The con man is a liar who can ascertain the truth of things, often better than the rest of us. He has to: if he is going to fleece his mark, he has to know who the mark is and who the mark would like to be. Working in that netherworld between fact and fantasy, the con man can gild the lily only if he sees the lily for what it is. But Rand had no desire to gild anything. The gilded lily was reality. What was there to add? She even sported a lapel pin to make the point: made of gold and fashioned in the shape of a dollar sign, it was bling of the most literal sort.

Since the nineteenth century, it has been the task of the left to hold up to liberal civilization a mirror of its highest values and to say, "You do not look like this." You claim to believe in the rights of man, but it is only the rights of property you uphold. You claim to stand for freedom, but it is only the freedom of the strong to dominate the weak. If you wish to live up to your principles, you must give way to their demiurge. Allow the dispossessed to assume power, and the ideal will be made real, the metaphor will be made material.

Rand believed that this meeting of heaven and earth could be arranged by other means. Rather than remake the world in the image of paradise, she looked for paradise in an image of the world. Political transformation wasn't necessary. Transubstantiation was enough. Say a few words, wave your hands and the ideal is real, the metaphor material. An idealist of the most primitive sort, Rand took a century of socialist dichotomies and flattened them. Small wonder so many have accused her of intolerance: When heaven and earth are pressed so closely together, where is there room for dissent?

Far from needing explanation, her success explains itself. Rand worked in that quintessential American proving ground—alongside the likes of Richard Nixon, Ronald Reagan, and Glenn Beck—where garbage achieves gravitas and bullshit gets blessed. There she learned that dreams don't come true. They are true. Turn your metaphysics into chewing gum, and your chewing gum is metaphysics. A is A.

4

Inside Out

"The 1960s are rightly remembered as years of cultural dissent and political upheaval, but they are wrongly remembered as years stirred only from the left," writes George Will in the foreword to a reissued edition of Barry Goldwater's *The Conscience of a Conservative*.[1] Several decades ago, such a claim would have elicited puzzled looks, if not catcalls and jeers. But in the years since, the publication of a slew of books, each advancing the notion that most of the political innovation of the last half-century has come from the right, has led historians to revise the conventional wisdom about postwar America, including the 1960s. The new consensus is reflected in the opening sentence of Ronald Story and Bruce Laurie's *The Rise of Conservatism in America, 1945–2000*: "The central story of American politics since World War II is the emergence of the conservative movement."[2] Yet for some reason Will still feels that his kinsmen are insufficiently appreciated and recognized.

This chapter originally appeared as a review of Barry Goldwater's *The Conscience of a Conservative* (Princeton, N.J.: Princeton University Press, 2007, 1960); *Rightward Bound: Making America Conservative in the 1970s*, ed. Bruce J. Schulman and Julian E. Zelizer (Cambridge, Mass.: Harvard University Press, 2008); and Jacob Heilbrunn's *They Knew They Were Right: The Rise of the Neocons* (New York: Doubleday, 2008) in *The Nation* (June 23, 2008): 25–33.

Will is hardly the first conservative to believe himself an exile in his own country. A sense of exclusion has haunted the movement from the beginning, when émigrés fled the French Revolution and Edmund Burke and Joseph de Maistre took up their cause. Born in the shadow of loss—of property, standing, memory, inheritance, a place in the sun—conservatism remains a gathering of fugitives. Even when assured of his position, the conservative plays the truant. Whether instrumental or sincere, this fusion of pariah and power is one of the sources of his appeal. As William F. Buckley wrote in the founding statement of *National Review*, the conservative's badge of exclusion has made him "just about the hottest thing in town."[3]

While David Hume and Adam Smith are often cited by the more genteel defenders of conservatism as the movement's leading lights, their writings cannot account for, as we have seen, what is truly bizarre about conservatism: a ruling class resting its claim to power upon its sense of victimhood, arguably for the first time in history. Plato's guardians were wise; Aquinas's king was good; Hobbes's sovereign was, well, sovereign. But the best defense of monarchy Maistre could muster was that his aspiring king had attended the "terrible school of misfortune" and suffered in the "hard school of adversity."[4] Maistre had good reason to offer this defense: playing the plebe, we now know, is a critical weapon in the conservative arsenal. Still, it's a confusing defense. After all, if the main offering a prince brings to the table is that he's really a pauper, why not seat the pauper instead?

Conservatives have asked us not to obey them, but to feel sorry for them—or to obey them because we feel sorry for them. Rousseau was the first to articulate a political theory of pity, and for that he has been called the "Homer of the losers."[5] But doesn't Burke, with his overwrought account of Marie Antoinette that we saw in chapter 1—"this persecuted woman," dragged "almost naked" by "the furies of hell" from her bedroom in Versailles and marched to "a Bastile for kings" in Paris—have some claim to the title, too?[6]

Marie Antoinette was a particular kind of loser, a person with everything who found herself utterly and at once dispossessed. Burke saw in her fall an archetype of classical tragedy, the great person laid low by fortune. But in tragedy, the most any hero can hope for is to understand his fate: the wheel of time cannot be reversed; suffering cannot be undone. Conservatives, however, are not content with illumination. They want restoration, an opportunity presented by the new forces of revolution and counterrevolution. Identifying as victims, they become the ultimate moderns, adept competitors in a political marketplace where rights and their divestiture are prized commodities.

Reformers and radicals must convince the subordinated and disenfranchised that they have rights and power. Conservatives are different. They are aggrieved and entitled—aggrieved because entitled—and already convinced of the righteousness of their cause and the inevitability of its triumph. They thus can play victim and victor with a conviction and dexterity the subaltern can only imagine. This makes them formidable claimants on our allegiance and affection. Whether we are rich or poor or somewhere in between, the conservative is, as Hugo Young said of Maggie Thatcher, one of us.[7]

But how do they convince us that we are one of them? By making privilege democratic and democracy aristocratic. The conservative does not defend the Old Regime; he speaks on behalf of old regimes—in the family, the factory, the field. There, ordinary men, and sometimes women, get to play the part of little lords and ladies, supervising their underlings as if they all belong to a feudal estate. Long before Huey Long cried, "Every man a king," a more ambiguous species of democrat spoke virtually the same words, though to different effect: the promise of democracy is to govern another human being as completely as a monarch governs his subjects. The task of this type of conservatism—democratic feudalism—becomes clear: surround these old regimes with fences and gates, protect them from meddlesome intruders like the state or a social movement, while descanting on mobility and innovation, freedom and the future.

Making privilege palatable to the masses is a permanent project of conservatism; but each generation must tailor that project to fit the contour of its times. Goldwater's challenge was set out in the title of his book: to show that conservatives had a conscience. Not a heart—he lambasted Eisenhower and Nixon for trying to prove that Republicans were compassionate[8]—or a brain, which liberals from John Stuart Mill to Lionel Trilling had doubted, but a conscience. Political movements often have to convince their followers that they can succeed, that their cause is just and their leaders are savvy, but rarely must they prove that theirs is a march of inner lights. Goldwater thought otherwise: to attract new voters and rally the faithful, conservatism had to establish its idealism and integrity, its absolute independence from the beck and call of wealth, from privilege and materialism—from reality itself. If they were to change reality, conservatives would have to divorce themselves, at least in their self-understanding, from reality.[9] (In this regard, he was not altogether different from Burke, who warned that while the ruling classes in Britain had "a vast interest to preserve" against the Jacobin threat and "great means of preserving it," they were like an "artificer . . . incumbered by his tools." Possessing vast "resources," Burke concluded, "may be among impediments" in the struggle against revolution.)[10] In recent years, it has become fashionable to dismiss today's Republican as a true believer who betrayed conservatism by abandoning its native skepticism and spirit of mild adjustment. Goldwater was independent and ornery, the argument goes, recoiling from anything so stultifying (and Soviet) as an ideology; Bush (or the neocon or Tea Partier) is rigid and doctrinaire, an enforcer of bright lines and gospel truths. But conservatism has always been a creedal movement—if for no other reason than to oppose the creeds of the left. "The other side have got an ideology," declared Thatcher. "We must have one as well."[11] To counter the left, the right has had to mimic the left. "As small as they are," John C. Calhoun wrote admiringly of the abolitionists, they "have acquired so much influence by the course they have pursued."[12]

Goldwater understood that. During the Gilded Age, conservatives had opposed unions and government regulation by invoking the freedom of workers to contract with their employer. Liberals countered that this freedom was illusory: workers lacked the means to contract as they wished; real freedom required material means. Goldwater agreed, only he turned the same argument against the New Deal: high taxes robbed workers of their wages, rendering them less free and less able to be free. Channeling John Dewey, he asked, "How can a man be truly free if he is denied the means to exercise freedom?"[13] Franklin Delano Roosevelt claimed that conservatives cared more about money than men. Goldwater said the same about liberals. Focusing on welfare and wages, they "look only at the material side of man's nature" and "subordinate all other considerations to man's material well being." Conservatives, by contrast, take in "the whole man," making his "spiritual nature" the "primary concern" of politics and putting "material things in their proper place."[14]

This romantic howl against the economism of the New Deal—similar to that of the New Left—was not a protest against politics or government; Goldwater was no libertarian. It was an attempt to elevate politics and government, to direct public discussion toward ends more noble and glorious than the management of creature comforts and material well-being. Unlike the New Left, however,

Goldwater did not reject the affluent society. Instead, he transformed the acquisition of wealth into an act of self-definition through which the "uncommon" man could distinguish himself from the "undifferentiated mass."[15] To amass wealth was not only to exercise freedom through material means, but also a way of lording oneself over others.

In his essay on conservative thought, Karl Mannheim argued that conservatives have never been wild about the idea of freedom. It threatens the submission of subordinate to superior. Because freedom is the lingua franca of modern politics, however, conservatives have had "a sound enough instinct not to attack" it. Instead, they have made freedom the stalking horse of inequality, and inequality the stalking horse of submission. Men are naturally unequal, they argue. Freedom requires that they be allowed to develop their unequal gifts. A free society must be an unequal society, composed of radically distinct, and hierarchically arrayed, particulars.[16]

Goldwater never rejected freedom; indeed, he celebrated it. But there is little doubt that he saw it as a proxy for inequality—or war, which he called "the price of freedom." A free society protected each man's "absolute differentness from every other human being," with difference standing in for superiority or inferiority. It was the "initiative and ambition of uncommon men"—the most different and excellent of men—that made a nation great. A free society would identify such men at the earliest stages of life and give them the resources they needed to rise to preeminence. Against those who subscribed to "the egalitarian notion that every child must have the same education," Goldwater argued for "an educational system which will tax the talents and stir the ambitions of our best students and . . . thus insure us the kind of leaders we will need in the future."[17]

Mannheim also argued that conservatives often champion the group—races or nations—rather than the individual. Races and nations have unique identities, which must, in the name of freedom, be preserved. They are the modern equivalents of feudal estates. They have distinctive, and unequal, characters and functions; they enjoy different, and unequal, privileges. Freedom is the protection of those privileges, which are the outward expression of the group's unique inner genius.[18]

Goldwater rejected racism (though not nationalism); but try as he might, when discussing freedom he could not resist the tug of feudalism. He called states' rights "the cornerstone" of liberty, "our chief bulwark against the encroachment of individual freedom" by the federal government. In theory, states protected individuals rather than groups. But who in 1960 were these individuals? Goldwater claimed that they were anyone and everyone, that states' rights had nothing to do with Jim Crow. Yet even he was forced to admit that segregation "is, today, the most conspicuous expression of the principle" of states' rights.[19] The rhetoric of states' rights threw up a cordon around white privilege. While surely the most noxious plank in the conservative platform—eventually, it was abandoned—Goldwater's argument for states' rights fits squarely within a tradition that sees freedom as a shield for inequality and a surrogate for mass feudalism.

Goldwater lost big in the 1964 presidential election. His children and grandchildren went on to win big—by broadening the circle of discontent beyond Southern whites to include husbands and wives, evangelicals and white ethnics, and by continuing to absorb and transmute the idioms of the left.[20] Adapting to the left didn't make American conservatism less reactionary—any more than Maistre's or Burke's recognition that the French Revolution had permanently changed Europe tempered conservatism there. Rather, it made conservatism suppler and more successful. The more it adapted, the more reactionary conservatism became.

Evangelical Christians were ideal recruits to the cause, deftly playing the victim card as a way of rejuvenating the power of whites. "It's time for God's people to come out of the closet," declared a Texas televangelist in 1980. But it wasn't religion that made evangelicals queer; it was religion combined with racism. One of the main catalysts of the Christian right was the defense of Southern private schools that were created in response to desegregation. By 1970, 400,000 white children were attending these "segregation academies." States like Mississippi gave students tuition grants, and until the Nixon administration overturned the practice, the IRS gave donors to these schools tax exemptions.[21] According to New Right and direct-mail pioneer Richard Viguerie, the attack on these public subsidies by civil rights activists and the courts "was the spark that ignited the religious right's involvement in real politics." Though the rise of segregation academies "was often timed exactly with the desegregation of formerly all-white public schools," writes one historian, their advocates claimed to be defending religious minorities rather than white supremacy (initially nonsectarian, most of the schools became evangelical over time). Their cause was freedom, not inequality—not the freedom to associate with whites, as the previous generation of massive resisters had claimed, but the freedom to practice their own embattled religion.[22] It was a shrewd transposition. In one fell swoop, the heirs of slaveholders became the descendants of persecuted Baptists, and Jim Crow a heresy the First Amendment was meant to protect.

The Christian right was equally galvanized by the backlash against the women's movement. Antifeminism was a latecomer to the conservative cause. Through the early 1970s, advocates of the Equal Rights Amendment (ERA) could still count Richard Nixon, George Wallace, and Strom Thurmond as supporters; even Phyllis Schlafly described the ERA as something "between innocuous and mildly helpful." But once feminism entered "the sensitive and intensely personal arena of relations between the sexes," writes historian Margaret Spruill, the abstract phrases of legal equality took on a more intimate and concrete meaning. The ERA provoked a counterrevolution, as we saw in chapter 1, led by Schlafly and other women, that was as grassroots and nearly as diverse as the movement it opposed.[23] So successful was this counterrevolution—not just at derailing the ERA, but at propelling the Republican Party to power—that it seemed to prove the feminist point. If women could be that effective as political agents, why shouldn't they be in Congress or the White House?

Schlafly grasped the irony. She understood that the women's movement had tapped into and unleashed a desire for power and autonomy among women that couldn't simply be quelled. If women were to be sent back to the exile of their homes, they would have to view their retreat not as a defeat, but as one more victory in the long battle for women's freedom and power. As we saw in chapter 1, she described herself as a defender, not an opponent, of women's rights. The ERA was "a takeaway of women's rights," she insisted, the "right of the wife to be supported and to have her minor children supported" by her husband. By focusing her argument on "the right of the wife in an ongoing marriage, the wife in the home," Schlafly reinforced the notion that women were wives and mothers first; their only need was for the protection provided by their husbands. At the same time, she described that relationship in the liberal language of entitlement rights. "The wife has the right to support" from her spouse, she claimed, treating the woman as a feminist claimant and her husband as the welfare state.[24]

Like their Catholic predecessors in eighteenth-century France, the Christian Right appropriated not just the ideas but the manners and mores of its opponents. Billy Graham issued an album called *Rap Session: Billy Graham and Students Rap on Questions of Today's Youth.* Evangelicals criticized the culture of narcissism— and then colonized it. James Dobson of the Focus on the Family got his start as a child psychologist at the University of Southern California, competing with Dr. Spock as the author of a bestselling child-rearing text. Evangelical bookstores, according to historian Paul Boyer, "promoted therapeutic and self-help books offering advice on finances, dating, marriage, depression, and addiction from an evangelical perspective." Most audacious of all was the film version of Hal Lindsey's book *The Late Great Planet Earth.* While the book popularized Christian prophecies of the End of Days, the film was narrated by Orson Welles, the original bad boy of the Popular Front.[25]

The most interesting cases of the right's appropriation of the left, however, came from big business and the Nixon administration. The business class saw the student movement as a critical constituency. Using hip and informal language, writes historian Bethany Moreton, corporate spokesmen left "their plaid suits in the closet" in order to sell capitalism as the fulfillment of sixties-style liberation, participation, and authenticity. Reeling from protests against the invasion of Cambodia (and the massacre of four students that ensued), students at Kent State formed a chapter of Students in Free Enterprise (SIFE), one of 150 across the country. They sponsored a "Battle of the Bands," for which one contestant wrote the following lyrics:

> *You know I could never be happy*
> *Just working some nine-to-five.*
> *I'd rather spend my life poor.*
> *Than living it as a lie.*
> *If I could just save my money*
> *Or maybe get a loan,*

I could start my own business
And make it on my own.

Small business institutes were set up on college campuses, casting "the businessman as a victim, not a bully." Business brought its Gramscian tactics to secondary schools as well. In Arkansas, SIFE performed classroom skits of Milton Friedman's PBS series *Free to Choose*. In 1971, Arizona passed a law requiring high school graduates to take a course in economics so that they would have "some foundation to stand on," according to the bill's sponsor, when they came up "against professors that are collectivists or Socialists." Twenty states followed suit. Arizona students could place out of the course if they passed an exam that asked them, among other things, to match the phrase "government intervention in a free enterprise system" with "is detrimental to the free market."[26]

The most ambidextrous of politicians, Nixon was the master of talking left while walking right. Nixon understood that the best response to the civil rights movement was not to defend whites against blacks, but to make whites into white ethnics burdened with their own histories of oppression and requiring their own liberation movements. Where immigrants from Southern and Eastern Europe had jumped into the melting pot and turned white, Nixon and the ethnic revivalists of the 1970s "provided Americans of European descent a new vehicle for asserting citizenship rights at a moment when it grew increasingly illegitimate to make claims on the state on the basis of whiteness," write historian Tom Sugrue and sociologist John Skrentny. Under Nixon's leadership, the Republican Party was transformed into a right-wing version of the Democratic urban machine. Poles and Italians were appointed to high-profile offices in his administration, and Nixon campaigned vigorously in white ethnic neighborhoods. He even told one crowd that "he felt like he had Italian blood." Nixon's efforts occasionally went beyond the symbolic—a 1971 proposal would have extended affirmative action to "members of certain ethnic groups, primarily of Eastern, Middle, and Southern European ancestry, such as Italians, Greeks, and Slavic groups"—but most were rhetorical. That didn't make them less potent: the new vocabulary of white ethnicity helped create "a romanticized past of hard work, discipline, well-defined gender roles, and tight-knit families," providing a new language for a new age—and a very old regime.[27]

Barry Goldwater's mother was a descendant of Roger Williams. His father, who converted to Episcopalianism, was a descendant of Polish Jews. When Goldwater ran in 1964, Harry Golden quipped, "I always knew the first Jew to run for president would be an Episcopalian."[28] If the history of conservatism is any guide, perhaps he should have run as a Jew.

5

The Ex-Cons

In the spring of 2000, Alex Star, editor of the now-defunct Lingua Franca, *commissioned me to write a profile of John Gray and Edward Luttwak, two conservative intellectuals who had moved to the left. Throughout the summer and fall, I interviewed Gray and Luttwak as well as other conservatives such as William F. Buckley, Irving Kristol, and Norman Podhoretz. It was a difficult time for the right. Bill Clinton was still president; 9/11 had not yet occurred. Prosperity was a given, war was a distant memory, and learned people still spoke of the end of history. The moment had a vastly different feel from today, and it affected how conservatives thought about their ideas and politics. While some of the references and statements in this article are now dated, and some of its claims I no longer believe, I have decided not to revise the piece in order to preserve the mood of that moment. In chapter 8, I revisit some of the issues discussed here in light of 9/11, the war on terror, and the Iraq War.*

There is another reason I have not revised this article. Though I had read Burke, Oakeshott, and Nozick in college and graduate school, researching and writing this article was my first sustained encounter with the worldview of the right. (It remains an unfortunate reality of American higher education that social scientists and historians can get through

This chapter originally appeared as an article in *Lingua Franca* (February 2001): 24–33.

*their training with only the most passing acquaintance with conserva-
tism.) This article became a kind of sentimental education for me, my introduction to the agony and the ecstasy of the conservative mind. While I
would certainly revise much of it today—particularly the underlying premise that the conservatives I discuss here are different from the mainstream—the article nevertheless provides the reader with a glimpse of
what first interested me about the right and how I came to write this book.*

According to popular myth, it was Winston Churchill who said,
"Any man under thirty who is not a liberal has no heart, and any
man over thirty who is not a conservative has no brains." He didn't
say it, but his imprimatur turned a clever quip of uncertain prove-
nance into an axiom of political biography: Radicalism is a privilege of youth, conservatism a responsibility of age, and every
thinking person eventually surrenders the first for the second.
From Max Eastman to Eugene Genovese, Whittaker Chambers to
Ronald Radosh, intellectuals migrate from left to right as if obeying
a law of nature.

Or do they? After all, John Stuart Mill published *The Subjection
of Women* when he was sixty-three. In the last ten years of his life,
Diderot hailed the American Revolution and blasted France as the
reincarnation of imperial Rome. And when George Bernard Shaw
addressed the question of politics and aging, he suggested just the
opposite of what Churchill is supposed to have said. "The most
distinguished persons," Shaw wrote in 1903, "become more revolutionary as they grow older."[1]

Since the end of the Cold War, several prominent conservatives
have followed Shaw's prescription and turned left. Michael Lind,
once a top editor at Irving Kristol's *The National Interest,* has
denounced his previous allies for prosecuting a "class war against
wage-earning Americans." Their market-driven theories, he writes,
are "unconvincing," their economic policies "appalling." Arianna

Huffington, erstwhile confederate of Newt Gingrich, now inveighs against a United States where the great majority is "left choking on the dust of Wall Street's galloping bulls."[2] Glenn Loury, an economist and former neoconservative darling, sports the signature emblem of left membership: he has become one of Norman Podhoretz's ex-friends. But today's most flamboyant expatriates are an Englishman, John Gray, and a Jewish émigré from Transylvania, Edward Luttwak.

In the 1970s, John Gray was a rising star of the British New Right. An Oxford-trained political philosopher, he penned prose poems to the free market, crisscrossed the Atlantic to fuel up on the high-octane libertarianism of American right-wing think tanks, and, says a longtime friend, enthralled his comrades late into the night with visions of the coming "anarcho-capitalist" Utopia. But after the Berlin Wall collapsed, Gray defected. First he criticized the Cold War triumphalism of Francis Fukuyama's "end of history" thesis and counseled against scrapping Britain's National Health Service. And then in 1998, from his newly established position as professor of European thought at the London School of Economics (LSE), he handed down *False Dawn,* a ferocious denunciation of economic globalization. Assailing the "shock troops of the free market," Gray warned that global capitalism could "come to rival" the former Soviet Union "in the suffering that it inflicts."[3] Now he is a regular contributor to *The Guardian* and *New Statesman,* Britain's principal left venues. So profound is his conversion that no less a figure than Margaret Thatcher has reportedly wondered, "Whatever became of John Gray? He used to be one of us."[4]

And what of Edward Luttwak? Once, he was one of Ronald Reagan's court intellectuals, a brilliant military hawk who mercilessly criticized liberal defense policies and provided the philosophical rationale for the American military buildup of the 1980s.

Liberal critics called him "Crazy Eddie," but cutting a figure that was part Dr. Strangelove and part Dr. Zhivago, Luttwak effortlessly parried their arguments, pressing the Cold War toward its conclusion.[5] Today, he is disillusioned by victory. He finds the United States a capitalist nightmare, "a grim warning" to leaders seeking to unleash free-market forces in their own countries. Deploying the same acerbic wit he once lofted against liberal peaceniks, he mocks the "Napoleonic pretensions" of American business leaders, challenges the conventional wisdom that capitalism and democracy are inevitable bedfellows (*"free markets* and *less free societies* go hand in hand"), and decries the savage inequalities produced by "turbo-capitalism." He excoriates European center-leftists like Tony Blair for abandoning their socialist roots and for their unwillingness "to risk any innovative action" on behalf of "ordinary workers." With their "disdain for the poor and other losers" and "contempt for the broad masses of working people," Luttwak writes, Clintonesque New Democrats and European Third Wayers "can yield only right-wing policies."[6]

In their original incarnations, Gray and Luttwak thrilled to two of conservatism's galvanizing passions—anticommunism and the free market. But since the fall of the Soviet Union, they have been posing questions about the market they once would never have dared ask.

Yet for all their disgust with unbridled capitalism, Gray and Luttwak find it hard to embrace any of the alternatives: The furthest Gray will go is to characterize himself as "center-left." Nor is the left too eager to claim either of them. One reviewer *of False Dawn* wrote in *In These Times* that Gray was merely a standard-bearer for the old regime, driven less by "a genuine hatred of inequality, injustice or poverty" than by "a deep fear of political instability."[7] With Communism in shambles and the market omnipotent, the agonistic passion that originally inspired Luttwak and Gray now finds itself without a home. They are today's most poignant exiles, lost in a diaspora of their own making.

Conservatives usually style themselves as chastened skeptics holding the line against political enthusiasm. Where radicals tilt toward the utopian, conservatives settle for world-weary realism. But, in reality, conservatives have been temperamentally antagonistic, politically insurgent, and utterly opposed to established moral convention. Ever since Edmund Burke, thinkers from Samuel Taylor Coleridge to Martin Heidegger have sought a more intense, almost ecstatic mode of experience in the spheres of religion, culture, and even the economy—all of which, they believe, are repositories of the mysterious and the ineffable. Indulging in political romanticism, they draw from the stock-in-trade of the counter-Enlightenment, celebrating the intoxicating vitality of struggle while denouncing the bloodless norms of reason and rights. As Isaiah Berlin observed of Joseph de Maistre:

> His violent preoccupation with blood and death belongs to a world different . . . from the slow, mature wisdom of the landed gentry, the deep peace of the country houses great and small. . . . The facade of Maistre's system may be classical, but behind it there is something terrifyingly modern, and violently opposed to sweetness and light.[8]

The battle in the twentieth century against Communism and social democracy provided the perfect vehicle for these conservative sensibilities. For figures like John Gray, the Soviet Union and the welfare state were the ultimate symbols of cold Enlightenment rationalism, and the free market was the embodiment of the romantic counter-Enlightenment. But revolutionary romantics ultimately suffer the fate of all romantics: disillusionment. And so today, with Communism in ruins and the free market triumphant, the dissident spirit that originally inspired Gray now fires an equally militant apostasy.

Gray was born in 1948 and grew up outside Newcastle, a port city near the North Sea in a coal-mining region only fifty miles from Scotland. In a country where accent is destiny, one still hears faint traces of his northeastern working-class origins, about which he is slightly defensive. His father was a carpenter; his entire family voted Labour. Gray arrived at Oxford in 1968, the annus mirabilis for young leftists throughout Europe. Sporting the costume of the period—"my hair was long, but everybody's hair was long"—he traveled to London to demonstrate against the Vietnam War. After receiving his degree in philosophy, politics, and economics, Gray stayed on at Oxford for graduate school, writing a thesis on John Stuart Mill and John Rawls, both sympathetic to a liberal socialism that Gray initially found attractive.

But as he muddled through Rawls's *A Theory of Justice,* Gray grew weary of the effort to extract socialist policies from liberal formulas. Part of his malaise was induced by Rawls's congested prose. "It's an almost unreadable book," he says. Rawls's plodding style seemed to mirror the deeper political ennui of social democracy. His work, says Gray, was "a transcendental deduction of the Labour Party in 1963." Like many New Leftists in the United States, Gray found the business of the welfare state dull and uninspired, the weak tea of colorless bureaucrats. As he would later describe it, the welfare state was the product of a "triangular collusion of employers, unions and government." It was a "colossal apparatus" extracting resources and energy from an enervated citizenry. Tepid compromise was the rule of the day; political leaders tried to be all things to all people. They refused "to admit the reality of conflicts," that "one equality, one demand of justice, may compete with another."[9] The welfare state, in short, was a far cry from the vital working-class radicalism that had produced it.

In Thatcherism, Gray caught a glimpse of revolutionary eternity. "There was a revolutionary, indeed a Bolshevik, aspect to the Thatcherite project at the start which I thought was both exciting and necessary," he says. Thatcher assumed the leadership of the Conservative Party at just about the time of Gray's conversion to capitalism. She promised to liberate Britain from the stifling routine of social democracy, and the free market from the chains of state planning. Though no egalitarian, Thatcher stoked the ambitions of middle- and working-class voters who saw the free market as a vehicle of upward mobility.

Her most impressive moment came in 1980, after her first year in power, when her policies seemed to be pushing the economy toward disaster. Having denounced her predecessor Edward Heath for executing his notorious "U-turn," when he capitulated to left-wing pressure after vowing a rollback of social democracy, Thatcher faced pressure from moderates within her own party—the Tory "Wets"—to reverse course. Instead of retreating, she defiantly faced down her temporizing critics, memorably declaring, "You turn if you want to. The lady's not for turning."[10] Conservatives were smitten. Norman Barry, another Thatcherite and until recently a close friend of Gray's, recalls, "I had thought she was just an election winner who wasn't Labour. But when she lifted exchange controls, I thought, 'This babe knows market economics.' So then I thought, 'Yeah!' And then she began privatization and other things. And then she wouldn't do a U-turn, I thought, 'This is for real.'"

Many Thatcherites thought of themselves as free-market revolutionaries, and Gray brought to their cause a romantic panache not often associated with neoclassical economics. In 1974, he began reading the work of Friedrich Hayek, the Austrian-born economist and fierce critic of state planning. Ten years later, Gray published *Hayek on Liberty,* which the master himself described as "the first survey of my work which not only fully understands but is able to carry on my ideas beyond the point at which I left off." The Hayek that Gray depicted was no antiseptic defender of property rights and low taxes. He was an exotic explorer of the subterranean, quasi-rational currents of human life, a Viennese voice that had more in common with Sigmund Freud and Ludwig Wittgenstein than with Milton Friedman or Robert Nozick. If *Hayek on Liberty* was an impassioned ode to the market, Gray was its yearning Byron.

Where many conservatives saw in Hayek the logical fulfillment of a calm, quintessentially British tradition of political economy extending back to Adam Smith, Gray detected an "uncompromising modernity" in Hayek's vision of the free market.[11] Intellectual ferment, political extremism, and social decay characterized fin-de-siècle Vienna, the milieu in which Hayek was born. Out of this whirlwind came psychoanalysis, fascism, and modern economics. Each challenged old orders of knowledge and politics. Hayek followed in the footsteps of the late-nineteenth-century Austrian school, claiming that "economic value—the value of an asset or resource—is conferred on it by the preferences or valuations of individuals and not by any of its objective properties."[12] While classical economists from David Ricardo to Karl Marx believed there had to be something *real*—most important, physical labor—behind the mysterious veil of prices, Hayek argued that it was only the eccentric preferences of particular human beings that gave value to goods in the world. An almost hyperactive subjectivity—comparable to Freud's anarchic id—haunted Gray's Hayek, reflecting Vienna's "experience of an apparently inexorable drift to dissolution."[13]

Against philosophers who elevated theoretical reason to the highest form of knowledge, Hayek, wrote Gray, believed that rational understanding was only the tip of the iceberg. Beneath it lay a murky stratum of thought "rarely expressible in theoretical or technical terms," and it was the free market's particular genius to harness these premonitions to everyday economic activity.[14]

Entrepreneurs were the sublime mediums of such "tacit knowledge," channeling its deep truths to other market actors. They were romantic heroes possessed by flashes of almost poetic vision. "Entrepreneurial insight or perception," explained Gray, was a matter not of book learning but of "serendipity and flair." It was "a creative activity insusceptible of formulation in hard and fast rules." Lying "beyond our powers of conscious control," the "entrepreneurial perception" appeared only infrequently, striking suddenly and without warning.[15] When it did appear, it reordered the universe.

The market, in short, provided a refuge for self-expression and creativity, a sanctuary for the rapturous counter-Enlightenment. Unimaginative writers were content to argue that markets "allocate scarce resources most efficiently" or that the market "allows for the motive of self-interest." But such defenses missed a more elemental truth: markets allowed for the expression of a "whole variety of human motives, in all of their complexity and mixtures."[16] The market supplied a theater for dramatic self-disclosure, a stage on which individuals could project their most irrepressible visions and strenuous desires.

All love affairs come to an end, but Gray's breakup with the market has been particularly venomous. He now denounces it as the scourge of civilization. In the United States, he writes, the free market has "generated a long economic boom from which the majority of Americans has hardly benefited." Americans suffer from "levels of inequality" that "resemble those of Latin American countries." The middle class enjoys the dubious charms of "asset-less economic insecurity that afflicted the nineteenth-century proletariat." The United States stands perilously close to massive social disruption, which has been held at bay only "by a policy of mass incarceration" of African Americans and other people of color. "The prophet of today's America," Gray claims, "is not Jefferson or Madison. . . . It is Jeremy Bentham"—the man who dreamed of a society "reconstructed on the model of an ideal prison."[17]

Even more appalling, writes Gray, global elites have sought to make American capitalism the model for the world. Even though market regimes vary by culture and country, the high priests of globalization impose a one-size-fits-all American model—with its minimal welfare state, weak business and environmental regulations, and low taxes. "According to the 'Washington consensus,'" writes Gray, "the manifold economic cultures and systems that the world has always contained will be redundant. They will be merged into a single universal free market" based on the "world's last great Enlightenment regime, the United States."[18]

When Gray first uttered these heresies, many of his conservative friends were shocked. Like Gray, Norman Barry is a political theorist who has written on Hayek. A professor at the University of Buckingham, the only wholly private university in Britain, he was the best man at Gray's second wedding but now rarely speaks with him. Barry cannot shake the suspicion that Gray's political turn was motivated by pure opportunism. "I believe in a proposition of neoclassical economics: Everybody's a utility maximizer," he explains. "It might have been a good career move to detach himself from libertarianism. I am speculating but not wildly. Libertarians don't get the best positions in universities." When Gray was only a fellow at a small Oxford college, claims Barry, "he used to say, 'Well, the way the world works I wouldn't get a chair.'. . . You don't get professorships at LSE if you're a free-market fanatic." The only continuity in Gray's position that Barry recognizes is his penchant for "philosophical promiscuity." Gray, says Barry, "was always flitting from person to person, philosopher to philosopher. . . . He couldn't form a steady relationship with any thinker. He tried a bit of Popper. Tried Hayek. Of course, he later dumped Hayek. Other writers he would try and dump."

Gray claims that he changed his mind for two reasons. During the late 1980s, he says, he began to suspect that political thinking on the right had stiffened into stale ideology—not unlike the dull Rawlsianism he fled so long ago. Gray had once thought of Thatcherism as tactically flexible and politically savvy, a movement sensitive to popular moods, its leader a Machiavellian virtuoso of political change. But he now believed that the movement had lost its artistry; supple thought had degenerated into rote incantation. Gray says, "What was striking about Bolshevism was that Lenin was so extraordinarily flexible. Then it hardened into Trotskyism. And similarly Thatcherism began to harden. . . . It was a habit of thought that I found deeply repugnant."

The collapse of the Soviet Union also forced Gray to question his free-market faith. Until 1989, Gray says, it made sense to think of the state as "the principal enemy of well-being," which was the attitude within "the admittedly hothouse atmosphere of the right-wing think thanks." But after the Soviet empire fell, the former Yugoslavia spiraled into genocidal civil war, and Western free-marketeers applied shock therapy to formerly Communist countries with disastrous results, Gray came to think that the state was a necessary evil, perhaps even a positive good. It was the only force that could prevent societies from sliding into total chaos, extreme inequality, and poverty.

But there is a deeper reason for Gray's turn: by itself, the market could not sustain his affections. Without the Soviet Union and the welfare state as diverting symbols of Enlightenment rationalism, Gray could no longer believe in the market as he once had. The market, he now had to admit, sponsors a "cult of reason and efficiency." It "snaps the threads of memory and scatters local knowledge." He used to think that the free market arose spontaneously and that state control of the economy was unnatural. But watching Jeffrey Sachs and the International Monetary Fund in Russia, he could not help but see the free market as "a product of artifice, design and political coercion." The market had to be created, often with the aid of ruthless state power. Today, he argues that Thatcher built the free market by crushing trade unions, hollowing out the Conservative Party, and disabling Parliament. She "set British society on a forced march into late modernity." Gray believes "Marxism-Leninism and free-market economic rationalism have much in common." Both, he writes, "exhibit scant sympathy for the casualties of economic progress."[19] There is only one difference: Communism is dead.

In an unguarded moment, Norman Barry confesses that he cannot fathom Gray's shift. "Maybe I just misunderstood him," he says, "but I thought that he did believe deeply. Nobody could have read that amount of stuff without believing some of it, anyway. I wonder whether he ever did." Gray did believe, but his belief was different from Barry's. Barry loves the market because it operates according to "the iron laws of economics." As he puts it, these may "take a little longer than Newtonian laws. If I drop this disk, it's down in a second. If I introduce rent control, it would take maybe six months to create homelessness." But, he adds, "it's just as decisive." By contrast, Gray once believed in capitalism precisely because he sought an escape from the laws of Newton. Having realized that the market inhibits passionate self-expression, Gray has been forced to acknowledge the truth of Irving Kristol's dictum: "Capitalism is the least romantic conception of a public order that the human mind has ever conceived."[20]

By the time Edward Luttwak was in his early forties, he had outrun Nazis, escaped Communists, and been shot at by leftist guerrillas in Central America. But to this day, he remembers his childhood move from Palermo to Milan as the most "traumatic" event of his life. Born in 1942 into a wealthy Jewish family in Romania, Luttwak grew up in southern Transylvania, which was briefly occupied by the Nazis in 1944. When he was five years old, his family fled an imminent Communist takeover and settled in Palermo. It was winter, Luttwak recalls, and "Paris and London were shivering. There was a fuel shortage. Milano was shivering. Things were pretty bleak." But in Palermo "the opera was in full swing." It was "the land of oranges and lemons," he says, where people could swim and ski almost year-round. Five years later, Luttwak's family moved again, this time to Milan, the industrial center of Italy. "Stuffy and fog-ridden," Milan made Luttwak miserable. "There was nowhere to play. The parks were a disgrace. I lost all my friends from Palermo. I found myself . . . amid a bunch of very bourgeois kids." The good life on the Mediterranean had come to an end, done in by dour industrialists to the north.

For most of his adult life, Luttwak waged a militant struggle against Communism. Inspired by a strategic military vision that connected the Gallic Wars to the civil wars of Central America, he worked closely with the U.S. Defense Department as a consultant, advising everyone from junior officers to the top brass. But Luttwak was more than a cold warrior. He was a *warrior*, or at least a fervent theorist of "the art of war." Where generals thought victory depended on aping management styles from IBM, Luttwak made the case for ancient battlefield tactics and forgotten maneuvers from the Roman Empire. Luttwak urged the military to look to Hadrian, not Henry Ford, for guidance. It was an arduous struggle, with officers more often acting like organization men than soldiers. Once again, Luttwak found his preferred way of life threatened by the culture of capitalism.

Luttwak first gained notoriety in Britain, where he settled after receiving his undergraduate degree in economics at the London

School of Economics. In 1968, he published *Coup d'État: A Practical Handbook*. The twenty-six-year-old author dazzled his readers with this audacious how-to guide, prompting a delighted John Le Carré to write, "Mr. Luttwak has composed an unholy gastronomic guide to political poison. Those brave enough to look into his kitchen will never eat quite as peacefully again." In 1970, Luttwak published an equally mischievous piece in *Esquire*, "A Scenario for a Military Coup d'État in the United States." Two years later, he moved to the United States to write a dissertation in political science and classical history at Johns Hopkins, conducting extensive research using original Latin, German, French, English, and Italian sources. The result was the widely praised *The Grand Strategy of the Roman Empire*. While in graduate school, Luttwak began to work as a consultant to various branches of the U.S. armed services, ultimately making recommendations on everything from how NATO should conduct tactical maneuvers to what kind of rifle soldiers in the El Salvadoran military should carry.

When Ronald Reagan ran for president in 1980, Luttwak was at the top of his game. A fellow at Georgetown's Center for Strategic and International Studies and a frequent contributor to *Commentary*, he argued that the United States should accelerate the high-tech arms race, forcing the Soviet Union into a contest it could not win. Reagan's closest advisers eagerly welcomed Luttwak to their inner circle. Just after Reagan's election, Luttwak attended a dinner party in Bethesda, along with Jeane Kirkpatrick, Fred Iklé, and other luminaries of the Republican defense establishment. Richard Allen, who would become Reagan's first national security adviser, worked the crowd, pretending to dispense positions in the administration as if they were party favors. As the *Washington Post* reported, Luttwak declined, explaining over chocolate Tia Maria pie, "I don't believe scribblers like myself should be involved in politics. It's like caviar. Very nice, but only in small quantities."

When pressed by Allen, he joked, "I only want to be vice-consul in Florence." Allen responded, "Don't you mean proconsul?"[21]

The prep-school gladiator bonhomie evaporated before the end of Reagan's first term. Luttwak may have been an invaluable asset when pushing for more defense spending, but he made enemies with his loud—and ever more sarcastic—criticisms of Pentagon mismanagement. In 1984, he published *The Pentagon and the Art of War,* where, among other things, he depicted Defense Secretary Caspar Weinberger as more of a slick used-car salesman than a genuine statesman. Military politicos struck back, dropping Luttwak from a roster of pro bono Pentagon consultants (he continued to do contract work elsewhere in the defense establishment). In 1986, Weinberger explained to the *Los Angeles Times* that Luttwak "just lost consulting positions from total incompetence, that's all."[22]

But it was more than Luttwak's criticisms of Weinberger that got him in trouble with the Defense Department. His real mistake in *The Pentagon and the Art of War* was to go after the military's conduct during the Vietnam War. Luttwak downplayed the armed forces' favorite explanations for their defeat in Vietnam—weak-willed politicians, the treasonous press, a defeatist public. He argued instead that America's warrior elite had simply lost the taste for blood. During the Vietnam War, he wrote, "deskbound officers" were always "far from combat." Their penchant for "out-right luxury" had a devastating effect on troop morale. Although Julius Caesar "retained both concubines and catamites in his rear-ward headquarters, ate off gold plate, and drank his Samian wine from jeweled goblets," when he was on the front lines with his soldiers he "ate only what they ate, and slept as they did—under a tent if the troops had tents, or merely wrapped in a blanket if they did not." By contrast, American officers refused "to share in the hardships and deadly risks of war."[23]

Pointy-headed bureaucrats also sapped the military's strength, according to Luttwak. Always looking to cut costs, Pentagon officials insisted that weapons, machinery, and research-and-development programs be standardized. But this only made the military vulnerable to enemy attack. Standardized weapons systems were easily overcome; having overwhelmed one, an enemy could overwhelm them all. When it came to the military, Luttwak concluded, "we need more 'fraud, waste, and mismanagement.'"[24]

Top generals were obsessed with efficiency partially because they learned the methods of business management instead of the art of war. For every officer with a degree in military history, there were a hundred more "whose greatest personal accomplishment is a graduate degree in business administration, management or economics." "Why should fighter pilots receive a full-scale university education," Luttwak asked in the *Washington Quarterly*, "instead of being taught how to hunt and kill with their machines?"[25]

The ultimate source of the military's dysfunction was its embrace of American corporate culture and business values. Like Robert McNamara, whom President Kennedy transferred to the Pentagon from the Ford Motor Company, most defense secretaries were in thrall to "corporate-style goals." They sought the least risky, most cost-effective means to a given end. They preferred gray suits, eschewing "personal eccentricities in dress, speech, manner, and style because any unusual trait may irritate a customer or a banker in the casual encounters common in business." Officers were merely "managers in uniform," Luttwak told *Forbes*. But, he noted, "what is good for business is not good for deadly conflict." Although "safely conservative dress and inoffensively conventional style" might work in an office, they could be deadly on the battlefield; they squelched bold initiatives and idiosyncratic genius.[26] Intimating that capitalism had colonized—indeed destroyed—spheres of society that were not strictly economic, Luttwak came perilously close to identifying himself with leading voices from the Marxist tradition—Jürgen Habermas, Georg Lukács, even Marx himself.

While the Soviet Union still existed, Luttwak was able to channel his contempt for managerial and corporate values into proposals for military reform. The struggle against Bolshevism fully captured his imagination, speaking to principles of individualism, independence, and personal dignity that he had learned as a child of Jewish atheists. Luttwak's parents taught him, he says, that "you wanted your shoulders out walking down the street. The master of your fate. Not to walk hunched, afraid that God will punish you if you eat a ham sandwich." He continues: "There was a certain contempt about piety. Piety was not seen as compatible with dignity." Dignity, he goes on, "is what we were defending in the Cold War. It was ideological. It was very fitting for me to be in the United States, to become an American, because the Americans were and are the ideological people. They were perfectly cast to be enlisted in an ideological struggle."

But now that the battle against Communism has been won, Luttwak has lost interest in most military matters; he no longer sees any compelling ideological reason to care about strategy and tactics. "Security problems and such have become peripheral, for all countries and for people, for myself as well. I don't engage my existence in something that is peripheral. . . . There was a compelling imperative to be involved. There isn't now."

Luttwak does occasionally muster energy for a specific project. During one of our interviews, he speaks by phone with a State Department official about doing consulting work for the war against the Colombian guerrillas. But when I ask him if the Colombian government is worth defending, he is uncharacteristically hesitant, finally confessing, "I don't know if anything is worth defending, but I think the guerrillas are worth fighting." I ask him why, and he responds that the guerrillas are aligned with drug traffickers who "do everything from taking people's places in restaurants in Medellín on a Saturday night—people are waiting to take seats and these guys come in and they grab their tables—everything from that to murder."

Military struggle may no longer hold any ideological allure for Luttwak, but his disaffection affords him the time and intellectual space to confront the enemy he has been shadowboxing his entire life: capitalism itself. "The market," he says, "invades every sphere of life," producing a "hellish society." In the same way that market values once threatened national security, they now threaten the economic and spiritual well-being of society. "An optimal production system is a completely inhuman production system," he explains, "because . . . you are constantly changing the number of people you employ, you're moving them around, you're doing different things, and that is not compatible with somebody being able to organize an existence for himself."

Although Luttwak writes in his 1999 book *Turbo-Capitalism,* "I deeply believe . . . in the virtues of capitalism," his opposition to the spread of market values is so acute that it puts him on the far end of today's political spectrum—a position that Luttwak congenially enjoys.[27] "Edward is a very perverse guy, intellectually and in many other ways," says former *Commentary* editor Norman Podhoretz, one of Luttwak's early champions during the 1970s. "He's a contrarian. He enjoys confounding expectations. But I frankly don't even know how serious he is in this latest incarnation." Luttwak insists that he is quite serious. He calls for socialized medicine. He advocates a strong welfare state, claiming, "If I had my druthers, I would prohibit any form of domestic charity." Charity is a "cop-out," he says: it takes dignity away from the poor.

The only thing that arouses Luttwak's ire more than untrammeled capitalism is its elite enthusiasts—the intellectuals, politicians, policy makers, and businessmen who claim that "just because the market is always more efficient, the market should always rule." Alan Greenspan earns Luttwak's special contempt: "Alan Greenspan is a Spencerian. That makes him an economic fascist." Spencerians like Greenspan believe that "the harshest economic pressures" will "stimulate some people to . . . economically heroic deeds. They will become great entrepreneurs or whatever else, and as for the ones who fail, let them fail." Luttwak's other bête noire is "Chainsaw Al" Dunlap, the peripatetic CEO who reaps unimaginable returns for corporate shareholders by firing substantial numbers of employees from companies. "Chainsaw does it," says Luttwak, referring to Dunlap's downsizing measures, "because he's simpleminded, harsh, and cruel." It's just "economic sadism." Against Greenspan and Dunlap, Luttwak affirms, "I believe that one ought to have only as much market efficiency as one needs, because everything that we value in human life is within the realm of inefficiency—love, family, attachment, community, culture, old habits, comfortable old shoes."

The defections of Luttwak and Gray suggest just how unkind the end of the Cold War has been to the conservative movement. It is increasingly clear that the fragile coalition of libertarians, traditionalists, and free-market enthusiasts once held together by the glue of anti-Communism will no longer stick. The end of the Soviet Union "deprived us of an enemy," Irving Kristol, the intellectual godfather of neoconservatism, tells me. "In politics, being deprived of an enemy is a very serious matter. You tend to get relaxed and dispirited. Turn inward." Notorious for his self-confidence, Kristol now confesses to a sad bewilderment in the post-Communist world. "That's one of the reasons I really am not writing much these days," he says. "I don't know the answers."

One might think the triumph of the free market would thrill right-wing intellectuals. But even the most revered conservative patriarchs worry that the market alone cannot sustain the flagging energies of the movement. After all, Reagan and Thatcher summoned conservatives to a political crusade, but the free-market ideology they unleashed is suspicious of all political faiths. The market's logic glorifies private initiative, individual action, the brilliance of the unplanned and random. Against that backdrop, it is difficult to think about politics at all—much less political transformation. William F. Buckley Jr. tells me, "The trouble with the emphasis in conservatism on the market is that it becomes rather boring. You hear it once, you master the idea. The notion of devoting your life to it is horrifying if only because it's so repetitious. It's like sex." Kristol adds, "American conservatism lacks for political imagination. It's so influenced by business culture and by business modes of thinking that it lacks any political imagination, which has always been, I have to say, a property of the left." He goes on, "If you read Marx, you'd learn what a political imagination could do."

But if conservatives are struggling to find a vision, can the ex-conservatives do much better? Unlike Kristol, who fled the left and launched the neoconservative movement, Luttwak and Gray have not formulated coherent alternatives, philosophical or political, to their former creeds. As Luttwak puts it: "Instead of proposing a whole counter-ideology, what I simply propose is society consciously saying that certain things should be protected from the market and kept out of the market." This, despite the fact that Luttwak remains temperamentally enamored, in his way, of the revolutionary impulse. "I prefer 'The Marseillaise' to the Mass," he says, "Mayakovski to the cross of St. George." He adds, "Revolutions are wonderful. People enjoying themselves. I was in Paris in 1968. . . . There was a wonderful feeling of possibility." But though Luttwak may long for a transformative politics, it remains beyond his reach, an object of nostalgia not just for him but for most intellectuals.

Except, it turns out, for William F. Buckley Jr., the original bad boy of the American right. At the end of our interview, I ask Buckley to imagine a younger version of himself, an aspiring political enfant terrible graduating from college in 2000, bringing to today's political world the same insurgent spirit that Buckley brought to his. What kind of politics would this youthful Buckley embrace? "I'd be a socialist," he replies. "A Mike Harrington socialist." He pauses. "I'd even say a communist."

Can he really imagine a young Communist Bill Buckley? He concedes that it's difficult. The original Bill Buckley had the benefit of the Soviet Union as an enemy; without its equivalent, his doppelgänger would confront a more complicated task. "This new Buckley would have to point to other things," he says. Buckley runs down a laundry list of left causes—global poverty, death from AIDS. But even he seems suddenly overwhelmed by the project of (in typical Buckleyese) "conjoining all of that into an arresting afflatus." Daunted by the challenge of thinking outside the free market, Buckley pauses, then finally says, "I'll leave that to you."

6

Affirmative Action Baby

Next to Clarence Thomas, Antonin Scalia is the most conservative justice on the Supreme Court. He also loves the television show *24*. "Boy, those early seasons," he tells his biographer, "I'd be up to two o'clock, because you're at the end of one [episode], and you'd say, 'No, I've got to see the next.'" Scalia is especially taken with Jack Bauer, the show's fictional hero played by Kiefer Sutherland. Bauer is a government agent at a Los Angeles counterterrorism unit who foils mass-murder plots by torturing suspects, kidnapping innocents, and executing colleagues. Refusing to be bound by the law, he fights a two-front war against terrorism and the Constitution. And whenever he bends a rule or breaks a bone, Scalia swoons.

> Jack Bauer saved Los Angeles. . . . He saved hundreds of thousands of lives. . . . Are you going to convict Jack Bauer? Say that criminal law is against him? You have the right to a jury trial? Is any jury going to convict Jack Bauer? I don't think so. So the question is really whether we really believe in these absolutes. And ought we believe in these absolutes?[1]

This chapter originally appeared as a review of Joan Biskupic's *American Original: The Life and Constitution of Supreme Court Justice Antonin Scalia* (New York: Farrar, Straus and Giroux, 2009) in the *London Review of Books* (June 10, 2010): 29–31.

Yet Scalia has spent the better part of his career as a lawyer, professor, and jurist telling us that the Constitution is an absolute, in which we must believe, even when—particularly when—it tells us something we do not want to hear. Scalia's Constitution is not a warming statement of benevolent purpose, easily adapted to our changing needs. His Constitution is cold and dead, its prohibitions and injunctions frozen in time. Phrases like "cruel and unusual punishment" mean what they meant when they were written into the Constitution. If that produces objectionable results—say, the execution of children and the mentally retarded—too bad. "I do not think," Scalia writes in *Nixon v. Missouri Municipal League*, that "the avoidance of unhappy consequences is adequate basis for interpreting a text."[2]

Scalia takes special pleasure in unhappy consequences. He relishes difficulty and dislikes anyone who would diminish or deny it. In *Hamdi v. Rumsfeld*, a plurality of the Court took what Scalia thought was a squishy position on executive power during wartime. The Court ruled that the Authorization for the Use of Military Force, passed by Congress after 9/11, empowered the president to detain U.S. citizens indefinitely as "illegal enemy combatants" without trying them in a court of law. It also ruled, however, that such citizens were entitled to due process and could challenge their detention before some kind of tribunal.

Scalia was livid. Writing against the plurality—as well as the Bush administration and fellow conservatives on the Court—he insisted that a government at war, even one as unconventional as the war on terror, had two, and only two, ways to hold a citizen: try him in a court of law or have Congress suspend the writ of habeas corpus. Live by the rules of due process, in other words, or suspend them. Take a stand, make a choice.

But the Court weaseled out of that choice, making life easier for the government and itself. Congress and the president could act as if habeas corpus were suspended, without having to suspend it, and the Court could act as if the writ hadn't been suspended thanks to a faux due process of military tribunals. More than coloring outside the lines of the Constitution, it was the Court's "Mr. Fix-It Mentality," in Scalia's words, its "mission to Make Everything Come Out Right," that enraged him.[3]

Scalia's mission, by contrast, is to make everything come out wrong. A Scalia opinion, to borrow a phrase from *New Yorker* writer Margaret Talbot, is "the jurisprudential equivalent of smashing a guitar on stage."[4] Scalia may have once declared the rule of law the law of rules—leading some to mistake him for a stereotypical conservative—but rules and laws have a particular frisson for him. Where others look to them for stabilizing checks or reassuring supports, Scalia looks for exhilarating impediments and vertiginous barriers. Where others seek security, Scalia seeks sublimity. Rules and laws make life harder, and harder is everything. "Being tough and traditional is a heavy cross to bear," he tells one reporter. *"Duresse oblige."*[5]

That, and not fidelity to the text or conservatism as it is conventionally understood, is the idée fixe of Scalia's jurisprudence—and the source of his apparent man-crush on Jack Bauer. Bauer never makes things easy for himself; indeed, he goes out of his way to make things as hard as possible. He volunteers for a suicide mission when someone else would do (and probably do it better); he turns himself into a junkie as part of an impossibly baroque plan to stop an act of bioterrorism; he puts his wife and daughter at risk, not once but many times, and then beats himself up for doing so. He loathes what he does but does it anyway. That is his nobility—some might say masochism—and why he warms Scalia's heart.

It means something, of course, that Scalia identifies the path of most resistance in fidelity to an ancient text, while Bauer finds it in betrayal of that text. But not as much as one might think: as we've come to learn from the marriages of our right-wing preachers and politicians, fidelity is often another word for betrayal.

Scalia was born in Trenton, New Jersey, in March 1936, but he was conceived the previous summer in Florence, Italy. (His father, a doctoral student in romance languages at Columbia, had won a fellowship to travel there with his wife.) "I hated Trenton," Scalia says; his heart belongs to Florence. A devotee of opera and hunting—"he loves killing unarmed animals," observes Clarence Thomas—Scalia likes to cut a Medicean profile of great art and great cruelty. He peppers his decisions with stylish allusions to literature and history. Once upon a time, he enjoys telling audiences, he was too "faint-hearted" an originalist to uphold the eighteenth century's acceptance of ear notching and flogging as forms of punishment. Not anymore. "I've gotten older and crankier," he says, ever the diva of disdain.[6]

When Scalia was six, his parents moved to the Elmhurst section of Queens. His lifelong conservatism is often attributed to his strict Italian Catholic upbringing there; alluding to Burke, he calls it his "little platoon." He attended Xavier High School, a Jesuit school in Manhattan, and Georgetown, a Jesuit university in Washington, D.C. In his freshman year at Georgetown, the senior class voted Senator Joseph McCarthy as the Outstanding American.[7]

But Scalia comes to his ethnicity and religion with an attitude, lending his ideology a defiant edge. (That defiance is often thought to be distinctive, out of keeping with conservative manners and mores; but as we have seen, it's not.) He claims he didn't get into Princeton, his first choice, because "I was an Italian boy from Queens, not quite the Princeton type." Later, after Vatican II liberalized the liturgy and practices of the Church, including his neighborhood church in suburban Washington, D.C., he insisted on driving his brood of seven children miles away to hear Sunday Mass in Latin. Later still, in Chicago, he did the same thing, only this time with nine children in tow. Commenting on how he and his wife managed to raise conservative children during the sixties and seventies—no jeans in the Scalia household—he says:

> They were being raised in a culture that wasn't supportive of our values, that was certainly true. But we were helped by the fact that we were such a large family. We had our own culture. . . . The first thing you've got to teach your kids is what my parents used to tell me all the time, "You're not everybody else. . . . We have our own standards and they aren't the standards of the world in all respects, and the sooner you learn that the better."[8]

Scalia's conservatism, it turns out, is less a little platoon than a Thoreauvian counterculture, a retreat from and rebuke to the mainstream, not unlike the hippie communes and groupuscules he once tried to keep at bay. It is not a conservatism of tradition or inheritance: his parents had only one child, and his mother-in-law often complained about having to drive miles and hours in search of the one true church. "Why don't you people ever seem to live near churches?" she would ask Scalia and his wife.[9] It is a conservatism of invention and choice, informed by the very spirit of rebellion he so plainly loathes—or thinks he loathes—in the culture at large.

In the 1970s, while teaching at the University of Chicago, Scalia liked to end the semester with a reading from *A Man for All Seasons*, Robert Bolt's play about Thomas More. While the play's anti-authoritarianism would seem at odds with Scalia's conservatism, its protagonist, at least as he is portrayed by Bolt, is not. Literally more Catholic than the pope, More is a true believer in the law who refuses to compromise his principles in order to accommodate the wishes of Henry VIII. He pays for his integrity with his life.

Scalia's biographer introduces this biographical tidbit with a revealing setup: "Yet even as Scalia in middle age was developing a more rigid view of the law, he still had bursts of idealism."[10] That "yet" is misplaced. Scalia's rigidity is not opposed to his idealism; it is his idealism. His ultraconservative reading of the Constitution reflects neither cynicism nor conventionalism; orthodoxy and piety are, for him, the essence of dissidence and iconoclasm. No charge grieves him more than the claim, rehearsed at length in his 1995 Tanner Lectures at Princeton, that his philosophy is "wooden," "unimaginative," "pedestrian," "dull," "narrow," and "hidebound."[11] Call him a bastard or a prick, a hound from hell or a radical in robes. Just don't say he's a suit.

Scalia's philosophy of Constitutional interpretation—variously called originalism, original meaning, or original public meaning—is often confused with original intention. While the first crew of originalists in the 1970s did claim that the Court should interpret the Constitution according to the intentions of the Framers, later originalists like Scalia wisely recast that argument in response to criticisms it received. The intentions of a single author are often unknowable, and in the case of many authors, practically indeterminate. And whose intentions should count: those of the 55 men who wrote the Constitution, the 1,179 men who ratified it, or the even greater number of men who voted for the men who ratified it? From Scalia's view, it is not intentions that govern us. It is the Constitution, the text as it was written and rewritten through amendment. That is the proper object of interpretation.

But how to recover the meaning of a text that can careen from terrifying generality in one sentence ("the executive Power shall be vested in a President") to an uneventful precision (presidential terms are four years) in the next? Look to the public meaning of the words at the time they were adopted, says Scalia. See how they were used: consult dictionaries, other usages in the text, influential writings of the time. Consider the context of their utterance, how they were received. From these sources, construct a bounded universe of possible meanings. Words don't mean one thing, Scalia concedes, but neither do they mean anything. Judges should read the Constitution neither literally nor loosely but "reasonably"—that is, in such a way that each word or phrase is construed "to contain all that it fairly means." And then, somehow or other, apply that meaning to our own much different times.[12]

Scalia justifies his originalism on two grounds, both negative. In a constitutional democracy it is the job of elected representatives to make the law, the job of judges to interpret it. If judges are not bound by how the law, including the Constitution, was understood at the time of its enactment—if they consult their own morals or their own interpretations of the country's morals—they are no longer judges but lawmakers, and often unelected lawmakers at that. By tying the judge to a text that does not change, originalism helps reconcile judicial review with democracy and protects us from judicial despotism.

If Scalia's first concern is tyranny from the bench, his second is anarchy on the bench. Once we abandon the idea of an unchanging Constitution, he says, we open the gates to any and all modes of interpretation. How are we to understand a Constitution that evolves? By looking at the polls, the philosophy of John Rawls, the teachings of the Catholic Church? If the Constitution is always changing, what constraints can we impose on what counts as an acceptable interpretation? None, Scalia says. When "every day" is "a new day" in the law, it ceases to be law.[13]

This mix of tyranny and anarchy is no idle fantasy, Scalia and other originalists insist. For a brief, terrible time—from the Warren Court of the 1960s to the Burger Court of the 1970s—it was a reality. In the name of a "living Constitution," left-wing judges remade (or tried to remake) the country in their own image, forcing an agenda of social democracy, sexual liberation, gender equality, racial integration, and moral relativism down the country's throat. Ancient words acquired new implications and insinuations: suddenly "due process of law" entailed a "right to privacy," code words for birth control and abortion (and later gay sex); "equal protection of the laws" required one man, one vote; the ban against "unreasonable searches and seizures" meant that evidence obtained unlawfully by the police could not be admitted in court; the proscription against the "establishment of religion" forbade school prayer. With each law it overturned and right it discovered, the Court seemed to invent a new ground of action. It was a constitutional Carnival, where exotic theories of adjudication were paraded with libidinous abandon. For originalists, what was most outrageous about this revolution from above—beyond the left-wing values it foisted upon the nation—was how out of keeping it was with how the Court traditionally justified its decisions to strike down laws.

Prior to the Warren Court, says Scalia, or the 1920s (it's never clear when exactly the rot set in), everyone was an originalist.[14] That's not quite true. Expansive constructions of Constitutional meaning are as old and august as the founding itself. And the theoretical self-consciousness Scalia and his followers bring to the table is a decidedly twentieth-century phenomenon. Scalia, in fact, often sounds like he's a comp lit student circa 1983. He says it is a "sad commentary" that "American judges have no intelligible theory of what we do most" and "even sadder" that the legal profession is "by and large . . . unconcerned with the fact that we have no intelligible theory."[15]

Conservatives used to mock that kind of theory fetishism as the mark of an inexperienced and artless ruling class; even an avowed originalist like Robert Bork concedes that "self-confident legal institutions do not require so much talking about." But Scalia and Bork forged their ideas in battle against a liberal jurisprudence that was self-conscious and theoretical, and, like so many of their predecessors on the right, they have come out of it looking more like their enemies than their friends. Bork, in fact, freely admits that it is not John Marshall or Joseph Story—the traditional greats of judicial review—to whom he looks for guidance; it is Alexander Bickel, arguably the most self-conscious of the twentieth-century liberal theoreticians, who "taught me more than anyone else about this subject."[16]

Like many originalists, Scalia claims that his jurisprudence has nothing to do with his conservatism. "I try mightily to prevent my religious views or my political views or my philosophical views from affecting my interpretation of the laws." Yet he has also said that he learned from his teachers at Georgetown never to "separate your religious life from your intellectual life. They're not separate." Only months before Ronald Reagan nominated him to the Supreme Court in 1986, he admitted that his legal views were "inevitably affected by moral and theological perceptions."[17]

And, indeed, in the deep grammar of his opinions lies a conservatism that, if it has little to do with advancing the immediate interests of the Republican Party, has even less to do with averting the threats of judicial tyranny and judicial anarchy. It is a conservatism that would have been recognizable to Social Darwinists of the late nineteenth century, that mixes freely of the premodern and the postmodern, the archaic and the advanced. It is not to be found in the obvious places—Scalia's opinions about abortion, say, or gay rights—but in a dissenting opinion about that most un-Scaliaesque of places, the golf course.

Casey Martin was a champion golfer (he's now an ex-golfer) who because of a degenerative disease could no longer walk the eighteen holes of a golf course. After the PGA Tour refused his request to use a golf cart in the final round of one of its qualifying tournaments, a federal court issued an injunction, based on the Americans with Disabilities Act (ADA), allowing Martin to use a cart. Title III of the ADA states that "no individual shall be discriminated against on the basis of disability in the full and equal enjoyment of the goods, services, privileges, advantages, or accommodations of any place of public accommodation by any person who owns, leases (or leases to), or operates a place of public accommodation." By the time the case reached the Supreme Court in 2001, the legal questions had boiled down to these: Is Martin entitled to the protections of Title III of the ADA? Would allowing Martin to use a cart "fundamentally alter the nature" of the game? Ruling 7–2 in Martin's favor—with Scalia and Thomas in dissent—the Court said yes to the first and no to the second.

In answering the first question, the Court had to contend with the PGA's claims that it was operating a "place of exhibition or entertainment" rather than a public accommodation, that only a customer of that entertainment qualified for Title III protections, and that Martin was not a customer but a provider of entertainment. The Court was skeptical of the first two claims. But even if they were true, the Court said, Martin would still be protected by Title III because he was in fact a customer of the PGA: he and the other contestants had to pay $3,000 to try out for the tournament. Some customers paid to watch the tournament, others to compete in it. The PGA could not discriminate against either.

Scalia was incensed. It "seems to me quite incredible," he began, that the majority would treat Martin as a "'custome[r]' of 'competition'" rather than as a competitor. The PGA sold entertainment, the public paid for it, the golfers provided it; the qualifying rounds were their application for hire. Martin was no more a customer than is an actor who shows up for an open casting call. He was an employee, or potential employee, whose proper recourse, if he had any, was not Title III of the ADA, which covered public accommodations, but Title I, which covered employment. But Martin wouldn't have that recourse, admitted Scalia, because he was essentially an independent contractor, a category of employee not covered by the ADA. Martin would thus wind up in a legal no man's land, without any protection from the law.

In the majority's suggestion that Martin was a customer rather than a competitor, Scalia saw something worse than a wrongly decided opinion. He saw a threat to the status of athletes everywhere, whose talent and excellence would be smothered by the bosomy embrace of the Court, and also a threat to the idea of competition more generally. It was as if the Homeric rivals of ancient Greece were being plucked from their manly games and forced to walk the aisles of a modern boutique.

Games hold a special valence for Scalia: they are the space where inequality rules. "The very nature of competitive sport is the measurement," he says, "of unevenly distributed excellence." That inequality is what "determines the winners and losers." In the noonday sun of competition, we cannot hide our superiority or inferiority, our excellence or inadequacy. Games make our unequal natures plain to the world; they celebrate "the uneven distribution of God-given gifts."

In the Court's transposition of competitor into customer, Scalia saw the forced entry of democracy (a "revolution," actually) into this antique preserve. With "Animal Farm determination"—yes, Scalia goes there—the Court had destroyed our one and only opportunity to see how unequal we truly are, how unfairly God has chosen to bestow his blessings upon us. "The year was 2001," reads the last sentence of Scalia's dissent, "and 'everybody was finally equal.'"

Like the Social Darwinists and Nietzsche, Scalia is too much a modernist, even a postmodernist, to pine for the lost world of feudal fixities. Modernity has seen too much flux to sustain a belief in hereditary status. The watermarks of privilege and privation are no longer visible to the naked eye; they must be identified, again and again, through struggle and contest. Hence the appeal of the game. In sports, unlike law, every day is a new day. Every competition is a fresh opportunity for mixing it up, for throwing our established hierarchies into anarchic relief and allowing a new face of supremacy or abjection to emerge. It thus offers the perfect marriage of the feudal and the fallible, the unequal and the unsettled.

To answer the second question—does riding in a golf cart "fundamentally alter the nature" of golf—the majority undertook a thorough history of the rules of golf. It then formulated a two-part test for determining whether riding in a cart would change the nature of golf. The dutifulness and care, the seriousness with which the majority took its task, both amused and annoyed Scalia.

> It has been rendered the solemn duty of the Supreme Court of the United States . . . to decide What Is Golf. I am sure that the Framers of the Constitution, aware of the 1457 edict of King James II of Scotland prohibiting golf because it interfered with the practice of archery, fully expected that sooner or later the paths of golf and government, the law and the links, would once again cross, and that the judges of this august Court would some day have to wrestle with that age-old jurisprudential question, for which their years of study in the law have so well prepared them: Is someone riding around a golf course from shot to shot really a golfer?

Scalia is clearly enjoying himself, but his mirth is a little mystifying. The ADA defines discrimination as

> a failure to make reasonable modifications in the policies, practices, or procedures, when such modifications are necessary

to afford such goods, services, facilities, privileges, advantages, or accommodations to individuals with disabilities, unless the entity can demonstrate that making such modifications would fundamentally alter the nature of such goods, services, facilities, privileges, advantages, or accommodations that the entity provides.

Any determination of discrimination requires a prior determination about whether the "reasonable modification" would "fundamentally alter the nature" of the good in question. The language of the statute, in other words, compels the Court to inquire into and decide What is Golf.

But Scalia won't have any of it. Refusing to be bound by the text, he prefers to meditate on the futility and fatuity of the Court's inquiry. In seeking to discover the essence of golf, the Court is looking for something that does not exist. "To say that something is 'essential,'" he writes, "is ordinarily to say that it is necessary to the achievement of a certain object." But games "have no object except amusement." Lacking an object, they have no essence. It's thus impossible to say whether a rule is essential. "All are arbitrary," he writes of the rules, "none is essential." What makes a rule a rule is either tradition or, "in more modern times," the edict of an authoritative body like the PGA. In an unguarded moment, Scalia entertains the possibility of there being "some point at which the rules of a well-known game are changed to such a degree that no reasonable person would call it the same game." But he quickly pulls back from his foray into essentialism. No Plato for him; he's with Nietzsche all the way.[18]

It is difficult to reconcile this almost Rortyesque hostility to the idea of golf's essence with Scalia's earlier statements about "the very nature of competitive sport" being the revelation of divinely ordained inequalities. (It's also difficult to reconcile Scalia's indifference to the language of the statute with his textualism, but that's another matter.) Left unresolved, however, the contradiction reveals the twin poles of Scalia's faith: a belief in rules as arbitrary impositions of power—reflecting nothing (not even the will or standing of their makers) but the flat surface of their locutionary meaning—to which we must nevertheless submit; and a belief in rules, zealously enforced, as the divining rod of our ineradicable inequality. Those who make it past these blank and barren gods are winners; everyone else is a loser.

In the United States, Tocqueville observed, a federal judge "must know how to understand the spirit of the age." While the persona of a Supreme Court Justice may be "purely judicial," his "prerogatives"—the power to strike down laws in the name of the Constitution—"are entirely political."[19] If he is to exercise those prerogatives effectively, he must be as culturally nimble and socially attuned as the shrewdest pol.

How then to explain the influence of Scalia? Here is a man who proudly, defiantly, proclaims his disdain for "the spirit of the age"— that is, when he is not embarrassingly ignorant of it. When the Court voted in 2003 to overturn state laws banning gay sex, Scalia saw the country heading down a slippery slope to masturbation.[20] In 1996, he told an audience of Christians that "we must pray for the courage to endure the scorn of the sophisticated world," a world that "will not have anything to do with miracles." We have "to be prepared to be regarded as idiots."[21] In a dissent from that same year, Scalia declared, "Day by day, case by case, [the Court] is busy designing a Constitution for a country I do not recognize."[22] As Maureen Dowd wrote, "He's so Old School, he's Old Testament."[23]

And yet, according to Elena Kagan, the newest member of the Court, appointed by Obama in 2010, Scalia "is the justice who has had the most important impact over the years on how we think and talk about the law." John Paul Stevens, the man Kagan replaced and until his retirement the most liberal Justice on the Court, says that Scalia has "made a huge difference, some of it constructive, some of it unfortunate." Scalia's influence, moreover, will in all likelihood extend into the future. "He is in tune with many of the current generation of law students," observes Ruth Bader Ginsburg, another Court liberal.[24] Give me a law student at an impressionable age, Jean Brodie might have said, and she is mine for life.

It is not Scalia's particular positions that have prevailed on the Court. Indeed, some of his most famous opinions—against abortion, affirmative action, and gay rights; in favor of the death penalty, prayer in school, and sex discrimination—are dissents. (With the addition of John Roberts to the Court in 2005 and Samuel Alito in 2006, however, that has begun to change.) Scalia's hand is more evident in the way his colleagues—and other jurists, lawyers, and scholars—make their arguments.

For many years, originalism was derided by the left. As William Brennan, the Court's liberal titan of the second half of the twentieth century, declared in 1985: "Those who would restrict claims of right to the values of 1789 specifically articulated in the Constitution turn a blind eye to social progress and eschew adaptation of overarching principles to changes of social circumstance." Against the originalists, Brennan insisted that "the genius of the Constitution rests not in any static meaning it might have had in a world that is dead and gone, but in the adaptability of its great principles to cope with current problems and current needs."[25]

Just a decade later, however, the liberal Laurence Tribe, paraphrasing the liberal Ronald Dworkin, would say, "We are all originalists now."[26] That's even truer today. Where yesterday's generation of constitutional scholars looked to philosophy— Rawls, Hart, occasionally Nozick, Marx, or Nietzsche—to interpret the Constitution, today's looks to history, to the moment when a word or passage became part of the text and acquired its meaning. Not just on the right, but also on the left: Bruce Ackerman, Akhil Amar, and Jack Balkin are just three of the most prominent liberal originalists writing today.

Liberals on the Court have undergone a similar shift. In his *Citizens United* dissent, Stevens wrote a lengthy excursus on the "original understandings," "original expectations," and "original public meaning" of the First Amendment with regard to corporate speech. Opening his discussion with a dutiful sigh of obligation— "Let us start from the beginning"—Stevens felt compelled by Scalia, whose voice and name were present throughout, to demonstrate that his position was consistent with the original meaning of freedom of speech.[27]

Other scholars and jurists have helped bring about this shift, but it is Scalia who has kept the flame at the highest reaches of the law. Not by tact or diplomacy. Scalia is often a pig, mocking his colleagues' intelligence and questioning their integrity. Sandra Day O'Connor, who sat on the Court from 1981 to 2006, was a frequent object of his ridicule and scorn. Scalia characterized one of her arguments as "devoid of content." Another, he wrote, "cannot be taken seriously." Whenever he is asked about his role in *Bush v. Gore* (2000), which put George W. Bush in the White House through a questionable mode of reasoning, he sneers, "Get over it!"[28] Nor, contrary to his camp followers, has Scalia dominated the Court by force of his intelligence. ("How bright is he?" exhales one representative admirer.)[29] On a Court where everyone is a graduate of Harvard, Yale, or Princeton, and Ivy League professors sit on either side of the bench, there are plenty of brains to go around.

Several other factors explain Scalia's dominance of the Court. For starters, Scalia has the advantage of a straightforward philosophy and nifty method. While he and his army march through the archives, rifling through documents on the right to bear arms, the commerce clause, and much else, the legal left remains "confused and uncertain," in the words of Yale law professors Robert Post and Reva Siegel, "unable to advance any robust theory of constitutional interpretation" of its own.[30] In an age when the left lacks certainty and will, Scalia's self-confidence can be a potent and intoxicating force.

Second, there's an elective affinity, even a tight fit, between the originalism of *duresse oblige* and Scalia's idea of the game. And that is Scalia's vision of what the good life entails: a daily and arduous struggle, where the only surety, if we leave things well enough alone, is that the strong shall win and the weak shall lose. Scalia, it turns out, is not nearly the iconoclast he thinks he is. Far from telling "people what they don't like to hear," as he claims, he tells the power elite exactly what they want to hear: that they are superior and that they have a seat at the table because they are superior.[31] Tocqueville, it seems, was right after all. It is not the alienness but the appositeness of Justice Scalia, the way he reflects rather than refracts the spirit of the age, that explains, at least in part, his influence.

But there may be one additional, albeit small and personal, reason for Scalia's outsized presence in our Constitutional firmament. And that is the patience and forbearance, the general decency and good manners, his liberal colleagues show him. While he rants and raves, smashing guitars and dive-bombing his enemies, they tend to respond with an indulgent shrug, a "that's just Nino," as O'Connor was wont to say.[32]

The fact may be small and personal, but the irony is large and political. For Scalia preys on and profits from the very culture of liberalism he claims to abhor: the toleration of opposing views, the generous allowances for other people's failings, the "benevolent compassion" he derides in his golf course dissent. Should his colleagues ever force him to abide by the same rules of liberal civility, or treat him as he treats them, who knows what might happen? Indeed, as two close observers of the Court have noted—in an article aptly titled "Don't Poke Scalia!"—whenever advocates before the bench subject him to the gentlest of gibes, he is quickly rattled and thrown off his game.[33] Prone to tantrums, coddled by a different set of rules: now that's an affirmative action baby.

Ever since the 1960s, it has been a commonplace of our political culture that liberal niceties depend upon conservative not-so-niceties. A dinner party on the Upper West Side requires a police force that doesn't know from Miranda, the First Amendment a military that doesn't know from Geneva. That, of course, is the conceit of *24* (not to mention a great many other Hollywood productions like *A Few Good Men*). But that formulation may have it exactly backward: without his more liberal colleagues indulging and protecting him, Scalia—like Jack Bauer—would have a much more difficult time. The conservatism of *duresse oblige* depends upon the liberalism of *noblesse oblige*, not the other way around. That is the real meaning of Justice Scalia.

PART 2 Virtues of Violence

7

A Color-Coded Genocide

On December 5, 1982, Ronald Reagan met Guatemalan president Efraín Ríos Montt in Honduras. It was a useful meeting for Reagan. "Well, I learned a lot," he told reporters on Air Force One. "You'd be surprised. They're all individual countries." It was also a useful meeting for Ríos Montt. Reagan declared him "a man of great personal integrity . . . totally dedicated to democracy." He also claimed that the Guatemalan strongman was getting "a bum rap" from human rights organizations for his military's campaign against leftist guerrillas. The next day, Daniel Wilkinson tells us in *Silence on the Mountain: Stories of Terror, Betrayal, and Forgetting in Guatemala*, one of Guatemala's elite platoons entered a jungle village called Las Dos Erres and killed 162 of its inhabitants, 67 of them children. Soldiers "grabbed" babies and toddlers by their legs, swung them in the air, and "smashed" their heads "against a wall." Older children and adults were forced to "kneel at the edge of a well," where a single "blow from a sledge hammer" sent them plummeting below. The platoon then raped a selection of women and girls it had "saved for last," pummeling their stomachs in

This chapter originally appeared as a review of Greg Grandin's *The Last Colonial Massacre: Latin America in the Cold War* (Chicago: University of Chicago Press, 2004) in the *London Review of Books* (November 18, 2004): 3–6.

order to force the pregnant among them to miscarry. They tossed the women into the well and filled it with dirt, burying an unlucky few alive. "The only human remains that [later] visitors would find" were "blood on the walls and placentas and umbilical cords on the ground."[1]

Amid the hagiography surrounding Reagan's death in 2004, it was probably too much to expect the media to mention his meeting with Ríos Montt. After all, it wasn't Reykjavik. But Reykjavik's shadow—or that cast by Reagan speaking in front of the Berlin Wall—does not entirely explain the silence about this encounter between presidents. While it is tempting to ascribe the omission to American amnesia, a more likely cause is the deep misconception about the Cold War under which most Americans labor. To the casual observer, the Cold War was a struggle between the United States and the Soviet Union, fought and won through stylish jousting at Berlin, antiseptic arguments over nuclear stockpiles, and the savvy brinkmanship of American leaders. Latin America seldom figures in popular or even academic discussion of the Cold War; and to the extent that it does, it is Cuba, Chile, and Nicaragua rather than Guatemala that earn most of the attention.

But Latin America was as much a battleground of the Cold War as Europe, and Guatemala was its front line. In 1954, the United States fought its first major contest against Communism in the Western hemisphere when it overthrew Guatemala's democratically elected president, Jacobo Arbenz, who had worked closely with the country's small but influential Communist Party. That coup sent a young Argentinean doctor fleeing to Mexico, where he met Fidel Castro. Five years later, Che Guevara declared that 1954 had taught him the impossibility of peaceful, electoral reform. He promised his followers that "Cuba will not be Guatemala." In 1966, Guatemala was again the pacesetter, this time pioneering the disappearances that would come to define the dirty wars of Argentina,

Uruguay, Chile, and Brazil. In a lightning strike, U.S.-trained security officials captured some thirty leftists, tortured and executed them, and then dropped most of their corpses into the Pacific. Explaining the operation in a classified memo, the CIA wrote: "The execution of these persons will not be announced and the Guatemalan government will deny that they were ever taken into custody." With the 1996 signing of a peace accord between the Guatemalan military and leftist guerrillas, the Latin American Cold War finally came to an end—in the same place it had begun—making the civil war in Guatemala the longest and most lethal in the hemisphere. Some 200,000 men, women, and children were dead, virtually all at the hands of the military: more than were killed in Argentina, Uruguay, Chile, Brazil, Nicaragua, and El Salvador combined, and roughly the same number as were killed in the Balkans. Because the victims were primarily Mayan Indians, Guatemala today has the only military in Latin America deemed by a United Nations–sponsored truth commission to have committed acts of genocide.[2]

When we talk about America's victory in the Cold War, we are talking about countries like Guatemala, where Communism was fought and defeated by means of the mass slaughter of civilians. But understanding the Cold War requires more than tallying body counts and itemizing atrocities. It requires us to locate this most global of contests in the smallest of places, to find beneath the dueling composure of superpower rivalry a bloody conflict over rights and inequality, to see behind a simple morality tale of good triumphing over evil the more ambivalent settlement that was—and is—the end of the Cold War. The task, in short, is to show how men and women made high politics and high politics made them, to show that the Cold War was waged not only in the airy game-rooms of nuclear strategists but, as Greg Grandin writes in *The Last Colonial Massacre*, "in the closed quarters of family, sex and community."[3]

Grandin opens his study with an epigraph from Sartre: "A victory described in detail is indistinguishable from a defeat."[4] The victory referred to here is singular and by now virtually complete: that of the United States over Communism. But the defeats are various, their consequences still unfolding. First is the defeat of the Latin American left, whose aspirations ranged from the familiar (armed seizure of state power) to the surprising (the creation of capitalism). Next is the defeat of a continental social democracy that would have allowed citizens to exercise a greater share of power—and to receive a greater share of its benefits—than historically had been their due. Finally, and most important, is the defeat of that still-elusive dream of men and women freeing themselves, thanks to their own reason and willed effort, from the bonds of tradition and oppression. This had been the dream of the transatlantic Enlightenment, and throughout the Cold War, American leaders argued on its behalf (or some version of it) in the struggle against Communism. But in Latin America, it was the left who took up the Enlightenment's banner, leaving the United States and its allies carrying the black bag of the counter-Enlightenment. More than foisting on the United States the unwanted burden of liberal hypocrisy, the Cold War inspired it to embrace some of the most reactionary ideals and revanchist characters of the twentieth century.

The Latin American left brought liberalism and progress to a land awash in feudalism. Well into the twentieth century, Guatemala's coffee planters presided over a regime of forced labor that was every bit as medieval as tsarist Russia. Using vagrancy laws and the lure of easy credit, the planters amassed vast estates and a workforce of peasants who essentially belonged to them. Reading like an excerpt from Gogol's *Dead Souls,* one advertisement from 1922 announced the sale of "5000 acres and many *mozos colonos* [indebted workers] who will travel to work on other plantations." While unionized workers elsewhere were itemizing what their employers could and could not ask of them, Guatemala's peasants were forced to provide a variety of compulsory services, including sex. Two planters in the Alta Verapaz region, cousins from Boston, used their Indian cooks and corn grinders to sire more than a dozen children. "They fucked anything that moved," a neighboring planter observed. Though plantations were mini-states—with private jails, stockades, and whipping posts—planters also depended on the army, judges, mayors, and local constables to force workers to submit to their will. Public officials routinely rounded up independent or runaway peasants, shipping them off to plantations or forcing them to build roads. One mayor had local vagrants paint his house. As much as anything, it is this view of political power as a form of private property that confirms Grandin's observation that by 1944 "only five Latin America countries—Mexico, Uruguay, Chile, Costa Rica and Colombia—could nominally call themselves democracies."[5]

And then, within two years, it all changed. By 1946, "only five countries—Paraguay, El Salvador, Honduras, Nicaragua and the Dominican Republic—could not" be called democracies. Turning the antifascist rhetoric of World War II against the hemisphere's old regimes, leftists overthrew dictators, legalized political parties, built unions, and extended the franchise. Galvanized by the New Deal and the Popular Front, reformers liked Guatemalan president Juan José Arévalo declared that "we are socialists because we live in the 20th century." The entire continent was fired by a combination of Karl Marx, the Declaration of Independence, and Walt Whitman, but Guatemala burned the brightest. There, a decades-long struggle to break the back of the coffee aristocracy culminated in the 1950 election of Arbenz, who with the help of a small circle of Communist advisers, instituted the Agrarian Reform of 1952. The legislation redistributed a million and a half acres to a hundred thousand families and also gave peasants a significant share of political power.

Local land reform committees, made up primarily of peasant representatives, bypassed the planter-dominated municipal government and provided peasants and their unions with a platform from which to make and win their claims for equity.[6]

Arguably the most audacious experiment in direct democracy the continent had ever seen, the Agrarian Reform entailed a central irony. The legislation's authors—most of them Communists—were not building socialism. They were creating capitalism. They were scrupulous about property rights and the rule of law. Peasants had to back their claims with extensive documentation; only unused land was expropriated; and planters were guaranteed multiple rights of appeal, all the way to the president. The Agrarian Reform imposed a regime of separated powers that was almost as cumbersome as James Madison's Constitution. (According to one of the bill's Communist authors, "it was a bourgeois law." When grassroots activists complained about the slowness of reform, Arbenz responded: "I don't care! You have to do things right!") The Agrarian Reform turned landless peasants into property owners, giving them the bargaining power to demand higher wages from their employers. According to Grandin, reformers hoped that the peasants would become "consumers of national manufactures," while "planters, historically addicted to cheap, often free labor and land," would be forced to "invest in new technologies" and thereby "make a profit."[7]

Guatemala's socialists did more than create democrats and capitalists. They also made peasants into citizens. While liberals and conservatives have long claimed that leftist ideologies reduce their adherents to automatons, leftist ideals and movements awakened peasants to their own power, giving them extensive opportunities to speak for themselves and to act on their own behalf. Efraín Reyes Maaz, for example, was a Mayan peasant organizer, born in the same year as the Bolshevik Revolution. "If I hadn't studied

Marx I would be *chicha ni limonada* [neither alcohol nor lemonade]," Reyes says. "I'd be nothing. But reading nourished me and here I am. I could die today and nobody could take that from me." Where other peasants seldom ventured beyond their plantations, the Communist Party inspired Reyes to travel to Mexico and Cuba, and he returned to Guatemala with the conviction that "every revolutionary carries around an entire world in his head." The Communist Party did not require Reyes to give up everything he knew; it gave him ample freedom to synchronize the indigenous and the European, making for a "Mayan Marxism" that was every bit as supple as the hybrid Marxism developed in Central Europe between the wars. When anti-Communists put an end to this democratic awakening in 1954, it was as much the peasant's newfound appetite for thinking and talking as the planter's expropriated land that they were worried about. As we saw in the introduction, Guatemala's archbishop complained that the Arbencistas sent peasants "gifted with facility with words" to the nation's capital, where they were "taught . . . to speak in public."[8]

Hoping to break this army of thought and talk, Guatemala's Cold Warriors fused a romantic aversion to the modern world with the most up-to-date technologies of propaganda and violence, making their effort more akin to fascism than to any fight for liberal democracy. Working through the Catholic Church, the regime that replaced Arbenz had prelates preach the gospel against Communism and socialism, and also against democracy, liberalism, and feminism. Reaching back to the rhetoric of opposition to the French Revolution, the Church fathers characterized the Cold War as a struggle between the City of God and "the city of the devil incarnate" and complained that Arbenz, "far from uniting our people in their advance toward progress," "disorganizes them into opposing bands." The Arbencistas, they claimed, were "professional corrupters of the feminine soul," elevating women with "gifts of proselytism or leadership" to "high and well-paid positions in official bureaucracy." Because the Church elders were sometimes too fastidious to whip up the masses, émigrés from Republican Spain, who were partial to Franco and Mussolini, frequently took their place, calling for a more ecstatic faith to counter Communism's appeal: "We do not want a cold Catholicism. We want holiness, ardent, great and joyous holiness . . . intransigent and fanatical."[9]

While the Cold Warriors' ideals looked backward, their weapons—furnished by the United States—and military strategies looked forward. (Indeed, one of the Americans' chief justifications for their interventions during the Cold War was that U.S. involvement would contain not only Communism but also, in the words of the State Department, a right-wing "counter-insurgency running wild." Instead of a savage "white terror," U.S.-trained security forces would work with the anti-Communist "democratic left" to fight a more "rational," "modern," and "professional" Cold War.) During the 1954 coup, the CIA turned to Madison Avenue, pop sociologies, and the literature of mass psychology to create the illusion of large-scale opposition to Arbenz. Radio shows spread rumors of an underground resistance, inciting wobbly army officers to abandon their oath to the democratically elected president. In subsequent decades, the CIA outfitted Guatemala with a centralized domestic intelligence agency, equipped with phones, radios, cameras, typewriters, carbon paper, filing cabinets, surveillance equipment—and guns, ammunition, and explosives. The CIA also brought together the military and the police in sleek urban command centers, where intelligence could be quickly analyzed, distributed, acted on, and archived for later use. After these efforts achieved their most spectacular results, with the 1966 disappearance of Guatemala's last generation of peaceful leftists, guerrillas began seriously to organize armed opposition in rural areas.

In response, the regime threw into the countryside an army so modernized—and so well trained and equipped by the United States—that by 1981 it was able to conduct the first color-coded genocide in history: "Military analysts marked communities and regions according to colors. White spared those thought to have no rebel influence. Pink identified areas in which the insurgents had limited presence; suspected guerrillas and their supporters were to be killed but the communities left standing. Red gave no quarter: all were to be executed and villages razed."[10]

Referring to a 1978 military massacre of Indians in Panzós, a river town in the Polochic Valley, the title of Grandin's book evokes this mixture of modern and antimodern elements. On May 29 of that year, roughly five hundred Mayan peasants assembled in the town center to ask the mayor to hear their complaints against local planters, which were to be presented by a union delegation from the capital. Firing on the protesters, a military detachment killed some-where between 34 and 100 men, women, and children. At first glance, the massacre seems like nothing so much as a repetition of Guate-mala's colonial past: humble Indian petitioners ask public officials to intercede on their behalf against local rulers; government forces in league with the planters respond with violence; Indians wind up floating down the river. On closer inspection, the massacre bears all the marks of the twentieth century. The Indians were led by leftist activists—one of them an indigenous woman—trained by clandes-tine Communist organizers. They worked with unions, based in the capital, reflecting the left's attempt to nationalize local grievances. For their part, the soldiers firing on the peasants were more than a local constabulary defending the interests of the planters. They were a contingent of Guatemala's newly trained army, spoke fluent anti-Communism, and wielded Israeli-made Galil assault rifles, suggest-ing not just the nationalization but the internationalization of Guatemala's traditional struggles over land and labor.[11]

Though the Cold War in Latin America began as a tense negotiation between American rationalism and Latin revanchism, it ended with the United States careening toward the latter. In a rerun of the fabled journey into the heart of darkness, U.S. officials returned from their travels south echoing the darkest voices of the counter-Enlightenment. One embassy officer wrote to his superiors back home: "After all hasn't man been a savage from the beginning of time so let us not be too queasy about terror. I have literally heard these arguments from our people." A CIA staffer urged his colleagues to abandon all attempts at mass persuasion in Guatemala and instead direct their efforts at the "heart, the stomach and the liver (fear)." Seeking to destabilize Allende's Chile, another CIA man proclaimed: "We cannot endeavor to ignite the world if Chile itself is a placid lake. The fuel for the fire must come from within Chile. Therefore, the station should employ every stratagem, every ploy, however bizarre, to create this internal resistance." As Grandin writes, "Will to set the world ablaze . . . faith in the night-side of the soul, contempt for democratic temperance and parliamentary procedure: these qualities are usually attributed to opponents of liberal civility, tolerance and pluralism—not their defenders."[12] With this plangent remark, Grandin concludes his remarkable tale, suggesting that the greatest defeat of the Cold War could be said to be that of America itself.

8

Remembrance of Empires Past

Busy giddy minds with foreign quarrels.

—**Henry IV, Part 2**

In 2000, I spent the better part of a late summer interviewing William F. Buckley and Irving Kristol. I was writing an article for *Lingua Franca* (see chapter 5) on the defections to the left of right-wing intellectuals and wanted to hear what the movement's founding fathers thought of their wayward sons. Over the course of our conversations, however, it became clear that Buckley and Kristol were less interested in these ex-conservatives than they were in the sorry state of the conservative movement and the uncertain fate of the United States as a global empire. The end of Communism and the triumph of the free market, they told me, were mixed blessings. While they were conservative victories, these developments had nevertheless rendered the United States ill-equipped for the post-Cold War era. Americans now possessed the most powerful empire in history. At the same time, they were possessed by one of the most antipolitical ideologies in history: the free market.

This chapter originally appeared as "Remembrance of Empires Past: 9/11 and the End of the Cold War," in *Cold War Triumphalism: The Misuse of History after the Fall of Communism*, ed. Ellen Schrecker (New York: New Press, 2004), 274–297.

According to its idealists, or at least one camp of its idealists, the free market is a harmonious order, promising an international civil society of voluntary exchange, requiring little more from the state than the occasional enforcement of laws and contracts. For Buckley and Kristol, this was too bloodless a notion upon which to found a national order, much less a global empire. It did not provide the passion and élan, the gravitas and authority, that the exercise of American power truly required, at home and abroad. It encouraged triviality and small-minded politics, self-interest over the national interest—not the most promising base from which to launch an empire. What's more, the right-wingers in charge of the Republican Party didn't seem to realize this.

"The trouble with the emphasis in conservatism on the market," Buckley told me, as we saw in chapter 5, "is that it becomes rather boring. You hear it once, you master the idea. The notion of devoting your life to it is horrifying if only because it's so repetitious. It's like sex." Conservatism, Kristol added, "is so influenced by business culture and by business modes of thinking that it lacks any political imagination, which has always been, I have to say, a property of the left." Kristol confessed to a deep yearning for an American empire: "What's the point of being the greatest, most powerful nation in the world and not having an imperial role? It's unheard of in human history. The most powerful nation always had an imperial role." But, he continued, previous empires were not "capitalist democracies with a strong emphasis on economic growth and economic prosperity." Because of its commitment to the free market, the United States lacked the fortitude and vision to wield imperial power. "It's too bad," Kristol lamented. "I think it would be natural for the United States . . . to play a far more dominant role in world affairs. Not what we're doing now but to command and to give orders as to what is be done. People need that. There are many parts of the world, Africa in particular, where an authority willing to use troops can make a very good difference, a healthy difference." But with public discussion moderated by accountants, Kristol thought it unlikely that the United States would take its rightful place as the successor to empires past. "There's the Republican Party tying itself into knots. Over what? Prescriptions for elderly people? Who gives a damn? I think it's disgusting that . . . presidential politics of the most important country in the world should revolve around prescriptions for elderly people. Future historians will find this very hard to believe. It's not Athens. It's not Rome. It's not anything."[1]

Since 9/11, I've had many occasions to recall these conversations. September 11, we were told in the aftermath, shocked the United States out of the complacent peace and prosperity that set in after the Cold War. It forced Americans to look beyond their borders, to understand at last the dangers that confront a world power. It reminded us of the goods of civic life and of the value of the state, putting an end to that fantasy of creating a public world out of private acts of self-interested exchange. It restored to our woozy civic culture a sense of depth and seriousness, of things "larger than ourselves." Most critical of all, it gave the United States a coherent national purpose and focus for imperial rule. A country that seemed for a time unwilling to face up to its international responsibilities was now prepared, once again, to bear any burden, pay any price, for freedom. This changed attitude, the argument went, was good for the world. It pressed the United States to create a stable and just international order. It was also good for the United States. It forced us to think about something more than peace and prosperity, reminding us that freedom was a fighting faith rather than a cushy perch.

Like any historical moment, 9/11—not the terrorist attacks or the day itself, but the new wave of imperialism it spawned—has multiple dimensions. Some part of this rejuvenated imperial political culture is the product of a surprise attack on civilians and the efforts of U.S. leaders to provide some measure of security to an apprehensive citizenry. Some part of it flows from the subterranean political economy of oil, from the desire of U.S. elites to secure access to energy reserves in the Middle East and Central Asia, and to wield oil as an instrument of geopolitics. But while these factors play a considerable role in determining U.S. policy, they do not explain entirely the politics and ideology of the imperial moment itself. To understand that dimension, we must look to the impact on American conservatives of the end of the Cold War, of the fall of Communism and the ascendancy of the free market as the organizing principle of the domestic and international order. For it was conservative dissatisfaction with that order that drove, in part, their effort to create a new one.

For neoconservatives who thrilled to Ronald Reagan's crusade against communism, all that was left after the Cold War was Reagan's other passion—his sunny entrepreneurialism and market joie de vivre—which found a welcome home in Bill Clinton's America. While neocons are certainly not opposed to capitalism, they do not believe the free market is the highest achievement of civilization. Their vision is more exalted. They aspire to the epic grandeur of Rome, the ethos of the pagan warrior—or moral crusader—rather than that of the comfortable bourgeois. Since the end of the Cold War, the imperial vision has received short shrift, eclipsed by the embrace of free markets and free trade. Undone by their own success, neoconservatives are not happy with the world they created. And so they have taken up the call of empire, providing the basso profundo to a swelling chorus. Though they have complete faith in American power, the neocons are uncomfortable using it for the mere extension of capitalism. They seek to create an international order that will be a monument for the ages, a world that is about something more than money and markets.

But as we have come to learn this envisioned imperium may not provide such an easy resolution to the challenges confronting the United States. Even before the war in Iraq went south, the American empire was coming up against daunting obstacles in the Middle East and Central Asia, suggesting how elusive the reigning idea of the neocon imperialists—that the United States can govern events, that it can make history—truly is. (Indeed, it was not so long ago that the Bush administration was telling journalists, "We're an empire now, and when we act, we create our own reality. And while you're studying that reality—judiciously as you will— we'll act again, creating other new realities, which you can study.")[2] Domestically, the cultural and political renewal that many imagined 9/11 would produce has proven a chimera, the victim of a free-market ideology that shows no sign of abating. As it turns out, 9/11 did not—and, in all truth, probably could not—fulfill the role ascribed to it by the neocons of empire.

Immediately following the attacks on the World Trade Center and the Pentagon, intellectuals, politicians, and pundits—not on the radical left, but mainstream conservatives and liberals—breathed an audible sigh of relief, almost as if they welcomed the strikes as a deliverance from the miasma Buckley and Kristol had been criticizing. The World Trade Center was still on fire and the bodies entombed there scarcely recovered when Frank Rich announced that "this week's nightmare, it's now clear, has awakened us from a frivolous if not decadent decade-long dream." What was that dream? The dream of prosperity, of surmounting life's obstacles with money. During the 1990s, Maureen Dowd wrote, we hoped "to overcome flab with diet and exercise, wrinkles with collagen and Botox, sagging skin with surgery, impotence with Viagra, mood swings with anti-depressants, myopia with laser surgery, decay with human growth hormone, disease with stem cell research and bioengineering." We "renovated our kitchens," observed David Brooks, "refurbished our home entertainment systems, invested in patio furniture, Jacuzzis and gas grills"—as if affluence might free us of tragedy and difficulty.[3] This ethos had terrible domestic consequences. For Francis Fukuyama, it encouraged "self-indulgent behavior" and a "preoccupation with one's own petty affairs." It also had international repercussions. According to Lewis "Scooter" Libby, the cult of peace and prosperity found its purest expression in Bill Clinton's weak and distracted foreign policy, which made "it easier for someone like Osama bin Laden to rise up and say credibly 'The Americans don't have the stomach to defend themselves. They won't take casualties to defend their interests. They are morally weak.'" According to Brooks, even the most casual observer of the pre-9/11 domestic scene, including Al Qaeda, "could have concluded that America was not an entirely serious country."[4]

But after that day in September, more than a few commentators claimed, the domestic scene was transformed. America was now "more mobilized, more conscious and therefore more alive" wrote Andrew Sullivan. George Packer remarked upon "the alertness, grief, resolve, even love" awakened by 9/11. "What I dread now," Packer confessed, "is a return to the normality we're all supposed to seek." For Brooks, "the fear that is so prevalent in the country" after 9/11 was "a cleanser, washing away a lot of the self-indulgence of the past decade." Revivifying fear eliminated the anxiety of prosperity, replacing a disabling emotion with a bracing passion. "We have traded the anxieties of affluence for the real fears of war."[5]

Now upscalers who once spent hours agonizing over which Moen faucet head would go with their copper farmhouse-kitchen sink are suddenly worried about whether the water coming out of pipes has been poisoned. People who longed for

Prada bags at Bloomingdales are suddenly spooked by unattended bags at the airport. America, the sweet land of liberty, is getting a crash course in fear.[6]

Today, Brooks concluded, "commercial life seems less important than public life. . . . When life or death fighting is going on, it's hard to think of Bill Gates or Jack Welch as particularly heroic."[7]

Writers repeatedly welcomed the galvanizing moral electricity now coursing through the body politic. A pulsing energy of public resolve and civic commitment, which would restore trust in government—perhaps, according to some liberals, even authorize a revamped welfare state—and bring about a culture of patriotism and connection, a new bipartisan consensus, the end of irony and the culture wars, a more mature, more elevated presidency.[8] According to a reporter at *USA Today*, President Bush was especially keen on the promise of 9/11, offering himself and his generation as Exhibit A in the project of domestic renewal. "Bush has told advisors that he believes confronting the enemy is a chance for him and his fellow baby boomers to refocus their lives and prove they have the same kind of valor and commitment their fathers showed in WWII." And while the specific source of Christopher Hitchens's elation may have been peculiarly his own, his self-declared schadenfreude assuredly was not: "I should perhaps confess that on September 11 last, once I had experienced all the usual mammalian gamut of emotions, from rage to nausea, I also discovered that another sensation was contending for mastery. On examination, and to my own surprise and pleasure, it turned out to be exhilaration. Here was the most frightful enemy—theocratic barbarism—in plain view. . . . I realized that if the battle went on until the last day of my life, I would never get bored in prosecuting it to the utmost."[9] With its shocking spectacle of fear and death, 9/11 offered a dead or dying culture the chance to live again.

Internationally, 9/11 forced the United States to reengage the world, to assume the burden of empires without embarrassment or confusion. Where the first George Bush and Bill Clinton had fumbled in the dark, searching for a doctrine to guide the exercise of U.S. power after the collapse of the Soviet Union, the mission of the United States was now clear: to defend civilization against barbarism, freedom against terror. As Condoleezza Rice told the *New Yorker*, "I think the difficulty has passed in defining a role. I think September 11th was one of those great earthquakes that clarify and sharpen. Events are in much sharper relief." An America thought to be lost in the quicksand of free markets, individualism, and isolation was now recalled to a consciousness of a world beyond its borders, and inspired to a commitment to sustain casualties on behalf of a U.S.-led global order. As Clinton's former undersecretary of defense concluded, "Americans are unlikely to slip back into the complacency that marked the first decade after the Cold War." They now understood, in the words of Brooks, that "evil exists" and that "to preserve order, good people must exercise power over destructive people."[10]

A decade later, it's difficult to recapture, let alone fathom, the mindset of that moment. Not just because it disappeared so quickly, with the country relapsing to its strange and sour partisanship—where the volume of rhetorical antagonism between the parties is matched only by the depth of their agreement about the economic fundamentals (in that respect, we're still living in Bill Clinton's America)—before Bush's first term had even ended. More bewildering is how so many writers and politicians could open their arms to the political fallout from mass death, taking 9/11 as an opportunity to express their apparently long-brewing contempt for the very peace and prosperity that preceded it. On September 12, one might have expected expressions of sorrow over the bursting of bubbles—economic, cultural, and political. Instead, many saw 9/11 as a thunderous judgment upon, and necessary corrective to, the frivolity and emptiness of the 1990s. We would have to reach back almost a century—to the opening days of World War I, when the "marsh gas of boredom and vacuity" enveloping another free-trading, globalizing fin de siècle exploded—to find a remotely exact parallel.[11]

To understand this spirit of exuberant relief, we must revisit the waning days of the Cold War, when American elites first saw that the United States would no longer be able to define its mission in terms of the Soviet menace. While the end of the Cold War unleashed a wave of triumphalism, it also provoked among elites an anxious uncertainty about U.S. foreign policy. With the defeat of Communism, many asked, how should the United States define its role in the world? Where and when should it intervene in foreign conflicts? How big a military should it field?

Underlying these arguments was a deep unease about the size and purpose of American power. The United States seemed to be suffering from a surfeit of power, which made it difficult for elites to formulate any coherent principles to govern its use. As Richard Cheney, then serving as the first President Bush's secretary of defense, acknowledged in February 1992, "We've gained so much strategic depth that the threats to our security, now relatively distant, are harder to define." Almost a decade later, the United States would still seem, to its leaders, a floundering giant. As Condoleezza Rice noted during the 2000 presidential campaign, "The United States has found it exceedingly difficult to define its 'national interest' in the absence of Soviet power." So uncertain about the national interest did political elites become that a top Clinton defense aide—and later dean of Harvard's Kennedy School—eventually threw up his hands in defeat, declaring the national interest to be whatever "citizens, after proper deliberation, say it is"—an abdication simply unthinkable during the Cold War reign of the Wise Men.[12]

When Clinton assumed office, he and his advisers took stock of this unparalleled situation—where the United States possessed so much power that it faced, in the words of Clinton National Security Advisor Anthony Lake, no "credible near-term threat to [its] existence"—and concluded that the primary concerns of American foreign policy were no longer military but economic. After summarily rehearsing the various possible military dangers to the United States, President Clinton declared in a 1993 address, "We still face, *overarching everything else*, this amorphous but profound challenge in the way humankind conducts its commerce." The great imperative of the post–Cold War era was to organize a global economy where citizens of the world could trade across borders. For that to happen, the United States had to get its own economic house in order—"renewal starts at home," said Lake—by reducing the deficit (in part through reductions in military spending), lowering interest rates, supporting high-tech industry, and promoting free trade agreements. Because other nations would also have to conduct a painful economic overhaul, Lake concluded that the primary goal of the United States was the "enlargement of the world's free community of market democracies."[13]

Clinton's assessment of the challenges facing the United States was partially inspired by political calculation. He had just won an election against a sitting president who not only had led the United States through victory in the Cold War, but also had engineered a stunning rout over the Iraqi military. A Southern governor with no foreign policy experience—and a draft-dodger to boot—Clinton concluded that his victory over Bush meant that questions of war and peace no longer resonated with American voters the way they might have in an earlier age.[14] But Clinton's vision also reflected a conviction, common to the 1990s, that the globalization of the free market had undermined the efficacy of military power and the viability of traditional empires. Force was no longer the sole, or most effective, instrument of national will. Power now hinged upon the dynamism and success of a nation's economy and the attractiveness of its culture. As Joseph Nye, Clinton's assistant secretary of defense, would come to argue, "soft power"—the cultural capital that made the United States so admired around the globe—was as important to national preeminence as military power. In perhaps a first for a U.S. official, Nye invoked Gramsci to argue that the United States would only maintain its position of hegemony if it persuaded—rather than forced—others to follow its example. "If I can get you to *want* to do what I want," wrote Nye, "then I do not have to force you to do what you do *not* want to do."[15] To maintain its standing in the world, the United States would have to out-compete other national economies, all the while ensuring the spread of its free market model and pluralist culture. The greatest danger confronting the United States was that it would not reform its economy or that it would abuse its military superiority and provoke international hatred. The problem was not that the United States did not have enough power, but that it had too much. To render the world safe for globalization, the United States would have to be defanged or, at a minimum, significantly curtailed in its imperial aspirations.

For conservatives who yearned for and then celebrated socialism's demise, Clinton's promotion of easygoing prosperity was a horror. Affluence produced a society without difficulty and adversity. Material satisfaction induced a loss of social depth and political meaning, a lessening of resolve and heroic verve. "In that age of peace and prosperity," David Brooks would write, "the top sitcom was *Seinfeld*, a show about nothing." Robert Kaplan emitted barb after barb about the "healthy, well fed" denizens of "bourgeois society," too consumed with their own comfort and pleasure to lend a hand—or shoulder a gun—to make the world a safer place. "Material possessions," he concluded, "encourage docility."[16] Throughout the 1990s, the lead item of intellectual complaint, across the political spectrum, was that the United States was insufficiently civic-minded or martial, its leaders and citizens too distracted by prosperity and affluence to take care of its inherited institutions, common concerns, and worldwide defense. Respect for the state was supposed to be dwindling, as was political participation and local volunteerism.[17] Indeed, one of the most telling signs of the waning imperative of the Cold War was the fact that the 1990s began and ended with two incidents—the Clarence Thomas–Anita Hill controversy and the Supreme Court decision *Bush v. Gore*—that cast scandalous suspicion on the nation's most venerated political institution.

For influential neocons, Clinton's foreign policy was even more anathema. Not because the neocons were unilateralists arguing against Clinton's multilateralism, or isolationists or realists critical of his internationalism and humanitarianism.[18] Clinton's foreign policy, they argued, was too driven by the imperatives of free market globalization. It was proof of the oozing decadence taking over the United States after the defeat of the Soviet Union, a sign of weakened moral fiber and lost martial spirit. In an influential manifesto published in 2000, Donald and Frederick Kagan could barely contain their contempt for "the happy international situation that emerged in 1991," which was "characterized by the spread of democracy, free trade, and peace" and which was "so congenial to America" with its love of "domestic comfort." According to Kaplan, "the problem with bourgeois societies" like our own "is a lack of imagination." The soccer mom, for instance, so insistently championed by Republicans and Democrats alike, does not care about the world outside her narrow confines. "Peace," he complained, "is pleasurable, and pleasure is about momentary satisfaction." It can be obtained "only through a form of tyranny, however subtle and mild." It erases the memory of bracing conflict, robust disagreement, the luxury of defining ourselves "by virtue of whom we were up against."[19]

Though conservatives are often reputed to favor wealth and prosperity, law and order, stability and routine—all the comforts of bourgeois life—Clinton's conservative critics hated him for his pursuit of these very virtues. Clinton's free-market obsessions betrayed an unwillingness to embrace the murky world of power and violent conflict, of tragedy and rupture. His foreign policy was not just unrealistic; it was insufficiently dark and brooding. "The striking thing about the 1990s zeitgeist," complained Brooks, "was the presumption of harmony. The era was shaped by the idea that there were no fundamental conflicts anymore." Conservatives thrive on a world filled with mysterious evil and unfathomable hatreds, where good is always on the defensive and time is a precious commodity in the cosmic race against corruption and decline. Coping with such a world requires pagan courage and an almost barbaric *virtú,* qualities conservatives embrace over the more prosaic goods of peace and prosperity. It is no accident that Paul Wolfowitz, the darkest of these dark princes of pessimism, was a student of Allan Bloom (in fact, Wolfowitz makes a cameo appearance in *Ravelstein,* Saul Bellow's novel about Bloom). For Bloom—like many other influential neoconservatives—was a follower of Leo Strauss, whose quiet odes to classical virtue and ordered harmony veiled his Nietzschean vision of torturous conflict and violent struggle.[20]

But there was another reason for the neocons' dissatisfaction with Clinton's foreign policy. Many of them found it insufficiently visionary and consistent. Clinton, they claimed, was reactive and ad hoc, rather than proactive and forceful. He and his advisers were unwilling to imagine a world where the United States shaped, rather than responded to, events. Breaking again with the usual stereotype of conservatives as nonideological pragmatists, figures like Wolfowitz, Libby, Kaplan, Perle, Frank Gaffney, Kenneth Adelman, and the father-and-son teams of Kagan and Kristol called for a more ideologically coherent projection of U.S. power, where the "benign hegemony" of American might would spread "the zone of democracy" rather than just extend the free market. They wanted a foreign policy that was, in words that Robert Kagan would later use to praise Senator Joseph Lieberman, "idealistic but not naïve, ready and willing to use force and committed to a strong military, but also committed to using American power to spread democracy and do some good in the world." As early as the first Bush administration, the neocons were insisting that the United States ought, in Cheney's words, "to shape the future, to determine the outcome of history," or, as the Kagans would later put it, "to intervene decisively in every critical region" of the world, "whether or not a visible threat exists there." They criticized those Republicans, in Robert Kagan's words, who "during the dumb decade of the 1990s" suffered from a "hostility to 'nation-building,' the aversion to 'international social work' and the narrow belief that 'superpowers don't do windows.'"[21] What these conservatives longed for was an America that was genuinely imperial—not just because they believed it would make the United States safer or richer, and not just because they thought it would make the world better, but because they literally wanted to see the United States *make* the world.

At the most obvious level, 9/11 confirmed what the conservatives had been saying for years: the world is a dangerous place, filled with hostile forces who will stop at nothing to see the United States felled. More important, 9/11 gave conservatives an opportunity to articulate, without embarrassment, the vision of imperial American power they had been quietly nourishing for decades. "People are now coming out of the closet on the word empire," Charles Kraut-hammer accurately observed soon after 9/11. Unlike empires past, this one would be guided by a benign, even beneficent vision of worldwide improvement. Because of America's sense of fair play and benevolent purpose—unlike Britain or Rome, the United States had no intention of occupying or seizing territory of its own—this new empire would not generate the backlash that all previous empires had generated. As a *Wall Street Journal* writer said, "we are an attractive empire, the one everyone wants to join." In the words of Rice, "Theoretically, the realists would predict that when you have a great power like the United States it would not be long before you had other great powers rising to challenge it. And I think what you're seeing is that there's at least a predilection this time to move to productive and cooperative relations with the United States, rather than to try to balance the United States."[22] In creating an empire, the United States would no longer have to respond to immediate threats, to "wait upon events while dangers gather," as President Bush put it in his 2002 state of the union address. It would now "shape the environment," anticipate threats, thinking not in months or years, but in decades, perhaps centuries. The goals were what Cheney, acting on the advice of Wolfowitz, first outlined in the early 1990s: to ensure that no other power ever arose to chal-lenge the United States and that no regional powers ever attained preeminence in their local theaters. The emphasis was on the pre-emptive and predictive, to think in terms of becoming, rather than in terms of being. As Richard Perle put it, vis-à-vis Iraq: "What is essential here is not to look at the opposition to Saddam as it is today, without any external support, without any realistic hope of removing that awful regime, but to look at what could be created."[23]

For conservatives, the two years after 9/11 were a heady time, a moment when their simultaneous commitment and hostility to the free market could finally be satisfied. No longer hamstrung by the numbing politics of affluence and prosperity, they believed they could count on the public to respond to the call of sacrifice and destiny, confrontation and evil. With "danger" and "security" the watchwords of the day, the American state would be newly sanctified—without opening the floodgates to economic redistribution. 9/11 and the American empire they hoped, would at last resolve the cultural contradictions of capitalism that Daniel Bell had noticed long ago but which had only truly come to the fore after the defeat of Communism.

What a difference a decade makes—or for that matter even a couple of years. Long before the United States would essentially have to declare victory in Iraq and (kind of) go home, long before George W. Bush left his office in disgrace, long before the war in Afghanistan proved to be far more than the American people could stomach, it was clear that the neocon imperium rested upon a shaky foundation. In late October and early November 2001, for example, after mere weeks of bombing had failed to dislodge the Taliban, critics started murmuring their fears that the war in Afghanistan would be a reprise of the Vietnam quagmire.[24] As soon as the war in Iraq seemed to be not quite the cakewalk its defenders had proclaimed it would be, Democrats began to probe, however tentatively, the edges of acceptable criticism. As early as the 2004 presidential campaign, voicing criticism of the war became something of a litmus test among the Democratic candidates.

None of these critics, of course, would challenge the full-throttle military premise of Bush's policies—and even under Obama, few would question the basic premises of America's global reach—but periodic appearance of such critics, particularly in times of trouble or defeat, suggests that the imperial vision is politically viable only so long as it is successful. This is as it must be: because the centerpiece of the imperial promise is that the United Stales can govern events, that it can determine the outcome of history, the promise stands or falls on success or failure. With any suggestion that events lie beyond the empire's control, the imperial vision blurs. Indeed, it only took a week in March 2002 of horrific bloodshed in Israel and the Occupied Territories—and the resulting accusations that "Bush fiddles in the White House or Texas, playing Nero as the Mideast burns"—for the planned empire to be called into question. No sooner had violence in the Middle East begun to escalate then even the administration's defenders began jumping ship, suggesting that any invasion of Iraq would have to be postponed indefinitely. As one of Reagan's high-level national security aides put it, "The supreme irony is that the greatest power the world has ever known has proven incapable of managing a regional crisis." The fact, this aide added, that the administration had been so maniacally "focused on either Afghanistan or Iraq"—the two key outposts of imperial confrontation—while the Middle East was going up in flames, "reflects either appalling arrogance or ignorance."[25]

Ironically, insofar as the Bush administration avoided those conflicts, such as that between the Israelis and Palestinians, where it might fail—and, indeed, as of this writing, the Obama administration seems to be following the same path with regard to Israel and Palestine—it was forced to forgo the very logic of imperialism that it sought to avow. Premised as it was on the ability of the United States to control events, the neocon imperial vision could not accommodate failure. But by avoiding failure, the imperialists were forced to acknowledge that they could not control events. As former Secretary of State Lawrence Eagleburger observed of the Israeli-Palestinian conflict, Bush realized "that simply to insert himself into this mess without any possibility of achieving any success is, in and of itself, dangerous, because it would demonstrate that in fact we don't have any ability right now to control or affect events"[26]—precisely the admission the neocons could not afford to make. This Catch-22 was no mere problem of logic or consistency: it betrayed the essential fragility of the imperial position itself.

That fragility also reflected the domestic hollowness of the neocons' imperial vision. Though the neocons saw and continue to see imperialism as the cultural and political counterpart to the free market, they have never come to terms—even ten years later—with how the conservative opposition to government spending and the commitment to tax cuts renders the United States unlikely to make the necessary investments in nation-building that imperialism requires.

Domestically, there is little evidence to suggest that the political and cultural renewal imagined by most commentators—the revival of the state, the return of shared sacrifice and community, the deepening of moral awareness—ever took place, even in the headiest days of the aftermath of 9/11. Of all the incidents one could cite from that time, two stand out. In March 2002, sixty-two senators, including nineteen Democrats, rejected higher fuel-efficiency standards in the automobile industry, which would have reduced dependence upon Persian Gulf oil. Missouri Republican Christopher Bond felt so unencumbered by the need to pay homage to state institutions in a time of war that he claimed on the Senate floor, "I don't want to tell a mom in my home state that she should not get an S.U.V. because Congress decided that would be a bad choice." Even more telling was how vulnerable proponents of higher standards were to these antistatist arguments. John McCain, for example, was instantly put on the defensive by the notion that the government would be interfering with people's private market choices. He was left to argue that "no American will be forced to drive any different automobile," as if that would have been a dreadful imposition in this new era of wartime sacrifice and solidarity.[27]

A few months earlier, Ken Feinberg, head of the September 11 Victims' Compensation Fund, announced that families of victims would receive compensation for their loss based in part on the salary each victim was earning at the time of his or her death. After the attacks on the World Trade Center and the Pentagon, Congress had taken the unprecedented step of assuming national responsibility for restitution to the families of the victims. Though the inspiration for this decision was to forestall expensive lawsuits against the airline industry, many observers took it as a signal of a new spirit in the land: in the face of national tragedy, political leaders were finally breaking with the jungle survivalism of the Reagan-Clinton years. But even in death, the market—and the inequalities it generates—was the only language America's leaders knew how to speak. Abandoning the notion of shared sacrifice, Feinberg opted for the actuarial tables to calculate appropriate compensation packages. The family of a single sixty-five-year-old grandmother earning $10,000 a year—perhaps a minimum-wage kitchen worker—would draw $300,000 from the fund, while the family of a thirty-year-old Wall Street trader would get $3,870,064. The men and women killed on September 11 were not citizens of a democracy; they were earners, and rewards would be distributed accordingly. Virtually no one—not even the commentators and politicians who denounced the Feinberg calculus for other reasons—criticized this aspect of his decision.[28]

Even within and around the military, the ethos of patriotism and shared destiny remained secondary to the ideology of the market. In a little-noticed October 2001 article in the *New York Times,* military recruiters confessed that they still sought to entice enlistees not with the call of patriotism or duty but with the promise of economic opportunity. As one recruiter put it, "It's just business as usual. We don't push the 'Help our country' routine." When the occasional patriot burst into a recruiting office and said,

"I want to fight," a recruiter explained, "I've got to calm them down. We're not all about fighting and bombing. We're about jobs. We're about education."[29] Recruiters admitted that they continued to target immigrants and people of color, on the assumption that it was these constituencies' lack of opportunity that drove them to the military. The Pentagon's publicly acknowledged goal, in fact, was to increase the number of Latinos in the military from 10 percent to 22 percent. Recruiters even slipped into Mexico, with promises of instant citizenship to poor noncitizens willing to take up arms on behalf of the United States. According to one San Diego recruiter, "It's more or less common practice that some recruiters go to Tijuana to distribute pamphlets, or in some cases they look for someone to help distribute information on the Mexican side."[30] In December 2002, as the United States prepared to invade Iraq, New York Democratic congressman Charles Rangel decided to confront this issue head-on by proposing a reinstatement of the draft. Noting that immigrants, people of color, and the poor were shouldering a greater percentage of the military burden than their numbers in the population warranted, Rangel argued that the United States should distribute the domestic costs of empire more equitably. If middle-class white kids were forced to shoulder arms, he claimed, the administration and its supporters might think twice before going to war. The bill went nowhere.

The fact that the war never imposed the sort of sacrifices on the population that normally accompany national crusades provoked significant concern among political and cultural elites. "The danger, over the long term," wrote the *Times*'s R. W. Apple before he died, "is loss of interest. With much of the war to be conducted out of plain sight by commandos, diplomats and intelligence agents, will a nation that has spent decades in easy self-indulgence stay focused?" Not long after he had declared the age of glitz and glitter over, Frank Rich found himself publicly agonizing that "you'd never guess this is a nation at war." Prior to 9/11, "the administration said we could have it all." Since 9/11, the administration had been saying much the same thing. A former aide to Lyndon Johnson told the *New York Times,* "People are going to have get involved in this. So far it's a government effort, as it should be, but people aren't engaged."[31] Without consecrating the cause in blood, observers feared, Americans would not have their commitment tested, their resolve deepened. As Doris Kearns Goodwin complained on *The News-Hour:*

> Well, I think the problem is we understand that it's going to be a long war but it's hard for us to participate in that war in a thousand and one ways the way we could in World War II. You could have hundreds of thousands joining the armed forces. They could go to the factories to make sure to get those ships, tanks, and weapons built. They could have victory gardens. They could feel not simply as we're being told: Go back to your ordinary lives. It's harder now. We don't have a draft in the same way we did although there's some indication I'd like to believe that that younger generation will want to participate. My own youngest son who just graduated from Harvard this June has joined the military. He wants that three-year commitment. He wants to be part of what this is all about instead of just going to work for a year and going to law school, he wants to be a part of this. And I suspect there will be a lot of others like that as well. But somehow you just keep wishing that the government would challenge us. Maybe we need a Manhattan Project for this antibiotics vaccine production. We were able to get cargo ships down from 365 days in World War II to one day by the middle with that kind of collective enterprise. And I think we need to be mobilized, our spirit, our productivity, much more than we were.[32]

In what may have been the strangest spectacle of the entire war, the nation's leaders wound up scrambling to find things for people to do—not because there was much to be done, but because without something to do, the ardor of ordinary Americans would grow cold. Since these tasks were unnecessary, and mandating them would have violated the norms of market ideology, the best the president and his colleagues could come up with was to announce Web sites and toll-free numbers where enterprising men and women could find information about helping out the war effort. As Bush declared in North Carolina the day after his 2002 state of the union address, "If you listened to the speech last night, you know, people were saying, 'Well, gosh, that's nice, he called me to action, where do I look?' Well, here's where: at usafreedomcorps. gov. Or you can call this number—it sounds like I'm making a pitch, and I am. This is the right thing to do for America. 1-877-USA-CORPS." The government couldn't even count on the citizenry to pay for the phone call. And what were the duties these volunteers were to perform? If they were doctors or health care workers, they could enlist to help out during emergencies. And everyone else? They could serve in neighborhood watch programs to guard against terrorist attacks—in North Carolina.[33]

Ever since the end of the Cold War, some might even say Vietnam, there has been a growing disconnect between the culture and ideology of U.S. business elites and that of political warriors like Wolfowitz and the other neocons. Where the Cold War saw the creation of a semicoherent class of Wise Men who brought together, however jaggedly, the worlds of business and politics—men like Dean Acheson and the Dulles brothers—the Reagan years and beyond have witnessed something altogether different. On the one hand, we have a younger generation of corporate magnates who, though ruthless in their efforts to secure benefits from the state, have none of the respect or passion for the state of their older counterparts. Certainly willing to take from the public till, they are contemptuous of politics and government. These new CEOs respond to their counterparts in Tokyo, London, and other global cities; so long as the state provides them with what they need and does not interfere unduly with their operations, they leave it to the apparatchiks.[34] Asked by Thomas Friedman how often he talks about Iraq, Russia, or foreign wars, one Silicon Valley executive said, "Not more than once a year. We don't even care about Washington. Money is extracted by Silicon Valley and then wasted by Washington. I want to talk about people who create wealth and jobs. I don't want to talk about unhealthy and unproductive people. If I don't care about the wealth destroyers in my own country, why should I care about the wealth destroyers in another country?"[35]

On the other hand, we have a new class of political elites who have little contact with the business community, whose primary experiences outside of government have been in academia, journalism, think tanks, or some other part of the culture industry. Men like Wolfowitz and Brooks, the Kagans and the Kristols, traffic in ideas and see the world as a landscape of intellectual projection. Unconstrained by even the most interested of interests, they see themselves as free to advance their cause, in the Middle East and elsewhere. Like their corporate counterparts, the neocons view the world as their stage; unlike their corporate counterparts, they are preparing for an altogether more theatrical, otherworldly drama. Their endgame, if they have one, is an apocalyptic confrontation between good and evil, civilization and barbarism—categories of pagan conflict diametrically opposed to the world-without-borders vision of America's free-trading, globalizing elite.

9

Protocols of Machismo

Men may dream in demonstrations, and cut out an illusory world
in the shape of axioms, definitions and propositions, with a final exclusion
of fact signed Q.E.D.

—George Eliot, *Daniel Deronda*

The twentieth century, it's often said, taught us a simple lesson
about politics: of all the motivations for political action, none is as
lethal as ideology. The lust for money may be distasteful, the desire
for power ignoble, but neither will drive its devotees to the criminal excess of an idea on the march. Whether the cause is the
working class or a master race, ideology leads to the graveyard.

Although moderate-minded intellectuals have repeatedly mobilized some version of this argument against the "isms" of right and
left, they have seldom mustered a comparable skepticism about
that other idée fixe of the twentieth century: national security.
Some writers criticize this war, others that one, but has anyone
ever penned, in the spirit of Daniel Bell, a book titled "The End of

This chapter originally appeared as a review of Michael Walzer's *Arguing about
War* (New Haven, Conn.: Yale University Press, 2004); Seymour M. Hersh's *Chain
of Command: The Road from 9/11 to Abu Ghraib* (New York: Harper Collins, 2004);
and *Torture,* ed. Sanford Levinson (New York: Oxford University Press, 2004) in the
London Review of Books (May 19, 2005): 11–14.

National Security"? Millions have been killed in the name of security; Stalin and Hitler claimed to be protecting their populations from mortal threats.[1] Yet no such book exists.

Consider the less than six degrees of separation between the idea of national security and the lurid crimes of Abu Ghraib. Each of the reasons the Bush administration gave for going to war against Iraq—the threat of weapons of mass destruction (WMD), Saddam's alleged links to Al Qaeda, even the promotion of democracy in the Middle East—referred in some way to protecting the United States. Getting good intelligence from informers is a critical element in defeating any insurgency. U.S. military intelligence believed (perhaps still does believe) that sexual humiliation is an especially useful instrument for extracting information from recalcitrant Muslim and Arab prisoners.[2]

Many critics have protested Abu Ghraib, but few have traced its outrages back to the idea of national security. Perhaps they believe such an investigation is unnecessary. After all, many of these individuals opposed the war on the grounds that U.S. security was not threatened by Iraq. Some of national security's most accomplished practitioners, such as Brent Scowcroft and Zbigniew Brzezinski, as well as theoreticians like Steven Walt and John Mearsheimer, claimed that a genuine consideration of U.S. security interests militated against the war. The mere fact, these critics could argue, that some politicians misused or abused the principle of national security need not call that principle into question. But when an idea routinely accompanies, if not induces, atrocities—Abu Ghraib was certainly not the first instance of a country committing torture in the name of security—second thoughts would seem to be in order. Unless, of course, defenders of the idea wish to join that company of ideologues they so roundly condemn, affirming their commitment to an ideal version of national security while disowning its actually existing variant.

In its ideal version, national security requires a clear-eyed understanding of a nation's interests and a sober assessment of the threats to them. Force, a counselor might say to his prince, is a tool a leader may use in response to those threats, but he should use it prudently and without emotion. Just as he should not trouble himself with questions of human rights or international law, he should not be excited by his use of violence. Analysts may add international norms to a leader's toolkit, but they are quick to point out, as Joseph Nye does in *The Paradox of American Power*, that these rules may have to give way to "vital survival interests," that "at times we will have to go it alone."[3] National security demands a monkish self-denial, where officials forego the comforts of conscience and pleasures of impulse in order to inflict when necessary the most brutal force and abstain from or abandon that force whenever it becomes counterproductive. It's an ethos that bears all the marks of a creed, requiring a mortification of self no less demanding than that expected of the truest Christian.

The first article of this creed, the national interest, gives leaders great wiggle room in identifying threats. What, after all, is the national interest? According to Nye, "the national interest is simply what citizens, after proper deliberation, say it is." Even if we assume that citizens are routinely given the opportunity to deliberate about the national interest, the fact is that they seldom, if ever, reach a conclusion about it. As Nye points out, Peter Trubowitz's exhaustive study of the way Americans defined the national interest throughout the twentieth century determined that "there is no single national interest. Analysts who assume that America has a discernible national interest whose defense should determine its relations with other nations are unable to explain the failure to achieve domestic consensus on international objectives."[4] This makes a good deal of sense: if an individual finds it difficult to determine his or her own interest, why should we expect a mass of individuals to do any better? But if a people cannot decide on its collective interest, how can it know when that interest is threatened? Faced with such confusion, leaders often fall back on the most obvious definition of a threat: imminent, violent assault from an enemy, promising to end the independent life of the nation. Leaders focus on cataclysmic futures, if for no other reason than that these are a convenient measure of what is or is not a threat, what is or is not security. But that ultimate threat often turns out to be no less illusory than the errant definition of security that inspired the invocation of the threat in the first place.

Hovering about every discussion of war and peace are questions of life and death. Not the death of some or even many people, but, as Michael Walzer proposes in *Arguing about War*, the "moral as well as physical extinction" of an entire people. True, it is only rarely that a nation will find its "ongoingness"—its ability "to carry on, and also to improve on, a way of life handed down" from its ancestors—threatened. But at moments of what Walzer, following Winston Churchill, calls "supreme emergency," a leader may have to commit the most obscene crimes in order to avert catastrophe.[5] The deliberate murder of innocents, the use of torture: the measures taken will be as many and almost as terrible as the evils a nation hopes to thwart.

For obvious reasons, Walzer maintains that leaders should be wary of invoking the supreme emergency, that they must have real evidence before they start speaking Churchillese. But a casual reading of the history of national security suggests not only that the rules of evidence will be ignored in practice, but also that the notion of catastrophe encourages, even insists on, these rules being flouted.

"In normal affairs," Richelieu declared at the dawn of the modern state system, "the administration of Justice requires authentic proofs; but it is not the same in affairs of state. . . . There, urgent conjecture must sometimes take the place of proof; the loss of the particular is not comparable with the salvation of the state."[6] As we ascend the ladder of threats, in other words, from petty crime to the destruction or loss of the state, we require less and less proof that each threat is real. The consequences of underestimating serious threats are so great, Richelieu suggests, that we may have no choice but to overestimate them. Three centuries later, Learned Hand invoked a version of this rule, claiming that "the gravity of the 'evil'" should be "discounted by its improbability."[7] The graver the evil, the higher degree of improbability we demand in order not to worry about it. Or, to put the matter another way, if an evil is truly terrible but not very likely to occur, we may still take pre-emptive action against it.

Neither statement was meant to justify great crimes of state, but both suggest an inverse relationship between the magnitude of a danger and the requirements of facticity. Once a leader starts pondering the nation's moral and physical extinction, he enters a world where the fantastic need not give way to the factual, where present benignity can seem like the merest prelude to future malignance. So intertwined at this point are fear and reason of state that early modern theorists, less shy than we about such matters, happily admitted the first as a proxy for the second: a nation's fear, they argued, could serve as a legitimate rationale for war, even a preventive one. "As long as reason is reason," Francis Bacon wrote, "a just fear will be a just cause of a preventive war."[8] That's a fairly good description of the logic animating the Cold War: fight them there—in Vietnam, Nicaragua, Angola—lest we must stop them here, at the Rio Grande, the Canadian border, on Main Street. It's also a fairly good description of the logic animating the Nazi invasion of the Soviet Union:

> We are fighting on such distant fronts to protect our own home-
> land, to keep the war as far away as possible, and to forestall
> what would otherwise be the fate of the nation as a whole and

what up to now only a few German cities have experienced or will have to experience. It is therefore better to hold a front 1,000 or if necessary 2,000 kilometers away from home than to have to hold a front on the borders of the Reich.[9]

These are by no means ancient or academic formulations. While liberal critics claim that the Bush administration lied about or deliberately exaggerated the threat posed by Iraq in order to justify going to war, the fact is that the administration and its allies were often disarmingly honest in their assessment of the threat, or at least honest about how they were going about assessing it. Trafficking in the future, they conjured the worst—"we don't want the smoking gun to be a mushroom cloud"[10]—and left it to their audience to draw the most frightful conclusions.

In his 2003 state of the union address, one of his most important statements in the run-up to the war, Bush declared: "Some have said we must not act until the threat is imminent. Since when have terrorists and tyrants announced their intentions, politely putting us on notice before they strike? If this threat is permitted to fully and suddenly emerge, all actions, all words and all recriminations would come too late."[11] Bush does not affirm the imminence of the threat; he implicitly disavows it, ducking behind the past, darting to the hypothetical, and arriving at a nightmarish, though entirely conjectured, future. He does not speak of "is" but of "if" and "could be." These words are conditional (which is why Bush's critics, insisting that he take his stand in the realm of fact or fiction, never could get a fix on him). He speaks in the tense of fear, where evidence and intuition, reason and speculation, combine to make the worst-case scenario seem as real as fact.

After the war had begun, the television journalist Diane Sawyer pressed Bush on the difference between the assumption, "stated as a hard fact, that there were weapons of mass destruction," and the hypothetical possibility that Saddam "could move to acquire those weapons." Bush replied: "So what's the difference?"[12] No offhand comment, this was Bush's most articulate statement of the entire war, an artful parsing of a distinction that has little meaning in the context of national security.

Probably no one in or around the administration better understood the way national security blurs the line between the possible and the actual than Richard Perle. "How far Saddam's gone on the nuclear weapons side I don't think we really know," Perle said on one occasion. "My guess is it's further than we think. It's always further than we think, because we limit ourselves, as we think about this, to what we're able to prove and demonstrate. . . . And, unless you believe that we have uncovered everything, you have to assume there is more than we're able to report."

Like Bush, Perle neither lies nor exaggerates. Instead, he imagines and projects, and in the process reverses the normal rules of forensic responsibility. When someone recommends a difficult course of action on behalf of a better future, he invariably must defend himself against the skeptic, who insists that he prove his recommendation will produce the outcome he anticipates. But if someone recommends an equally difficult course of action to avert a hypothetical disaster, the burden of proof shifts to the skeptic. Suddenly she must defend her doubt against his belief, her preference for politics as usual against his politics of emergency. And that, I suspect, is why the Bush administration's prewar mantra, "the absence of evidence is not evidence of absence"—laughable in the context of an argument for, say, world peace—could seem surprisingly cogent in an argument for war. "Better to be despised for too anxious apprehensions," Burke noted, "than ruined by too confident a security."[13]

As Walzer suggests, an entire people can face annihilation. But the victims of genocide tend to be stateless or powerless, and the world has difficulty seeing or acknowledging their destruction, even when the evidence is undeniable. The citizens and subjects of great powers, on the other hand, rarely face the prospect of "moral as well as physical extinction." (Walzer cites only two cases.) Yet their leaders seem to imagine that destruction with the greatest of ease.

We get a taste of this indulgence of the state and its concerns—and a corresponding skepticism about non-state actors and their concerns—in Walzer's own ruminations on war and peace. Throughout *Arguing about War*, Walzer wrestles with terrorists who claim that they are using violence as a last resort and antiwar activists who claim than governments should go to war only as a last resort. Walzer is dubious about both claims. But far from revealing a dogged consistency, his skepticism about the "last resort" suggests a double standard. It sets the bar for using force much higher for non-state actors than it does for state actors—not because terrorists target civilians while the state does not, but because Walzer refuses to accept the terrorist's "last resort" while he is ready to lend credence to the government's, or at least is ready to challenge critics of the government who insist that war truly be a last resort.

For Walzer, the last resort argument of antiwar activists is often a ruse designed to make a government's going to war impossible—and a muddy ruse at that. For "lastness," he says, "is a metaphysical condition, which is never actually reached in real life; it is always possible to do something else, or to do it again, before doing whatever it is that comes last." We can always ask for "another diplomatic note, another United Nations resolution, another meeting," we can always dither and delay. Though Walzer acknowledges the moral power of the last resort argument—"political leaders must cross this threshold [going to war] only with great reluctance and trepidation"—he suspects that it is often "merely an excuse for postponing the use of force indefinitely." As a result, he says, "I have always resisted the argument that force is a last resort."[14]

But when non-state actors argue that they are resorting to terrorism as a last resort, Walzer suspects them of bad faith. For such individuals, "it is not so easy to reach the 'last resort.'" To get there, one must indeed try everything (which is a lot of things) and not just once. Even "under conditions of oppression and war," he insists, "it is by no means clear when" the oppressed or their spokespersons have truly "run out of options." Walzer acknowledges that a similar argument might be applied to government officials, but the officials he has in mind are those who "kill hostages or bomb peasant villages"—not those who claim they must go to war.[15] Thus, Walzer entertains the possibility that governments, with all their power, may find themselves racing against time, while insisting that terrorists, and the people they claim to represent, invariably will have all the time in the world.

What is it about being a great power that renders the imagining of its own demise so potent? Why, despite all the strictures about the prudent and rational use of force, are those powers so quick to resort to it? Perhaps it is because there is something deeply appealing about the idea of disaster, about manfully confronting and mastering catastrophe. For disaster and catastrophe can summon a nation, at least in theory, to plumb its deepest moral and political reserves, to have its mettle tested, on and off the battlefield. However much leaders and theorists may style themselves the cool adepts of realpolitik, war remains the great romance of the age, the proving ground of self and nation.

Exactly why the strenuous life should be so attractive is anyone's guess, but one reason may be that it counters what conservatives since the French Revolution have believed to be the corrosions of liberal democratic culture: the softened mores and weakened will, the subordination of passion to rationality, of fervor to rules. As an antidote to the deadening effects of contemporary life—reason, bureaucracy, routine, anomie, ennui—war is modernity's great answer to itself. "War is inescapable," Yitzhak Shamir declared, not because it ensures security but because "without this, the life of the individual has no purpose."[16] Though this sensibility seeps across the political spectrum, it is essentially an ideal of the conservative counter-Enlightenment, which found its greatest fulfillment during the years of Fascist triumph ("war is to men," Mussolini said, "as maternity is to women")—and is once again, it seems, prospering in our own time as well.[17]

Nowhere in recent memory has this romanticism been more apparent than in the neoconservative arguments during the Bush years about prewar intelligence, how to prosecute the wars in Afghanistan and Iraq, and whether or not to use torture. Listening to the neocon complaints about U.S. intelligence during the run-up to the war, one could hear distant echoes of Carlyle's assault on the "Mechanical Age" ("all is by rule and calculated contrivance") and Chateaubriand's despair that "certain eminent faculties of genius" will "be lost, and imagination, poetry and the arts perish."[18] Perle was not alone in his impatience with what Hersh calls the intelligence community's "susceptibility to social science notions of proof." Before he became secretary of defense, Donald Rumsfeld criticized the refusal of intelligence analysts to use their imaginations, "to make estimates that extended beyond the hard evidence they had in hand." Once in office, he mocked analysts' desire to have "all the dots connected for us with a ribbon wrapped around it." His staffers derided the military quest for "actionable intelligence," for information solid enough to warrant assassinations and other preemptive acts of violence. Outside the government, David Brooks blasted the CIA's "bloodless compilations of data by anonymous technicians" and praised those analysts who make "novelistic judgments" informed by "history, literature, philosophy and theology."[19]

Rumsfeld's war on the rule-bound culture and risk aversion of the military revealed a deep antipathy to law and order—not something stereotypically associated with conservatives but familiar enough to any historian of twentieth-century Europe (and, indeed, any historian of conservative thought more generally). Issuing a secret directive that terrorists should be captured or killed, Rumsfeld went out of his way to remind his generals that the goal was "not simply to arrest them in a law-enforcement exercise." Aides urged him to support operations by U.S. Special Forces, who could conduct lightning strikes without approval from generals. Otherwise, they warned, "the result will be decision by committee." One of Rumsfeld's advisers complained that the military had been "Clintonized," which could have meant anything from becoming too legalistic to being too effeminate. (Throughout the Bush years, there was an ongoing struggle within the security establishment over the protocols of machismo.) Geoffrey Miller, the man who made "Gitmo-ize" a household word, relieved a general at Guantanamo for being too "soft—too worried about the prisoners' well-being."[20] By now it seems self-evident that the neocons were drawn into Iraq for the sake of a grand idea: not the democratization of the Middle East, though that undoubtedly had some appeal, or even the creation of an American empire, but rather an idea of themselves as a brave and undaunted army of transgression. The gaze of the neocons, like that of America's perennially autistic ruling classes, does not look outward nearly as much as it looks inward: at their restless need to prove themselves, to demonstrate that neither their imagination nor their actions will be constrained by anyone or anything—not even by the rules and norms they believe are their country's gift to the world.

If *Torture*, Sanford Levinson's edited collection of essays, is any indication of contemporary sensibilities, neocons in the Bush

White House are not the only ones in thrall to romantic notions of danger and catastrophe. Academics are too. Every scholarly discussion of torture, and the essays collected in *Torture* are no exception, begins with the ticking-time-bomb scenario. The story goes something like this: a bomb is set to go off in a densely populated area in the immediate future; the government doesn't know exactly where or when, but it knows that many people will be killed; it has in captivity the person who planted the bomb, or someone who knows where it is planted; torture will yield the needed information; indeed, it is the only way to get the information in time to avert the catastrophe. What to do?

It's an interesting question. But given that it is so often posed in the name of realism, we might consider a few facts before we rush to answer it. First, as far as we know, no one at Guantanamo, Abu Ghraib, or any of the other prisons in America's international archipelago has been tortured in order to defuse a ticking time bomb. Second, at the height of the war in Iraq, anywhere between 60 and 90 percent of American-held prisoners there either were in jail by mistake or posed no threat at all to society. Third, many U.S. intelligence officials opted out of torture sessions precisely because they believed torture did not produce accurate information.[21] These are the facts, and yet they seldom, if ever, make an appearance in these academic exercises in moral realism.

The essays in *Torture* pose one other difficulty for those interested in reality: none of the writers who endorse the use of torture by the United States ever discusses the specific kinds of torture actually used by the United States. The closest we get is an essay by Jean Bethke Elshtain, in which she writes:

> Is a shouted insult a form of torture? A slap in the face? Sleep deprivation? A beating to within an inch of one's life? Electric prods on the male genitals, inside a woman's vagina, or in a

person's anus? Pulling out fingernails? Cutting off an ear or a breast? All of us, surely, would place every violation on this list beginning with the beating and ending with severing a body part as forms of torture and thus forbidden. No argument there. But let's turn to sleep deprivation and a slap in the face. Do these belong in the same torture category as bodily amputations and sexual assaults? There are even those who would add the shouted insult to the category of torture. But, surely, this makes mincemeat of the category.[22]

Distinguishing the awful from the acceptable, Elshtain never mentions the details of Abu Ghraib or the Taguba report, making her list of do's and don'ts as unreal as the ticking time bomb itself. Even her list of taboos is stylized, omitting actually committed crimes for the sake of repudiating hypothetical ones. Elshtain rejects stuffing electric cattle prods up someone's ass. What about a banana? She rejects cutting off ears and breasts. What about "breaking chemical lights and pouring the phosphoric liquid on detainees"? She condemns sexual assault. What about forcing men to masturbate or wear women's underwear on their heads? She endorses "solitary confinement and sensory deprivation." What about the "bitch in the box," where prisoners are stuffed in a car trunk and driven around Baghdad in 120° heat? She supports "psychological pressure," quoting from an article that "the threat of coercion usually weakens or destroys resistance more effectively than coercion itself." What about threatening prisoners with rape? When it comes to the Islamists, Elshtain cites the beheading of Daniel Pearl. When it comes to the Americans, she muses on Laurence Olivier's dentistry in *Marathon Man*.[23] Small wonder there's "no argument there": there is no *there* there.[24]

The unreality of Elshtain's analysis is not incidental or peculiar to her. Even writers who endorse torture but remain squeamish about it can't escape such abstractions. The more squeamish they are, in fact, the more abstractions they indulge in. Sanford Levinson, for example, tentatively discusses Alan Dershowitz's proposal that government officials should be forced to seek warrants from judges in order to torture terrorist suspects. Hoping to make the reality of torture, and the pain of its victims, visible and concrete, Levinson insists that "the person the state proposes to torture should be in the courtroom, so that the judge can take no refuge in abstraction." But then Levinson asks us to consider "the possibility that anyone against whom a torture warrant is issued receives a significant payment as 'just compensation' for the denial of his or her right not to be tortured."[25] Having just counseled against abstraction, Levinson resorts to the greatest abstraction of all—money—as payback for the greatest denial of rights imaginable.

If the unreality of these discussions sounds familiar, it is because they are watered by the same streams of conservative romanticism that coursed in and out of the White House during the Bush years. Notwithstanding Dershowitz's warrants and Levinson's addenda, the essays endorsing torture are filled with hostility to what Elshtain variously calls "moralistic code fetishism" and "rule-mania" and what we might simply call "the rule of law."[26] But where the Bush White House sought to be entirely free of rules and laws—and here the theoreticians depart from the practitioners—the contemplators of torture seek to make the torturers true believers in the rules.

There are two reasons. One reason, which Walzer presents at great length in a famous essay from 1973, reprinted in *Torture*, is that the absolute ban on torture makes possible—or forces us to acknowledge—the problem of "dirty hands." Like the supreme emergency, the ticking time bomb forces a leader to choose between two evils, to wrestle with the devil of torture and the devil of innocents dying. Where other moralists would affirm the ban on torture and allow innocents to die, or adopt a utilitarian calculus and order torture to proceed, Walzer believes the absolutist and the utilitarian wash their hands too quickly; their consciences come too clean. He wishes instead "to refuse 'absolutism' without denying the reality of the moral dilemma," to admit the simultaneous necessity for—and evil of—torture. Why? To make space for a moral leader, as Walzer puts it in *Arguing about War*, "who knows that he can't do what he has to do—and finally does" it. It is the familiar tragedy of two evils, or two competing goods, that is at stake here, a reminder that we must "get our hands dirty by doing what we ought to do," that "the dilemma of dirty hands is a central feature of political life."[27] The dilemma, rather than the solution, is what Walzer wishes to draw attention to. Should torturers be free of all rules save utility, or constrained by rights-based absolutism, there would be no dilemma, no dirty hands, no moral agon. Torturers must be denied their Kant and Bentham—and leave us to contend with the brooding spirit of the counter-Enlightenment, which insists that there could never be one moral code, one set of "eternal principles," as Isaiah Berlin put it, "by following which alone men could become wise, happy, virtuous and free."[28]

But there is another reason some writers insist on a ban on torture they believe must also be violated. How else to maintain the frisson of transgression, the thrill of Promethean criminality? As Elshtain writes in her critique of Dershowitz's proposal for torture warrants, leaders "should not seek to legalize" torture. "They should not aim to normalize it. And they should not write elaborate justifications of it. . . . The tabooed and forbidden, the extreme nature of this mode of physical coercion must be preserved so that it never becomes routinized as just the way we do things around here." What Elshtain objects to in Dershowitz's proposal is not the routinizing of *torture*; it is the *routinizing* of torture, the possibility of reverting to the "same moralistic-legalism" she hoped violations of the torture taboo would shatter.[29] This argument too is redolent of the conservative counter-Enlightenment, which always suspected, again quoting Berlin, that "freedom involves breaking rules, perhaps even committing crimes."[30]

But if the ban on torture must be maintained, what is a nation to do with the torturers who have violated it, who have, after all, broken the law? Naturally the nation must put them on trial; "the interrogator," in Elshtain's words, "must, if called on, be prepared to defend what he or she has done and, depending on context, pay the penalty."[31] In what may be the most fantastic move of an already fantastic discussion, several of writers on torture—even Henry Shue, an otherwise steadfast voice against the practice—imagine the public trial of the torturer as similar to that of the civil disobedient, who breaks the law in the name of a higher good, and throws himself on the mercy or judgment of the court. For only through a public legal proceeding, Levinson writes, will we "reinforce the paradoxical notion that one must condemn the act even if one comes to the conclusion that it is indeed justified in a particular situation," a notion, he acknowledges, that is little different from the comment of Admiral Mayorga, one of Argentina's dirtiest warriors: "The day we stop condemning torture (although we tortured), the day we become insensitive to mothers who lose their guerrilla sons (although they are guerrillas) is the day we stop being human beings."[32]

By now it should be clear why we use the word "theater" to denote the settings of both stagecraft and statecraft. Like the theater, national security is a house of illusions. Like stage actors, political actors are prone to a diva-like obsession, gazing in the mirror, wondering what the next day's—or century's—reviews will bring. It might seem difficult to imagine Liza Minnelli playing Henry Kissinger, but I'm not sure the part would be such a stretch. And what of the intellectuals who advise these leaders or the philosophers who analyze their dilemmas? Are they playwrights or critics, directors or audiences? I'm not entirely sure, but the words of their greatest spiritual predecessor might give us a clue. "I love my native city more than my own soul," cried Machiavelli, quintessential teacher of the hard ways of state.[33] Change "native city" to "child," replace "my own soul" with "myself," and we have the justification of every felonious stage mother throughout history, from the Old Testament's rule-breaking Rebecca to *Gypsy*'s ball-busting Rose.

10

Potomac Fever

The year 1948, John Cheever once wrote, was "the year everybody in the United States was worried about homosexuality." And nobody was more worried than the federal government, rumored to be teeming with gays and lesbians. One might think that Washington's attentions would have been focused elsewhere—on the Soviet Union, say, or on Communist spies. But in 1950 President Truman's advisers warned him that "the country is more concerned about the charges of homosexuals in the government than about Communists." The executive branch responded immediately. That year, the State Department fired "perverts" at the rate of one a day, more than twice the figure for suspected Communists. Charges of homosexuality ultimately accounted for a quarter to a half of all dismissals in the State Department, the Commerce

This chapter originally appeared as a review of David K. Johnson's *The Lavender Scare: The Cold War Persecution of Gays and Lesbians in the Federal Government* (Chicago: University of Chicago Press, 2004); David Cole's and James Dempsey's *Terrorism and the Constitution: Sacrificing Civil Liberties in the Name of National Security* (New York: New Press, 2006); Nancy Baker's *General Ashcroft: Attorney at War* (Lawrence: University Press of Kansas, 2006); James Risen's *State of War: The Secret History of the CIA and the Bush Administration* (New York: Free Press, 2006); and Eric Boehlert's *Lapdogs: How the Press Rolled Over for Bush* (New York: Free Press, 2006) in the *London Review of Books* (October 19, 2006): 10–12.

Department and the CIA. Only 25 percent of Joseph McCarthy's fan letters complained of "red infiltration"; the rest fretted about "sex depravity."[1]

The Lavender Scare, as it's been called, lasted from 1947 through the 1970s, and thousands lost their jobs. It was an exercise in humiliation—and hilarity. For the men and women charged with rinsing the pink from the Potomac were astonishingly ignorant about their quarry. Senator Clyde Hoey, head of the first congressional inquiry into the threat, had to ask an aide: "Can you please tell me, what can two women possibly do?" Senator Margaret Chase Smith asked one Hoey committee witness whether there wasn't a "quick test like an X-ray that discloses these things."[2]

The official justification for the purge was that homosexuals were vulnerable to blackmail and could be turned into Soviet spies. But investigators never found a single instance of this kind of blackmail during the Cold War. The best they could come up with was a dubious case from before World War I, when the Russians allegedly used the homosexuality of Austria's top spy to force him to work for them.[3]

The real justification was even more suspect: gays were social misfits whose pathology made them susceptible to Communist indoctrination. Many conservatives also believed that the Communist Party was a movement of and for libertines, and the Soviet Union a haven of free love and open marriage. Gays, they concluded, couldn't resist the temptation of freedom from bourgeois constraint. Drawing parallels with the decline of the Roman Empire, McCarthy regarded homosexuality as a cultural degeneracy that could only weaken the United States. It was, as one tabloid put it, "Stalin's Atom Bomb."[4]

How could a nation confronting so many foreign threats allow itself to be so distracted? (This is not just a question for historians: throughout the first decade of the twenty-first century, while the

United States was supposedly confronting a threat to its very existence, the U.S. military devoted considerable energy to purging its gay and lesbian service members. As of 2009, the military had fired at least sixty Arabic speakers for being gay.[5] One case was uncovered after investigators asked a soldier if he had ever participated in community theater.) With the Soviets in possession of the bomb and Korea on the march, why was Secretary of State Dean Acheson dispatched to Congress to defend his heterosexuality and that of his "powder puff diplomats"?[6] Didn't he have more important things to do than host rowdy gatherings of politicians and journalists that were

> reminiscent of "stag parties," featuring copious amounts of Scotch and bourbon, and smiling women "whose identity remained undisclosed." As one senator remarked, "It reminded me somewhat of the fraternity rushing season at college." Dean Acheson tried to appear as "one of the boys," slapping senators on the back. A journalist reported that "his hair was rumpled, his tie awry. The stiff and precise manner and speech which have antagonized many of us had disappeared. He even seemed to have removed the wax from his moustache."[7]

The Lavender Scare offers an instructive parable about that proverbial balance between freedom and security, which so vexes us today. It suggests that not only do we seldom strike the right balance between freedom and security, but that the metaphor of balance may itself be deeply flawed.

The first problem with the metaphor of balance between freedom and security is its assumption that security is a transparent concept, unsullied by ideology and self-interest. Because security benefits everyone—"the most vital of all interests," John Stuart Mill called it, which no one can "possibly do without"—it is immune to politics.[8] Yet, as Arnold Wolfers wrote years ago, security is an "ambiguous symbol," which "may not have any precise meaning at all."[9] Under the banner of a seemingly neutral, universal value, political elites are allowed, indeed encouraged, to pursue partisan and ideological courses of action they would ordinarily find hard to justify.

The actions of the U.S. government during the war on terror bear out this claim. According to two official commissions, one of the reasons U.S. intelligence agencies did not anticipate 9/11 was that turf wars prevented them from sharing information. The "obstacles to information sharing were more bureaucratic than legal" and had little to do "with the constitutional principles of due process, accountability, or checks and balances."[10] But while the government rides roughshod over Constitutional principles, it has done little to remove these bureaucratic obstacles. Even the Department of Homeland Security, which was supposed to unite competing agencies, "is bogged down by bureaucracy" and a "lack of strategic planning," according to one wire report.[11]

In the counterterrorism community, to cite another example, it is widely acknowledged that the preemptive arrest and preventive detention of suspected terrorists frustrates the gathering of intelligence. Yet since 9/11 the United States government consistently has relied on such policies. In the two years following 9/11, federal authorities preemptively rounded up more than 5,000 foreign nationals. As of 2006 not a single one of those individuals stood "convicted of any terrorist crime."[12]

The pattern is clear: measures that would improve security are not taken, while the measures that are taken, either fail to improve security or undermine it. There are several explanations for this paradox, including the blinkered interests of the intelligence bureaucracy. But a key factor is that conservatives view national security through the lens of their ongoing *Kulturkampf* against the 1960s.

This belief influences Republican policies, as we saw during the Bush years, but it also affects Democrats, who are perennially on the defensive against the charge that they are insufficiently hawkish.

Consider the career of John Ashcroft, Bush's first attorney general, who helped design so many of the draconian measures of the war on terror. As attorney general in Missouri, Ashcroft nearly got cited for contempt—not usually a good career move in American politics—for fighting the court-ordered desegregation of schools in St. Louis and Kansas City. As a senator, he received an honorary degree from Bob Jones University, which has barred interracial dating, and gave a friendly interview to *Southern Partisan*, a magazine sympathetic to the Old Confederacy. Like the biblical kings, he had his father anoint his head with oil when he became a governor and then a senator. After his father's death, he had Clarence Thomas do the honors when Bush appointed him attorney general. Convinced that calico cats were signs of the devil, he reportedly had his team make sure that the International Court at The Hague had none on its premises.[13]

Ashcroft's peculiar notions reflect the broader discontent of his party with the political culture bequeathed to or foisted on the United States in the 1960s and 1970s. During those years, liberals and leftists not only toppled legalized racial and gender hierarchies; they also attempted to rein in the security apparatus. They limited executive power, championed an activist judiciary, increased the rights of dissenters and criminals, and separated law enforcement from intelligence gathering. Though these reforms proved short-lived—they were significantly undermined by Reagan and Clinton—the legal legacy of the 1960s has come to stand for the larger culture of freedom that conservatives have loathed and liberals have loved for years.

Conservatives like to eschew any talk of terrorism's "root causes," but when it comes to the decadent liberalism that has allegedly hampered the government's ability to fight evildoers at home and abroad, they are willing to make an exception. Constitutional rights, Ashcroft insisted after 9/11, are "weapons with which to kill Americans." Terrorists "exploit our openness." According to Republican Senator Orrin Hatch, terrorists "would like nothing more than the opportunity to use all our traditional due process protections to drag out the proceedings."[14] For conservatives, 9/11 was a thunderous judgment on thirty years of treason—as if the attacks on the Pentagon and the World Trade Center were caused not by Al Qaeda but by reading criminals their Miranda rights— and a golden opportunity to move in the opposite direction: to expand the power of the presidency at the expense of Congress and the courts, and to blur the lines between intelligence gathering, political surveillance, and law enforcement.[15]

This synergy between national security and conservative anxiety is hardly new. The Lavender Scare reflected a general backlash against the loosening of sexual mores and gender roles that resulted from the New Deal and World War II. Roosevelt's welfare state, conservatives argued, sapped the nation's energy and patriarchal vigor. Instead of sturdy husbands and firm fathers controlling their wives and children, lisping bureaucrats and female social workers were now running the show. World War II exacerbated the problem: with so many men away at the front, and women working in the factories, male authority was further eroded. Citing these "social and family upheavals," J. Edgar Hoover argued that "the wartime spirit of abandon and 'anything goes' led to a decline of morals among people of all ages."[16]

Washington was the center of this cultural revolution. A boom town for young single people in the 1930s and 1940s, it had a tight housing market, forcing men to bunk with men, and offered women plentiful opportunities to support themselves through government jobs. What with the anonymous cruising sites of

Lafayette Park (right in front of the White House) and the company of tolerant female colleagues in the federal bureaucracy, homosexuals managed to turn Washington into a "very gay city." Hoover grew up in Washington, when it was a racist backwater of the Old South, and despite his own ambiguous sexuality, he was not happy about these changes.[17]

After the war, conservatives stirred a panic about gender roles. "A great emphasis," according to Cheever, "by way of defense, was put upon manliness, athletics, hunting, fishing and conservative clothing, but the lonely wife wondered, glancingly, about her husband at his hunting camp, and the husband wondered with whom he shared a rude bed of pines. Was he? Had he? Did he want to? Had he ever?" In generating that panic, conservatives deftly turned the public against a government bent on making everyone gay. The New Deal, they claimed, was a Queer Deal; America was run by "fairies and Fair Dealers."[18] Because of this ungodly union of Democrats, Communists, and fags, the United States was now vulnerable to the Soviet Union.

Today's conservatives believe that decades of domestic reform, driven this time by an excessive tenderness about the Constitution, have created a devitalized society that lacks the will and wherewithal to face down foreign threats. That is why Bush promised after 9/11 that there would be "no yielding. No equivocation. No lawyering this thing to death." It's also why Ashcroft bridled at the notion that the U.S. government should read Al Qaeda "the Miranda rights, hire a flamboyant defense lawyer, bring them back to the United States to create a new cable network of Osama TV."[19] It's not clear who, if anyone, was recommending such a policy, but that Ashcroft felt compelled to denounce it gives an indication of what he finds at issue when he talks about security. Conservatives certainly believe the Patriot Act and other restrictions of civil liberties will protect the American people—whether it's terrorism they're being protected from is another question.

There is a second problem with the notion of a balance between freedom and security. Ever since warfare became the business of peoples rather than kings, the compass of security has steadily expanded beyond the barracks and high command of the military. Frederick II waged war, Lukács wrote, "in such a manner that the civilian population simply would not notice it." Modern war insinuates itself into "the inner life of a nation."[20] It requires the full mobilization of a country's resources and active support of its citizenry. Limiting freedom in the most remote parts of society can thus be justified as a legitimate act of national defense. One can find a clear and present danger in the nation's political economy, its schools and popular culture, even in its beds, and resolve to suppress liberty there in order to avert the threat. When liberals and conservatives affirm the priority of security over freedom in wartime, they are not just endorsing government restrictions on what the press reports about the military; they are also licensing the suppression of all manner of dissent, throughout the entire social order.

Consider the National Security Agency's (NSA) surveillance of telecommunications traffic in the United States, which was first reported in the *New York Times* in 2005. As James Risen, who helped break the story, writes, the NSA is "the largest organization in the United States intelligence community, double the size of the CIA and truly the dominant electronic spy service in the world." Thanks to a secret order issued by Bush in 2002, it "is now eavesdropping on as many as five hundred people in the United States at any given time and potentially has access to the phone calls and emails of millions more. It does this without court-approved search warrants and with little independent oversight."[21]

The Bush administration's justification for this program, which may be "the largest domestic spying operation since the 1960s," is that, in order to monitor international traffic between terrorists, it must tap into the domestic network. "The switches carrying calls from Cleveland to Chicago . . . may also be carrying calls from Islamabad to Jakarta," with the result that "it is now difficult to tell where the domestic telephone system ends and the international network begins." The administration authorized the NSA to work secretly with telecommunications companies to spy on this international traffic and encouraged them to route more of it through the United States. If they aren't already, the NSA and its helpers in private industry may soon be spying not only on America but on Europe and Asia as well.[22]

The expansion of the security domain into all areas of society does more than curtail freedom in the abstract: it also empowers the conservative forces of political repression. Influential conservatives argue that national unity is an essential weapon of war, that opposition undermines the war effort, and that dissenters are dangerous, subversive, or traitorous. After antiwar candidate Ned Lamont's victory over Joe Lieberman in the 2006 Connecticut Democratic senatorial primary, Vice President Cheney declared that Lamont's election would only embolden "the al Qaeda types," who were "betting on the proposition that ultimately they can break the will of the American people."[23]

The Patriot Act, passed by Congress six weeks after 9/11, takes the equation of dissent with subversion a step further, suggesting that opponents of the war on terror are not just helping terrorists but may be terrorists themselves. Section 802 of the Act defines "domestic terrorism" as "acts dangerous to human life that are a violation of the criminal laws" and that "appear, to be intended . . . to influence the policy of a government by intimidation or coercion."[24] A definition as broad and vague as this could easily be used against demonstrators marching without a permit (a protest might make it impossible for ambulances or other emergency vehicles to get through).[25] After antiwar protesters caused a disruption in Portland, Oregon, in the autumn of 2002, state legislators drafted an antiterrorism bill along these lines. They defined terrorism as, among other things, any act intended "by at least one of its participants" to disrupt "commerce or the transportation systems of the State of Oregon."[26]

During the Republican National Convention in September 2004, the New York City Police Department arrested 1,800 antiwar protesters on various charges, most of which were later thrown out of court. Justifying these arrests, the city's mayor, Michael Bloomberg, said: "Some people think that we shouldn't allow people to express themselves. That's exactly what the terrorists did, if you think about it, on 9/11. Now this is not the same kind of terrorism, but there's no question that these anarchists are afraid to let people speak out."[27]

Because war mobilizes all spheres of society, defenders of the social order claim that any disruption to that order—from, say, striking labor unions—is as threatening to the war effort as opposition to the war itself. It was on these grounds that in 1950 the Supreme Court upheld the federal government's denial of labor protection to Communist-led unions. These union leaders, the court argued, might use their positions of power "at a time of external or internal crisis" to call "political strikes" and disrupt the channels of commerce.[28] In January 2003, the office of Tom DeLay, then the House majority leader, sent out a fundraising letter to supporters of the National Right to Work Foundation, a business group seeking to rid America of unions. Claiming that the labor movement "presents a *clear-and-present-danger* to the security of the United States at home and the safety of our Armed Forces Overseas," the letter denounced "Big Labor Bosses . . . willing to harm freedom-loving workers, the war effort and the economy to acquire more power!"[29]

Republicans in Congress also worked closely with Bush to deny union rights and whistle-blower protections to 170,000 employees in the Department of Homeland Security. Even though many of them are clerical workers, and even though employees in the Defense Department are not denied these rights, the administration claimed that eliminating these rights and protections would make the department as "agile and aggressive as the terrorists themselves." After Congress passed the antiunion bill in November 2002, a White House official declared it to be a model for all federal employees.[30]

The expansive nature of security authorizes the government not only to deploy these weapons but also to share them with private employers, who are often better positioned to use and abuse them. Because employers aren't subject to the constraints of the First Amendment, they are generally free to use their powers of hiring and firing, promotion and demotion, to silence dissent. During the McCarthy years, for example, the government imprisoned fewer than two hundred men and women for political reasons. But anywhere between 20 and 40 percent of the workforce was monitored for signs of ideological nonconformity, which included support for civil rights and labor unions.[31]

The effects of this outsourcing of repression are particularly visible in the media, for the U.S. media practices a form of censorship that must be the envy of tyrants everywhere. Without the government lifting a finger, informal pressure and newsroom careerism are enough to make reporters toe the line. The former CBS news anchor Dan Rather claims that conservatives are "all over your telephones, all over your email." As a result, "you say to yourself: 'You know, I think we're right on this story. I think we've got it in the right context, I think we've got it in the right perspective, but we better pick another day.'"[32] Those at the bottom get the message fast. The television reporter Sam Donaldson, who covered the White House during the Reagan years, tells Eric Boehlert:

> Today, not all the bosses support their reporters. So if you're a reporter at the White House and you're thinking about further successes in the business and you're nervous about your boss getting a call, maybe you pull your punches because of the career track.[33]

Journalists afraid for their careers aren't likely to question their government in time of war. And they haven't. ABC's Ted Koppel, one of the most aggressive interviewers in the business, admits that "we were too timid before the war" in Iraq. The PBS anchor Jim Lehrer says: "It would have been difficult to have had debates [about occupying Iraq] . . . you'd have had to have gone against the grain." The few journalists who bucked the trend were swiftly punished. After criticizing the media for its coverage of the war, Ashleigh Banfield was "taken to the woodshed" by her bosses, according to a *Newsday* report, and her career at NBC was finished. A *Wall Street Journal* reporter sent a personal email describing the terrible situation in Iraq: her editors pulled her out of the country and off the story.[34]

The last problem with the notion of a balance between freedom and security is that it mistakenly assumes that the benefits and burdens of freedom and security will be distributed equally among all members of society. But it is always some members of society, often the most marginalized and despised—gays and leftists during the Cold War, Arabs and Muslims (and still gays and leftists, albeit to a lesser degree) today—who are forced to give up their freedoms so that the rest can enjoy their security. Indeed, it is precisely because these groups are powerless, and not because they are dangerous, that the powerful can require them to bear the cost. (Even though 2 percent of American men aged 18 to 21 are arrested for drunk driving, the Supreme Court has ruled that this fact does not justify denying men of that age the right to buy alcohol. Many fewer than 2 percent of Arabs and Muslims in the United States are engaged in terrorist activity but the U.S. government has denied these groups far more fundamental rights.)[35] What the metaphor of balance between freedom and security conceals is the fundamental imbalance of power between groups in society; unequal costs are paid in return for unequal gains.

In *No Equal Justice* (1999), David Cole turned a commonplace—that white and/or wealthy Americans get better treatment from the cops and courts than black and/or poor citizens—into a startling theorization of a dual justice system in America. Granting maximal rights to all citizens would have a high cost in terms of safety, he observed, while denying those rights would have a high cost in terms of freedom. So what does America do? It does both: it formally grants rights to all, but systematically denies them to blacks and the poor. White, wealthy America gets maximal freedom and maximal safety, and "sidesteps the difficult question of how much constitutional protection we could afford if we were willing to ensure that it was enjoyed equally by all people."[36]

In *Enemy Aliens* and *Terrorism and the Constitution*, Cole extends this argument to noncitizens in wartime. Ever since the Alien Act of 1798 America's first impulse when faced with a foreign threat has been to restrict the rights of immigrants. The attraction of such measures is similar to the attraction of the dual system of criminal justice. It is a "politically tempting way to mediate the tension between liberty and security. Citizens need not forgo their rights" in order to be—or to feel—protected. Noncitizens forgo theirs, and because they "have no direct voice in the democratic process by which to register their objections," few people complain.[37]

After 9/11, security measures that would have affected all citizens—such as Operation TIPS, in which utility employees, delivery men, and other individuals were to spy on their fellow citizens, or the Pentagon's Total Information Awareness program, a massive surveillance project of public and private computer records—were quickly blocked, even by leading Republicans. But measures affecting noncitizens, particularly Muslims and Arabs, received overwhelming public support. Perhaps that is why a year after 9/11, only 7 percent of Americans believed themselves to have sacrificed basic rights and liberties.[38]

But there is one difference between the treatment of aliens in wartime and the treatment of blacks and the poor in peacetime. Wartime measures inflicted on noncitizens eventually influence measures against U.S. citizens, especially liberals or progressives. In 1942, the federal government put Japanese noncitizens and Japanese Americans in internment camps (on the assumption that even if they were citizens, their racial heritage made them aliens). Several years later, the FBI compiled a secret list of 12,000 citizens to be detained in the event of a national emergency—an initiative ratified in 1950 by the passage of the Internal Security Act, which remained on the books until 1971.[39] Whether or not a similar mutation will occur in the war on terror is anyone's guess, but the evidence so far is not encouraging.

What a fuller analysis of the metaphor reveals is that the items being balanced on the scale are not freedom and security but power and powerlessness. It thus makes perfect sense for conservatives to use the metaphor, for it conceals and protects their natural constituency. The real question is: why do liberals oblige them?

Perhaps it is because it was liberals who invented the argument. It was liberals who first argued that individuals should be free to say and do whatever they wish, as long as they don't harm anyone else. Liberal democracies should use coercion only to punish acts or attempted acts of harm, including threats to the security of the nation. One can see variants of this argument in Locke's account of religious toleration, which could be sacrificed only for "the safety and security of the commonwealth"; Mill's theory of liberty, which could be limited only to avert harm; and Oliver Wendell Holmes's defense of freedom of speech, which could be abridged only to thwart "a clear and present danger."[40]

The problem with these arguments is that it is nearly impossible to define harm—or danger, threat, menace—in a neutral way. Every definition of harm and its national security cognates rests on ideological assumptions about human nature, morality, and the good life. And in this regard, liberals are as guilty as conservatives. The only difference is that they often have less power to act on their convictions—and to stop their opponents from acting on theirs.

As a philosophical footnote to the Lavender Scare, we might recall that at the very moment the United States was conducting its purge of gays and lesbians, two Englishmen—conservative jurist Patrick Devlin and liberal philosopher H. L. A. Hart—were engaged in a debate of surprising relevance to events across the water. It began in 1957, when the Wolfenden Committee in the United Kingdom recommended, among other things, that gay sex between consenting adults in private be decriminalized. Speaking at the British Academy in March 1959, Devlin bridled at the committee's contention that there is "a realm of private morality and immorality which is, in brief and crude terms, not the law's business" and that only concrete acts of injury or harm should be prosecuted and punished by law. Not so, said Devlin: "What makes a society of any sort is community of ideas, not only political ideas but also ideas about the way its members should behave and govern their lives." Any challenge to those ideas—no matter how private, incidental, or symbolic—undermined social cohesion and posed as great a threat to the civic order as treason. In the same way that treason could lead to the overthrow of a government, homosexuality could produce a "loosening of moral bonds," which "is often the first stage of disintegration." Thus, "the suppression of vice is as much the law's business as the suppression of subversive activities."[41]

Hart's response was fast—he took to the airwaves in July, delivering a lecture on BBC Radio that was subsequently published in *The Listener*—and furious.[42] "It is grotesque," he declared, "to think of the homosexual behaviour of two adults in private as in any way like treason or sedition." Not just grotesque but obtuse: Devlin mistakenly assumed "that deviation from a general moral code is bound to affect that code, and to lead not merely to its modification but to its destruction." If one man's private acts did alter a society's beliefs—a big if, Hart insisted—such a shift would constitute not a collapse but a transformation of social morality. The proper political analogue to gay sex, then, was not treason but "a peaceful change" in a form of government.[43]

Critics tend to think that Hart got the better of Devlin. But I wonder. Hart, after all, never defined harm with any precision or persuasiveness, and it's not clear that he could have. So what was to stop Devlin from claiming that homosexuality was as harmful as treason—or, as his American counterparts claimed, that homosexuality *was* treason? Very little, it seems, either politically or philosophically. For when harm comes in shades of grey, someone, somewhere, will inevitably see it in lavender and pink—or any other disfavored color of the rainbow.

11

Easy to Be Hard

I enjoy wars. Any adventure's better than sitting in an office.

—Harold Macmillan

Despite the support among self-identified conservative voters and politicians for the death penalty, torture, and war, intellectuals on the right often deny any affinity between conservatism and violence.[1] "Conservatives," writes Andrew Sullivan, "hate war."

> Their domestic politics is rooted in a loathing of civil wars and violence, and they know that freedom is always the first casualty of international warfare. When countries go to war, their governments invariably get bigger and stronger, individual liberties are whittled away, and societies which once enjoyed the pluralist cacophony of freedom have to be marshaled into a single, collective note to face down an external foe. A state of permanent warfare—as George Orwell saw—is a virtual invitation to domestic tyranny.[2]

This chapter originally appeared as "Easy to Be Hard: Conservatism and Violence," in *Performances of Violence*, ed. Austin Sarat, Carleen Basler, and Thomas L. Dumm (Amherst: University of Massachusetts Press, 2011), 18–42.

Channeling a tradition of skepticism from Oakeshott to Hume, the conservative identifies limited government as the extent of his faith, the rule of law his one requirement for the pursuit of happiness. Pragmatic and adaptive, disposed rather than committed, such a sensibility—and it is a sensibility, the conservative insists, not an ideology—is not interested in violence. His endorsements of war, such as they are, are the weariest of concessions to reality. Unlike his friends on the left—conservative that he is, he values friendship more than agreement—he knows we live and love in the midst of great evil. This evil must be resisted, sometimes by violent means. All things being equal, he would like to see a world without violence. But all things are not equal, and he is not in the business of seeing the world as he'd like it to be.

The historical record of conservatism—not only as a political practice, which is not my primary concern here, but as a theoretical tradition—suggests otherwise. Far from being saddened, burdened, or vexed by violence, the conservative has been enlivened by it. I don't mean in a personal sense, though many a conservative, like Harold Macmillan quoted above or Winston Churchill quoted below, has expressed an unanticipated enthusiasm for violence. My concern is with ideas and argument rather than character or psychology. Violence, the conservative intellectual has maintained, is one of the experiences in life that makes us feel the most alive, and violence is an activity that makes life, well, lively.[3] Such arguments can be made nimbly—"Only the dead have seen the end of war," as Douglas MacArthur once put it[4]—or laboriously, as in the case of Treitschke:

> To the historian who lives in the world of will it is immediately clear that the demand for a perpetual peace is thoroughly reactionary; he sees that with war all movement, all growth, must be struck out of history. It has always been the tired,

unintelligent, and enervated periods that have played with the dream of perpetual peace. . . . However, it is not worth the trouble to discuss this matter further; the living God will see to it that war constantly returns as a dreadful medicine for the human race.[5]

Pithy or prolix, the case boils down to this: war is life, peace is death.

This belief can be traced back to Edmund Burke's *A Philosophical Enquiry into the Origin of Our Ideas of the Sublime and the Beautiful*. There Burke develops a view of the self desperately in need of negative stimuli of the sort provided by pain and danger, which Burke associates with the sublime. The sublime is most readily found in two political forms: hierarchy and violence. But for reasons that shall become clear, the conservative—again, consistent with Burke's arguments—often favors the latter over the former. Rule may be sublime, but violence is more sublime. Most sublime of all is when the two are fused, when violence is performed for the sake of creating, defending, or recovering a regime of domination and rule. But as Burke warned, it's always best to enjoy pain and danger at a remove. Distance and obscurity enhance sublimity; nearness and illumination diminish it. Counterrevolutionary violence may be the Everest of conservative experience, but one should view it from afar. Get too close to the mountaintop, and the air becomes thin, the view clouded. At the end of every discourse on violence, then, lies a waiting disappointment.

The Sublime and the Beautiful begins on a high note, with a discussion of curiosity, which Burke identifies as "the first and simplest emotion." The curious race "from place to place to hunt out something new." Their sights are fixed, their attention is rapt. Then the world turns gray. They begin to stumble across the same things, "with less and less of any agreeable effect." Novelty diminishes: how much, really, is there new in the world? Curiosity "exhausts" itself. Enthusiasm and engagement give way to "loathing and weariness."[6] Burke moves on to pleasure and pain, which are supposed to transform the quest for novelty into experiences more sustaining and profound. But rather than a genuine additive to curiosity, pleasure offers more of the same: a moment's enthusiasm, followed by dull malaise. "When it has run its career," Burke says, pleasure "sets us down very nearly where it found us." Any kind of pleasure "quickly satisfies; and when it is over, we relapse into indifference."[7] Quieter enjoyments, less intense than pleasure, are equally soporific. They generate complacency; we "give ourselves over to indolence and inaction."[8] Burke turns to imitation as another potential force of outward propulsion. Through imitation, we learn manners and mores, develop opinions, and are civilized. We bring ourselves to the world, and the world is brought to us. But imitation contains its own narcotic. Imitate others too much and we cease to better ourselves. We follow the person in front of us "and so on in an eternal circle." In a world of imitators, "there never could be any improvement." Such "men must remain as brutes do, the same at the end that they are at this day, and that they were in the beginning of the world."[9]

Curiosity leads to weariness, pleasure to indifference, enjoyment to torpor, and imitation to stagnation. So many doors of the psyche open onto this space of inertial gloom we might well conclude that it lurks not at the edge, but at the center of the human condition. Here, in this dark courtyard of the self, all action ceases, creating an ideal environment for "melancholy, dejection, despair, and self-murder."[10] Even love, the most outward of raptures, carries the self back to a state of internal dissolution.[11] Suicide, it seems, is the inevitable fate awaiting anyone who takes pleasure in the world as it is.

For a certain type of conservative theorist, passages like these pose something of a challenge. Here is the inventor of the conservative tradition articulating a vision of the self dramatically at odds with the imagined self of conservative thought. The conservative self, as we have repeatedly seen, claims to prefer "the familiar to the unknown . . . the tried to the untried, fact to mystery, the actual to the possible, the limited to the unbounded, the near to the distant, the sufficient to the superabundant, the convenient to the perfect, present laughter to utopian bliss."[12] He is partial to things as they are not because he finds things just or good, but because he finds them familiar. He knows them and is attached to them. He wishes neither to lose them nor to have them taken away. Enjoying what he has, rather than acquiring something better, is his highest good. But should the self of *The Sublime and the Beautiful* be assured of his attachments and familiars, he would quickly find himself confronting the specter of his own extinction, more than likely at his own hand.

Perhaps it is this lethal ennui, lurking just beneath the surface of conservative discourse, that explains the failure of the conservative politician to follow the lead of the conservative theorist. Far from embracing the cause of quiet enjoyments and secure attachments, the conservative politician has consistently opted for an activism of the not-yet and the will-be. Ronald Reagan's first inaugural address was a paean to the power of dreams: not small dreams but big, heroic dreams, of progress and betterment, and not dreams for their own sake, but dreams as a necessary and vital prod to action. Three months later, in an address before Congress, Reagan drove the point home with a quote from Carl Sandburg: "Nothing happens unless first a dream." And nothing happening, or too few things happening, or things not happening quickly enough, is what the conservative in politics dislikes. Reagan could scarcely contain his impatience with the dithering of politicians:

"The old and comfortable way is to shave a little here and add a little there. Well, that's not acceptable anymore." Old and comfortable was the indictment, no "half-measures" the verdict.[13]

Reagan was hardly the first conservative to act for the sake of the invisible and the ideal as against the material and the real. In his acceptance speech to the 1964 Republican National Convention, Barry Goldwater could find no more potent charge to level at the welfare state than that it had made a great nation "becalmed." Thanks to the New Deal, the United States had lost its "brisk pace" and was now "plodding along." Calm, slow, and plodding are usually welcomed by the conservative theorist as signs of present bliss. But to the conservative politician, they are evils. He must declare war, rallying his armies against the listless and the languid with talk of "causes," "struggle," "enthusiasm," and "devotion."[14]

That crusading zeal is not peculiar to American conservatism. It is found in Europe as well, even in England, the land that made moderation the moniker of conservatism. "Whoever won a battle," scoffed Margaret Thatcher, "under the banner 'I stand for Consensus'?"[15] And then there is Winston Churchill, traveling to Cuba in 1895 to report on the Spanish war against Cuban independence.[16] Ruminating on the disappointments of his generation—latecomers to the Empire, they were deprived of the opportunity for imperial conquest (as opposed to administration)—he arrived in Havana. This is what he had to say (looking back on the experience in 1930):

> The minds of this generation, exhausted, brutalized, mutilated and bored by War, may not understand the delicious yet tremulous sensations with which a young British Officer bred in the long peace approached for the first time an actual theatre of operations. When first in the dim light of early morning I saw the shores of Cuba rise and define themselves

from dark-blue horizons, I felt as if I sailed with Long John Silver and first gazed on Treasure Island. Here was a place where real things were going on. Here was a scene of vital action. Here was a place where anything might happen. Here was a place where something would certainly happen. Here I might leave my bones.[17]

Whatever the relationship between theory and practice in the conservative tradition, it is clear from *The Sublime and the Beautiful* that if the self is to survive and flourish it must be aroused by an experience more vital and bracing than pleasure or enjoyment. Pleasure and enjoyment act like beauty, "relaxing the solids of the whole system."[18] That system, however, must be made taut and tense. The mind must be quickened, the body exerted. Otherwise, the system will soften and atrophy, and ultimately die.

What most arouses this heightened state of being is the confrontation with non-being. Life and health are pleasurable and enjoyable, and that is what is wrong with them: "they make no such impression" on the self because "we were not made to acquiesce in life and health." Pain and danger, by contrast, are "emissaries" of death, the "king of terrors." They are sources of the sublime, "the strongest"—most powerful, most affecting—"emotion which the mind is capable of feeling."[19] Pain and danger, in other words, are generative experiences of the self.

Pain and danger are generative because they have the contradictory effect of minimizing and maximizing our sense of self. When sensing pain or danger, our mind "is so entirely filled with its object, that it cannot entertain any other." The "motions" of our soul "are suspended," as harm and the fears it arouses "rush in upon the mind." In the face of these fears, "the mind is hurried out of itself." When we experience the sublime, we feel ourselves evacuated, overwhelmed by an external object of tremendous power and threat. Everything that gave us a sense of internal being and vitality ceases to exist. The external is all, we are nothing. God is a good example, and the ultimate expression, of the sublime: "Whilst we contemplate so vast an object, under the arm, as it were, of almighty power, and invested upon every side with omnipresence, we shrink into the minuteness of our own nature, and are, in a manner, annihilated before him."[20]

Paradoxically, we also feel our existence to an extent we never have felt it before. Seized by terror, our "attention" is roused and our "faculties" are "driven forward, as it were, on their guard." We are pulled out of ourselves. We are cognizant of the immediate terrain and our presence upon it. Before, we barely noticed ourselves or our surroundings. Now we spill out of ourselves, inhabiting not only our bodies and minds but the space around us. We feel "a sort of swelling"—a sense that we are greater, our perimeter extends further—that "is extremely grateful to the human mind." But this "swelling," Burke reminds us, "is never more perceived, nor operates with more force, than when without danger we are conversant with terrible objects."[21]

In the face of the sublime, the self is annihilated, occupied, crushed, overwhelmed; in the face of the sublime, the self is heightened, aggrandized, magnified. Whether the self can truly occupy such opposing, almost irreconcilable, poles of experience at the same time—it is this contradiction, the oscillation between wild extremes, that generates a strong and strenuous sense of self. As Burke writes elsewhere, intense light resembles intense darkness not only because it blinds the eye and thus approximates darkness, but also because both are extremes. And extremes, particularly opposing extremes, are sublime because sublimity "in all things abhors mediocrity."[22] The extremity of opposing sensations, the savage swing from being to nothingness, makes for the most intense experience of selfhood.

The question for us, which Burke neither poses nor answers, here nor in his other work, is: What kind of political form entails this simultaneity of—or oscillation between—self-aggrandizement and self-annihilation? One possibility would be hierarchy, with its twin requirements of submission and domination; the other is violence, particularly warfare, with its rigid injunction to kill or be killed. Perhaps not coincidentally, both are of great significance to conservatism as a theoretical tradition and a historical practice.

Rousseau and John Adams are not usually thought of as ideological bedfellows, but on one point they agreed: social hierarchies persist because they ensure that everyone, save those at the very bottom and the very top, enjoys the opportunity to rule and be ruled in turn. Not, to be sure, in the Aristotelian sense of self-governance, but in the feudal sense of reciprocal governance: each person dominates someone below him in exchange for submitting to someone above him. "Citizens only allow themselves to be oppressed to the degree that they are carried away by blind ambition," writes Rousseau. "Since they pay more attention to what is below them than to what is above, domination becomes dearer to them than independence, and they consent to wear chains so that they may in turn give them to others. It is very difficult to reduce to obedience anyone who does not seek to command."[23] The aspirant and the authoritarian are not opposing types: the will to rise precedes the will to bow. More than thirty years later, Adams would write that every man longs "to be observed, considered, esteemed, praised, beloved, and admired."[24] To be praised, one must be seen, and the best way to be seen is to elevate oneself above one's circle. Even the American democrat, Adams reasoned, would rather rule over an inferior than dispossess a superior. His passion is for supremacy, not equality, and so long as he is assured an audience of lessers, he will be content with his lowly status:

Not only the poorest mechanic, but the man who lives upon common charity, nay the common beggars in the streets . . . court a set of admirers, and plume themselves on that superiority which they have, or fancy they have, over some others. . . . When a wretch could no longer attract the notice of a man, woman or child, he must be respectable in the eyes of his dog. "Who will love me then?" was the pathetic reply of one, who starved himself to feed his mastiff, to a charitable passenger who advised him to kill or sell the animal.[25]

One can see in these descriptions of social hierarchy lineaments of the sublime: annihilated from above, aggrandized from below, the self is magnified and miniaturized by its involvement in the practice of rule. But here's the catch: once we actually are assured of our power over another being, says Burke, our inferior loses her capacity to harm or threaten us. She loses her sublimity. "Strip" a creature "of its ability to hurt," and "you spoil it of every thing sublime."[26] Lions, tigers, panthers, and rhinoceroses are sublime not because they are magnificent specimens of strength but because they can and will kill us. Oxen, horses, and dogs are also strong but lack the instinct to kill or have had that instinct suppressed. They can be made to serve us and in the case of dogs even love us. Because such creatures, however strong, cannot threaten or harm us, they are incapable of sublimity. They are objects of contempt, contempt being "the attendant on a strength that is subservient and innoxious."[27]

We have continually about us animals of a strength that is considerable, but not pernicious. Amongst these we never look for the sublime: it comes upon us in the gloomy forest, and in the howling wilderness. . . . Whenever strength is only useful, and employed for our benefit or our pleasure, then it is never sublime; for nothing can act agreeably to us, that does not act in conformity to our will; but to act agreeably to our will, it must be subject to us; and therefore can never be the cause of a grand and commanding conception.[28]

At least one-half, then, of the experience of social hierarchy—not the experience of being ruled, which carries the possibility of being destroyed, humiliated, threatened, or harmed by one's superior, but the experience of easily ruling another—is incompatible with, and indeed weakens, the sublime. Confirmed of our power, we are lulled into the same ease and comfort, undergo the same inward melting, we experience while in the throes of pleasure. The assurance of rule is as debilitating as the passion of love.

Burke's intimations about the perils of long-established rule reflect a surprising strain within conservatism: a persistent, if unacknowledged, discomfort with power that has ripened and matured, authority that has grown comfortable and secure. Beginning with Burke himself, conservatives have expressed a deep unease about ruling classes so assured of their place in the sun that they lose their capacity to rule: their will to power dissipates; the muscles and intelligence of their command attenuate.

As we saw in chapter 1, Burke believes that the Old Regime is beautiful. For that reason, it is also "sluggish, inert, and timid." It cannot defend itself "from the invasions of ability," with ability standing in for the new men of power that the Revolution brings forth. The moneyed interest, also allied with the Revolution, is stronger than the landed interest because it is "more ready for any adventure" and "more disposed to new enterprises of any kind."[29] The Old Regime is beautiful, static, weak; the Revolution is ugly, dynamic, strong. "It is a dreadful truth," Burke admits in the second of his *Letters on a Regicide Peace*, "but it is a truth that cannot be concealed; in ability, in dexterity, in the distinctness of their views, the Jacobins are our superiors."[30]

Joseph de Maistre was less tactful than Burke in his condemnations of the Old Regime, perhaps because he took its failings more personally. Long before the Revolution, he claims, the leadership of the Old Regime had been confused and bewildered. Naturally, the ruling classes were unable to comprehend, much less resist, the onslaught unleashed against them. Impotence, physical and cognitive, was—and remains—the Old Regime's great sin. The aristocracy cannot understand; it cannot act. Some portion of the nobility may be well meaning, but they cannot see their projects through. They are foppish and foolish. They have virtue but not *virtú*. The aristocracy "fails ridiculously in everything it undertakes." The clergy has been corrupted by wealth and luxury. The monarchy consistently has shown that it lacks the will "to punish" that is the hallmark of every real sovereign.[31] Faced with such decadence, the inevitable outgrowth of centuries in power, Maistre concludes it is a good thing the counterrevolution has not yet triumphed (he is writing in 1797). The Old Regime needs several more years in the wilderness if it is to shed the corrupting influences of its once beautiful life:

> The restoration of the throne would mean a sudden relaxation of the driving force of the state. The black magic working at the moment would disappear like mist before the sun. Kindness, clemency, justice, all the gentle and peaceful virtues, would suddenly reappear and would bring with them a general meekness of character, a certain cheerfulness entirely opposed to the rigours of the revolutionary regime.[32]

A century later, a similar case will be made by Georges Sorel against the *belle époque*. Sorel is not usually seen as an emblematic figure of the right—then again, even Burke's conservatism remains a subject of dispute[33]—and, indeed, his greatest work, *Reflections on*

Violence, is often thought of as a contribution, albeit minor, to the Marxist tradition. Yet Sorel's beginnings are conservative and his endings proto-fascist, and even in his Marxist phase his primary worry is decadence and vitality rather than exploitation and justice. The criticisms he lodges against the French ruling classes at the end of the nineteenth century are not dissimilar to those made by Burke and Maistre at the end of the eighteenth. He even makes the comparison explicit: the French bourgeoisie, Sorel writes, "has become almost as stupid as the nobility of the eighteenth century." They are "an ultra-civilized aristocracy that demands to be left in peace." Once, the bourgeoisie was a race of warriors. "Bold captains," they were "creators of new industries" and "discovers of unknown lands." They "directed gigantic enterprises," inspired by that "conquering, insatiable and pitiless spirit" that laid railroads, subdued continents, and made a world economy. Today, they are timid and cowardly, refusing to take the most elemental steps to defend their own interests against unions, socialists, and the left. Rather than unleash violence against striking workers, they surrender to the workers' threat of violence. They lack the ardor, the fire in the belly, of their ancestors. It is difficult not to conclude that "the bourgeoisie is condemned to death and that its disappearance is only a matter of time."[34]

Carl Schmitt formalized Sorel's contempt for the weaknesses of the ruling classes into an entire theory of politics. According to Schmitt, the bourgeois was as he was—risk-averse, selfish, uninterested in bravery or violent death, desirous of peace and security—because capitalism was his calling and liberalism his faith. Neither provided him with a good reason for dying for the state. In fact, both gave him good reasons, indeed an entire vocabulary, not to die for the state. Interest, freedom, profit, rights, property, individualism, and other such words had created one of the most self-absorbed ruling classes in history, a class that enjoyed privilege but did not feel itself obliged to defend that privilege. After all, the premise of liberal democracy was the separation of politics from economics and culture. One could pursue profit, at someone else's expense, and think freely, no matter how subversive the thoughts, without disrupting the balance of power. The bourgeoisie, however, were confronting an enemy that very much understood the connections between ideas, money, and power, that economic arrangements and intellectual arguments were the stuff of political combat. Marxists got the friend-enemy distinction, which is constitutive of politics; the bourgeoisie did not.[35] The spirit of Hegel used to reside in Berlin; it has long since "wandered to Moscow."[36]

Sorel identified one exception to this rule of capitalist decadence: the robber barons of the United States. In the Carnegies and the Goulds of American industry, Sorel thought he saw "the indomitable energy, the audacity based on an accurate appreciation of strength, the cold calculation of interests, which are the qualities of great generals and great capitalists." Unlike the pampered bourgeoisie of France and Britain, the millionaires of Pittsburgh and Pittston "lead to the end of their lives a galley-slave existence without ever thinking of leading a nobleman's life, as the Rothschilds do."[37]

Sorel's spiritual counterpart across the Atlantic, Teddy Roosevelt, was not so sanguine about American industrialists and financiers. (Burkean anxiety about the ruling classes is common to the European and American conservative.) The capitalist, Roosevelt declared, sees his country as a "till," always weighing the "the honor of the nation and the glory of the flag" against a "temporary interruption of money-making." He is not "willing to lay down his life for little things" like the defense of the nation. He cares "only whether shares rise or fall in value."[38] He shows no interest in great affairs of state, domestic or international, unless they impinge upon his own. It was no accident, Roosevelt claimed, perhaps with a nod to Carnegie, that such men opposed the great imperial expedition that was the Spanish-American War.[39] Complacent and comfortable, assured of their riches by the success of the labor wars of previous decades and the election of 1896, these were not men who could be counted upon to defend the nation or even themselves. "We may some day have bitter cause," Roosevelt declared, "to realize that a rich nation which is slothful, timid, or unwieldy is an easy prey" for other, more martial peoples. The danger facing a ruling class, and a ruling nation, that has grown "skilled in commerce and finance" is that it "loses the hard fighting virtues."[40]

Roosevelt was hardly the first American conservative to worry about ruling classes gone soft and hierarchies overripe with power. Nor would he be the last. Throughout the 1830s, we saw in chapter 1, as the abolitionists began pressing their cause, John C. Calhoun drove himself into a rage over the easy living and willed cluelessness of his comrades on the plantation. They had grown lazy, fat, and complacent, so roundly enjoying the privileges of their position that they could not see the coming catastrophe. Or, if they could, the Southern planters couldn't do anything to fend it off, their political and ideological muscles having atrophied long ago.[41] Barry Goldwater likewise expressed contempt for the Republican Establishment.[42] And throughout the 1990s—to jump ahead by another three decades—one could hear Roosevelt's heirs on the right direct the same venom against the American capitalist at the masters of the universe on Wall Street and the geeky entrepreneurs of Silicon Valley.[43]

If the ruling class is to be vigorous and robust, the conservative has concluded, its members must be tested, exercised, and challenged. Not just their bodies, but also their minds, even their souls. Echoing Milton—"I cannot praise a fugitive and cloistered virtue, unexercised and unbreathed, that never sallies out and sees her adversary, but slinks out of the race. . . . That which purifies us is trial, and trial is by what is contrary"[44]—Burke believes that adversity and difficulty, the confrontation with affliction and suffering, make for stronger, more virtuous beings.

> The great virtues turn principally on dangers, punishments, and troubles, and are exercised rather in preventing mischiefs, than in dispensing favours; and are therefore not lovely, though highly venerable. The subordinate turn on reliefs, gratifications, and indulgences; and are therefore more lovely, though inferior in dignity. Those persons who creep into the hearts of most people, who are chosen as the companions of their softer hours, and their reliefs from care and anxiety, are never persons of shining qualities, nor strong virtues.[45]

Perhaps we see here the origins of the conservative preference for warfare over the welfare state, but that is another topic for another day). But where Milton and other like-minded republicans believe that impurity and corruption await the complacent and the comfortable, Burke espies the more terrifying specter of dissipation, degeneration, and death. If the powerful are to remain powerful, if they are to remain alive at all, their power, indeed the credibility of their own existence, must be continuously challenged, threatened, and defended.

One of the more arresting—though I hope by now intelligible—features of conservative discourse is the fascination, indeed appreciation, one finds for the conservative's enemies, particularly for their use of violence against him and his allies. Maistre's most rapturous comments in his *Considerations on France* are reserved for the Jacobins, whose brutal will and penchant for violence—their "black magic"—he plainly envies. Thanks to their efforts, France has been purified and restored to its rightful pride of place among the family of nations. They have rallied the people against foreign invaders, a "prodigy" that "only the infernal genius of Robespierre could accomplish." Unlike the monarchy, the Revolution has the will to punish.[46]

From the perspective of the Burkean sublime, however, Maistre's argument only goes so far. The Revolution rejuvenates the Old Regime by forcing it from power and purifying the people through violence. It delivers a clarifying shock to the system. But Maistre never contemplates, or at least never discusses, the revivifying effect that wresting power back from the Revolution might have on the leaders of the Old Regime. And indeed, once he gets around to describing how he thinks the counterrevolution will occur, the final battle turns out to be a stunningly anticlimactic affair, with scarcely a shot fired at all. "How Will the Counter-Revolution Happen if it Comes?" Maistre asks. "Four or five persons, perhaps, will give France a king." Not exactly the stuff of a virile, transformed ruling class, battling its way back to power.[47]

Maistre never contemplated the restorative possibilities of hand-to-hand combat between the Old Regime and the Revolution; for this one must turn to Sorel. And while Sorel's allegiances in the war between the rulers and the ruled of the late nineteenth century are more ambiguous than Maistre's, his account of the effect of the violence of the ruled upon the rulers is not. The French bourgeoisie has lost its fighting spirit, Sorel claims, but that spirit is alive and well among the workers. Their battlefield is the workplace, their weapon is the general strike, and their aim is the overthrow of the state. It is the last that most impresses Sorel, for the desire to overthrow the state signals just how unconcerned the workers are about "the material profits of conquest." Not only do they not seek higher wages and other improvements in their well-being; instead they have set their sights on the most improbable of goals—overthrowing the state by a general strike. It is that improbability, the distance between means and ends, that makes the violence of the proletariat so glorious. The proletarians are like Homeric warriors, absorbed in the grandeur of the battle and indifferent to the aims of the war: Who really has ever overthrown a state by a general strike? Theirs is a violence for its own sake, without concern for costs, benefits, and the calculations in between.[48] As Ernst Jünger wrote a generation later, it "is not what we fight for but how we fight."[49]

But what grips Sorel is not the proletariat but the rejuvenating effects it might have on the bourgeoisie. Can the violence of the general strike "give back to the bourgeoisie an ardour which is extinguished?" Certainly the vigor of the proletariat might reawaken the bourgeoisie to its own interests and the threats its withdrawal from politics has posed to those interests. More tantalizing to Sorel, however, is the possibility that the violence of workers will "restore to [the bourgeoisie] the warlike qualities it formerly possessed," forcing the "capitalist class to remain ardent in the industrial struggle." Through the struggle against the proletariat, in other words, the bourgeoisie may recover its ferocity and ardor. And ardor is everything. From ardor alone, that splendid indifference to reason and self-interest, an entire civilization, drowning in materialism and complacency, will be reawakened. A ruling class, threatened by violence from the ruled, roused to its own taste for violence—that is the promise of the civil war in France.[50]

For the conservative, no matter how modulated or moderate, a renewed vigor has always been the promise of civil war. For between the easy cases of a Catholic reactionary like Maistre and a proto-fascist like Sorel stands the more difficult but ultimately more revealing example of Alexis de Tocqueville. His drift from the moderation of the July Monarchy to the revanchism of 1848 demonstrates how easily and inexorably the Burkean conservative will swing from the beautiful to the sublime, how the music of prudence and moderation gives way to the march of violence and vitriol.[51]

Publicly presenting himself as the consummate realist, discriminating and judicious, with little patience for enthusiasm of any sort, Tocqueville was actually a closet romantic. He confessed to his brother that he shared their father's "devouring impatience," his "need for lively and recurring sensations." Reason, he said, "has always been for me like a cage," behind which he would "gnash [his] teeth." He longed for "the sight of combat." Looking back on the French Revolution, which he missed (he was born in 1805), he lamented the end of the Terror, claiming that "men thus crushed can not only no longer attain great virtues, but they seem to have become almost incapable of great crimes." Even Napoleon, scourge of conservatives, moderates, and liberals everywhere, earned Tocqueville's admiration as the "most extraordinary being who has appeared in the world for many centuries." Who, by contrast, could find inspiration in the parliamentary politics of the July Monarchy, that "little democratic and bourgeois pot of soup"?

Yet once he set upon a career in politics, it was into that little bourgeois pot of soup that Tocqueville jumped. Predictably, it was not to his taste. Tocqueville may have mouthed the words of moderation, compromise, and the rule of law, but they did not move him. Without the threat of revolutionary violence, politics was simply not the grand drama he imagined it had been between 1789 and 1815. "Our fathers observed such extraordinary things that compared with them all of our works seem commonplace." The politics of moderation and compromise produced moderation and compromise; it did not produce politics, at least not as Tocqueville understood the term. During the 1830s and 1840s, "what was most wanting . . . was political life itself." There was "no battlefield for contending parties to meet upon." Politics had been "deprived" of "all originality, of all reality, and therefore of all genuine passions."

Then came 1848. Tocqueville didn't support the Revolution. Indeed, he was among its most vociferous opponents. He voted for the full suspension of civil liberties, which he happily announced was done "with even more energy than had been done under the Monarchy." He welcomed talk of a dictatorship—to protect the very regime he had spent the better part of two decades disparaging. And he loved it all: the violence, the counterviolence, the battle. Defending moderation against radicalism, Tocqueville was given a chance to use radical means for moderate ends, and it is not entirely clear which of the two most stirred him.

> Let me say, then, that when I came to search carefully into the depths of my own heart, I discovered, with some surprise, a certain sense of relief, a sort of gladness mingled with all the griefs and fears to which the Revolution had given rise. I suffered from this terrible event for my country, but clearly not for myself; on the contrary, I seemed to breathe more freely than before the catastrophe. I had always felt myself stifled in the atmosphere of the parliamentary world which had just been destroyed: I had found it full of disappointments, both where others and where I myself was concerned.

A self-styled poet of the tentative, the subtle, and the complex, Tocqueville burned with enthusiasm upon waking up to a world divided into two camps. Timid parliaments sowed a gray confusion; civil war forced upon the nation a bracing clarity of black and white. "There was no field left for uncertainty of mind: on this side lay the salvation of the country; on that, its destruction. . . . The road seemed dangerous, it is true, but my mind is so constructed that it is less afraid of danger than of doubt." For this member of the ruling class, sublimity welling up from the violence of the lower orders offered an opportunity to escape the stifling beauty of life on the bourgeois Parnassus.

Francis Fukuyama is perhaps the most thoughtful of recent writers to pursue this conservative line of argument about violence. Unlike Maistre, however, or Tocqueville and Sorel—all of whom wrote in the midst of battle, when the outcome was unclear—Fukuyama writes from the vantage of victory. It is 1992, and the capitalist classes have beaten their socialist opponents in the long civil war of the short twentieth century. It is not a pretty sight, at least not for Fukuyama. For the revolutionary was one of the few thymotic men of the twentieth century. Thymotic man is like Sorel's worker: he who risks his life for the sake of an improbable principle, who is unconcerned with his own material interests and cares only for honor, glory, and the values for which he fights. After a strange but brief homage to the Bloods and the Crips as thymotic men, Fukuyama looks back fondly to men of purpose and power like Lenin, Trotsky, and Stalin, "striving for something purer and higher" and possessed of "greater than usual hardness, vision, ruthlessness, and intelligence." By virtue of their refusal to accommodate themselves to the reality of their times, they were the "most free and therefore the most human of beings." But somehow or other, these men and their successors lost the civil war of the twentieth century, almost inexplicably, to the forces of "Economic Man." For Economic Man is "the true *bourgeois*." Such a man would never be "willing to walk in front of a tank or confront a line of soldiers" for any cause, even his own. Yet Economic Man is the victor, and far from rejuvenating or restoring him to his primal powers, the war seems only to have made him more bourgeois. Conservative that he is, Fukuyama can only chafe at the triumph of Economic Man and "the life of rational consumption" he has brought about, a life that is "in the end, *boring*."[52]

Far from being exceptional, Fukuyama's disappointment about the actual—as opposed to anticipated or fantasized—effect of violence on a dissipated ruling class is emblematic. "The aims of battle and the fruits of conquest are never the same," E. M. Forster observed in *A Passage to India*. "The latter have their value and only the saint rejects them, but their hint of immortality vanishes as soon as they are held in the hand."[53] Deep within the conservative discourse lurks an element of anticlimax that cannot be contained. While the conservative turns to violence as a way of liberating himself, or the ruling classes, from the deadening ennui and softening atrophy that comes with power, virtually every encounter in conservative discourse with actual violence entails disillusion and deflation.

Recall Teddy Roosevelt, brooding on the materialism and weakness of America's capitalist classes. Where, he wondered, could one find an example of the "strenuous life"—the thrill of difficulty and danger, the strife that made for progress—in contemporary America? Perhaps in the foreign wars and conquests America had undertaken at the end of the century. Yet even here Roosevelt encountered frustration. Though his reports from the Spanish-American War were filled with bravery and bravado, a careful reading of his adventures in Cuba suggests that his exploits there were a fiasco. Each of the famous charges Roosevelt led up or down a hill was an anticlimax. The first culminated with him seeing exactly two Spanish soldiers felled by his men: "These were the only Spaniards I actually saw fall to aimed shots by any one of my men," he wrote, "with the exception of two guerillas in trees." The second found him leading an army that neither heard nor followed him. So it was with a grim appreciation that he recited the dyspeptic comments of one of the army's leaders in Cuba, a certain General Wheeler, who "had been through too much heavy fighting in the Civil War to regard the present fight as very serious."[54]

In the bloody occupations that followed the Spanish-American War, however, Roosevelt thought he saw the true bliss it was in that dawn to be alive. Roosevelt was sure that America's occupations of the Philippines and elsewhere were as close to a replay of the Civil War—that noble crusade of unsullied virtue—as he and his countrymen were ever likely to see. "We of this generation do not have to face a task such as that our fathers faced," he declared in 1899, "and woe to us if we fail to perform them! . . . We cannot avoid the responsibilities that confront us in Hawaii, Cuba, Porto [sic] Rico, and the Philippines." Here—in the islands of the Caribbean and the Pacific—was the confluence of blood and purpose he had been searching for his entire life. The task of imperial uplift, of educating the natives in "the cause of civilization," was arduous and violent, imposing a mission upon America that would take years, God willing, to fulfill. If the imperial mission succeeded—and even if it failed—it would create a genuine ruling class in America, hardened and made strenuous by battle, nobler and less grubby-minded than Carnegie's minions.[55]

It was a beautiful dream. But it too could not bear the weight of reality. Though Roosevelt hoped the men who ruled the Philippines would be "chosen for signal capacity and integrity," running "the provinces on behalf of the entire nation from which they come, and for the sake of the entire people to which they go," he worried that America's colonial occupiers would come from the same class of selfish financiers and industrialists that had driven him abroad in the first place. And so his paeans to imperialism ended on a sour note of warning, even doom. "If we permit our public service in the Philippines to become the prey of the spoils politicians, if we fail to keep it up to the highest standard, we shall be guilty of an act, not only of wickedness, but of weak and short-sighted folly, and we shall have begun to tread the path which was trod by Spain to her own bitter humiliation."[56]

But if his dream ended badly, Roosevelt at least had the advantage of being able to say that he always suspected it would. The same could not be said of the Fascists of Italy, whose self-deception about the wresting of power from the left persisted for decades, testifying to an inability to confront their own disappointment. For years, the Fascists celebrated the 1922 March on Rome as the violent and glorious triumph of will over adversity. October 28, the day of the Blackshirts' arrival in Rome, became a national holiday; it was declared the first day of the Fascist New Year upon the introduction of the new calendar in 1927. The story of Mussolini's arrival in particular—wearing the proverbial black shirt—was repeated with awe. "Sire," he supposedly said to King Victor Emmanuel III, "forgive my attire. I come from the battlefields." In actual fact, Mussolini traveled by train overnight from Milan, where he had been conspicuously attending the theater, snoozing comfortably in the sleeping car. The only reason he even made it into Rome was that a timid establishment, led by the king, telephoned him in Milan with a request that he form a government. Barely a shot was fired, on either side.[57] Maistre could not have written it better.

We can see a similar phenomenon at play in the war on terror. Though many view the Bush administration and neoconservatism as departures from proper conservatism—the most recent statement of this thesis being Sam Tanenhaus's *The Death of Conservatism*[58]—the neocon project of imperial adventurism traces the Burkean arc of violence from beginning to end. I have already discussed, in chapter 8, how the neoconservatives saw 9/11 and the war on terror as a chance to escape from the decadent and deadening peace and prosperity of the Clinton years, which they believed had weakened American society. Oozing in comfort, Americans—and more important their leaders—had supposedly lost the will, the desire and ability, to govern the world. Then 9/11 happened, and suddenly it seemed as if they could.

That dream, of course, now lies in tatters, but one of its more idiosyncratic aspects is worth noting, for it presents a wrinkle in the long saga of conservative violence. According to many conservatives, and not just the neocons, one of the recent sources of American decadence, traceable back to the Warren Court and the rights revolutions of the 1960s, is the liberal obsession with the rule of law. This obsession, in the eyes of the conservative, takes many forms: the insistence on due process in criminal procedure; a partiality to litigation over legislation; an emphasis on diplomacy and international law over war; attempts to restrain executive power through judicial and legislative oversight. However unrelated these symptoms may seem, conservatives see in them a single disease: a culture of rules and laws slowly disabling and devitalizing the blond beast of prey that is American power. These are signs of a Nietzschean unhealthiness, and 9/11 was the inevitable result.

If another 9/11 is to be prevented, that culture of rights and rules must to be repudiated and reversed. As the reporting of Seymour Hersh and Jane Mayer makes clear, the war on terror—with its push for torture, for overturning the Geneva Conventions, for refusing the restrictions of international law, for illegal surveillance, and for seeing terrorism through the lens of war rather than of crime and punishment—reflects as much, if not more, these conservative sensibilities and sensitivities as it does the actual facts of 9/11 and the need to prevent another attack.[59] "She's soft—too soft," says now-retired Lieutenant General Jerry Boykin about the United States, pre- and post-9/11. The way to make her hard is not merely to undertake difficult and strenuous military action but also to violate the rules—and the culture of rules—that made her soft in the first place. The United States must learn how to "live on the edge," says former NSA director Michael Hayden. "There's nothing we won't do, nothing we won't try," former CIA director George Tenet helpfully adds.[60]

The great irony of the war on terror is that far from emancipating the blond beast of prey, the war has made law, and lawyers, far more critical than one might imagine. As Mayer reports, the push for torture, unbridled executive power, the overthrow of the Geneva Conventions, and so on came not from the CIA or the military; the driving forces were lawyers in the White House and the Justice Department like David Addington and John Yoo. Far from Machiavellian virtuosos of transgressive violence, Addington and Yoo are fanatics about the law and insist on justifying their violence through the law. Lawyers, moreover, consistently oversee the actual practice of torture. As Tenet wrote in his memoir, "Despite what Hollywood might have you believe, in situations like this [the capture, interrogation, and torture of Al Qaeda logistics chief Abu Zubayda] you don't call in the tough guys; you call in the lawyers." Every slap on the face, every punch in the gut, every shake of the body—and much, much worse—must first be approved by higher-ups in the various intelligence agencies, inevitably in consultation with attorneys. Mayer compares the practice of torture to a game of "Mother, May I?" As one interrogator states, "Before you could lay a hand on him [the torture victim], you had to send a cable saying, 'He's uncooperative. Request permission to do X.' And permission would come, saying 'You're allowed to slap him one time in the belly with an open hand.'"[61]

Rather than free the blond beast to roam and prey as he wishes, the removal of the ban on torture and the suspension of the Geneva Conventions have made him, or at least the lawyers who hold his leash, more anxious. How far can he go? What can he do? Every act of violence, as this exchange between two Pentagon lawyers reveals, becomes a law school seminar:

What did "deprivation of light and auditory stimuli" mean? Could a prisoner be locked in a completely dark cell? If so, could he be kept there for a month? Longer? Until he went blind? What, precisely, did the authority to exploit phobias permit? Could a detainee be held in a coffin? What about using dogs? Rats? How far could an interrogator push this? Until a man went insane?[62]

Then there is the question of combining approved techniques of torture. May an interrogator withhold food from the prisoner and turn down the temperature of his cell at the same time? Does the multiplying effect of pains doubled and tripled cross a never-defined line?[63] As Orwell taught, the possibilities for cruelty and violence are as limitless as the imagination that dreams them up. But the armies and agencies of today's violence are vast bureaucracies, and vast bureaucracies need rules. Eliminating the rules does not Prometheus unbind; it just makes for more billable hours.

"No yielding. No equivocation. No lawyering this thing to death." That was George W. Bush's vow after 9/11 and his description of how the war on terror would be conducted. Like so many of Bush's other declarations, it turned out to be an empty promise. This thing was lawyered to death. But, and this is the critical point, far from minimizing state violence—which was the great fear of the neocons—lawyering has proven to be perfectly compatible with violence. In a war already swollen with disappointment and disillusion, the realization that inevitably follows—the rule of law can, in fact, authorize the greatest adventures of violence and death, thereby draining them of sublimity—must be, for the conservative, the greatest disillusion of all.

Had they been closer readers of Burke, the neoconservatives—like Fukuyama, Roosevelt, Sorel, Schmitt, Tocqueville, Maistre, Treitschke, and so many more on the American and European right—could have seen this disillusion coming. Burke certainly did. Even as he wrote of the sublime effects of pain and danger, he was careful to insist that should those pains and dangers "press too nearly" or "too close"—that is, should they become realities rather than fantasies, should they become "conversant about the present destruction of the person"—their sublimity would disappear. They would cease to be "delightful" and restorative and become simply terrible.[64] Burke's point was not merely that no one, in the end, really wants to die or that no one enjoys unwelcome, excruciating pain. It was that sublimity of whatever kind and source depends upon obscurity: get too close to anything, whether an object or experience, see and feel its full extent, and it loses its mystery and aura. It becomes familiar. A "great clearness" of the sort that comes from direct experience "is in some sort an enemy to all enthusiasms whatsoever."[65] "It is our ignorance of things that causes all our admiration, and chiefly excites our passions. Knowledge and acquaintance make the most striking causes affect but little."[66] "A clear idea," Burke concludes, "is therefore another name for a little idea."[67] Get to know anything, including violence, too well, and it loses whatever attribute—rejuvenation, transgression, excitement, awe—you ascribed to it when it was just an idea.

Earlier than most, Burke understood that if violence were to retain its sublimity, it had to remain a possibility, an object of fantasy—a horror movie, a video game, an essay on war. For the actuality (as opposed to the representation) of violence was at odds with the requirements of sublimity. Real, as opposed to imagined, violence entailed objects getting too close, bodies pressing too near, flesh upon flesh. Violence stripped the body of its veils; violence made its antagonists familiar to each other in a way they had never been before. Violence dispelled illusion and mystery, making things drab and dreary. That is why, in his discussion in the *Reflections* of the revolutionaries' abduction of Marie Antoinette, Burke takes such pains to emphasize her "almost naked" body and turns so effortlessly to the language of clothing—"the decent drapery of life," the "wardrobe of the moral imagination," "antiquated fashion," and so on—to describe the event.[68] The disaster of the revolutionaries' violence, for Burke, was not cruelty; it was the unsought enlightenment.

Since 9/11, many have complained, and rightly so, about the failure of conservatives—or their sons and daughters—to fight the war on terror themselves. For those on the left, that failure is symptomatic of the class injustice of contemporary America. But there is an additional element to the story. So long as the war on terror remains an idea—a hot topic on the blogs, a provocative op-ed, an episode of *24*—it is sublime. As soon as the war on terror becomes a reality, it can be as cheerless as a discussion of the tax code and as tedious as a trip to the DMV.

Conclusion

Conservatism has dominated American politics for the past forty years. Just as the Republican administrations of Dwight Eisenhower and Richard Nixon demonstrated the resilience of the New Deal, so have the Democratic administrations of Bill Clinton and Barack Obama demonstrated the resilience of Reaganism. The conservative embrace of unregulated capitalism and imperial power still envelops our two parties. Consistent with this book's argument about the private life of power, the most visible effort of the GOP since the 2010 midterm election has been to curtail the rights of employees and the rights of women. While the right's success in these campaigns is by no means assured, the fact that the Republicans have taken aim at the last redoubt of the labor movement and the entirety of Planned Parenthood gives some indication of how far they've come. The end (in both senses of the word) of the right's long march against the twentieth century may be in sight.

The success of the right, however, is not an unmixed blessing. As conservatives have long noted, there is a dialectical synergy between the left and the right, in which the progress of the former spurs on the innovations of the latter. "It is ironic, although not historically unprecedented," wrote Frank Meyer, the intellectual architect of the fusionist strategy that brought together the libertarian and traditionalist wings of modern conservatism, "that such a burst of creative energy on the intellectual level" on the right "should occur simultaneously with a continuing spread of the influence of Liberalism in the practical political sphere." Across the Atlantic, Roger Scruton, a more traditional type of British Tory, wrote that "in times of crisis . . . conservatism does its best," while Friedrich Hayek observed that the defense of the free market "became stationary when it was most influential" and "progressed" when it was "on the defensive."[1] True, these were intellectuals writing about ideas; conservative operatives might be less sanguine about the prospect of trading four more years for a few good books. Even so, if the ultimate fate of a party is tied to the strength of its ideas—not the truth of its ideas, but the resonance and pertinence of those ideas, their cultural purchase and ability to travel across the political landscape—it should be a cause of concern on the right that its ideas have so roundly succeeded. As Burke warned long ago, victory may simply be a way station to death.

Several recent books of conservative introspection suggest that many on the right are indeed concerned about the state of conservative ideas.[2] But most of these attempts at self-criticism seem motivated by a simple fear of defeat at the polls. Oriented as they are to the electoral cycle or to the pros and cons of particular policies, they don't see that conservatism, like any party, can lose elections yet still control public debate. More important, these writers don't understand that failure is the wellspring of conservative renewal. They imagine that conservatism can simply be reinvented or retooled to meet the needs of a changing electorate or the hobbyhorses of its theoreticians. But that is not how conservatism works. Conservatism requires defeat; failure is its most potent source of inspiration. Not failure in the brooding, romantic sense that Andrew Sullivan articulates in his paean to loss, but failure in the simultaneously threatening and galvanizing sense.[3] Loss—real social loss, of power and position, privilege and prestige—is the mustard seed of conservative innovation. What the right suffers from today is not loss but success, and until a significant dominant group in society is forced to suffer loss—of the kind experienced by employers during the 1930s, white supremacists during the 1960s, or husbands in the 1970s—it will remain a philosophically flabby movement. Politically powerful, but intellectually moribund.

Which leads me to wonder about the long-term prospects of the Tea Party, the latest variant of right-wing populism. Has the Tea Party given conservatism a new lease on life? Or is the Tea Party like the New Politics of the late 1960s and early 1970s, the last spark of a spent force, its frantic energies a mask for the decline of the larger movement of which it is a part? It's impossible to say, but this much is clear: So long as there are social movements demanding greater freedom and equality, there will be a right to counter them. With the exception of the gay rights movement, there are today no threatening social movements of the left. Once they arise, a new right will arise with them—not a right that needs to invent bogeymen like Obama's socialism but a right with real monsters to destroy. Until then, we can chalk up the current state of the right not to its failures of imagination or excess of spleen—as some have done[4]—but to its overwhelming success.

Modern conservatism came onto the scene of the twentieth century in order to defeat the great social movements of the left. As far as the eye can see, it has achieved its purpose. Having done so, it now can leave. Whether it will, and how much it will take with it on its way out, remains to be seen.

Introduction

1. At the turn of the twentieth century, 98% of the overwhelmingly Republican—and anti-union—federal judiciary came from "the very top of the nation's class and status hierarchies." William E. Forbath, *Law and the Shaping of the American Labor Movement* (Cambridge, Mass.: Harvard University Press, 1991), 33.

2. Even today, marital rape is punished with less severity—and requires prosecutors to mount greater obstacles—than nonmarital rape. According to one scholar, "The marital rape exemption survives in some substantial form in a majority of states." Jill Elaine Hasday, "Contest and Consent: A Legal History of Marital Rape," *California Law Review* 88 (October 2000): 1375, 1490; Rebecca M. Ryan, "The Sex Right: A Legal History of the Marital Rape Exemption," *Law & Social Inquiry* 20 (Autumn 1995): 941–942, 992–995; Nancy F. Cott, *Public Vows: A History of Marriage and the Nation* (Cambridge, Mass.: Harvard University Press, 2000), 211.

3. It should be pointed out that before the marital rape exemption was eliminated, sexual violence had come to be considered one of the few legitimate grounds for divorce. Hasday, "Contest and Consent," 1397–1398, 1475–1484; Ryan, "Sex Right," 941; Cott, *Public Vows*, 195, 203.

4. Karen Orren, *Belated Feudalism: Labor, the Law, and Liberal Development in the United States* (New York: Cambridge University Press, 1991); Robert J. Steinfeld, *Coercion, Contract, and Free Labor in the Nineteenth Century* (New York: Cambridge University Press, 2001); Forbath, *Shaping of the American Labor Movement*.

5. Greg Grandin, *The Last Colonial Massacre: Latin America in the Cold War* (Chicago: University of Chicago Press, 2004), 56–57. The outbreak of political speech among those without power was also, according to a disgruntled Democrat writing to liberal Senator Paul Douglas in the 1960s, the great evil of the Great Society: "I feel Mr. Johnson is much responsible for the present riot by his constant encouragement for the Negro to take any measure to assert himself & DEMAND his rights." Rick Perlstein, *Nixonland: The Rise of a President and the Fracturing of America* (New York: Scribner, 2008), 117.

6. John C. Calhoun, "Speech on the Admission of California—and the General State of the Union" (March 4, 1850), in *Union and Liberty: The Political Philosophy of John C. Calhoun*, ed. Ross M. Lence (Indianapolis: Liberty Fund, 1992), 583–585.

7. Alexander Keyssar, *The Right to Vote: The Contested History of Democracy in the United States* (New York: Basic, 2000), 112.

8. Jeremy Brecher, *Strike!* (Cambridge, Mass.: South End Press, 1997), 34, 126. Also see Kim Phillips-Fein, *Invisible Hands: The Businessmen's Crusade against the New Deal* (New York: Norton, 2009), 87–114.

9. Forbath, *Shaping of the American Labor Movement*, 65.

10. James Boswell, *Life of Johnson*, ed. R. W. Chapman and J. D. Fleeman (New York: Oxford University Press, 1998), 1017.

11. Edmund Burke, *Reflections on the Revolution in France*, ed. J. C. D. Clark (Stanford, Calif.: Stanford University Press, 2001), 205–206.

12. Ibid., 217–218.

13. Cited in Daniel T. Rodgers, *Age of Fracture* (Cambridge, Mass.: Harvard University Press, 2011), 207.

14. Friedrich Hayek, *Law, Legislation and Liberty*, vol. 2, *The Mirage of Social Justice* (Chicago: University of Chicago Press, 1976), 84–85; Robert Nozick, *Anarchy, State, and Utopia* (New York: Basic Books, 1974), 235–238.

15. G. A. Cohen, *Self-Ownership, Freedom, and Equality* (New York: Cambridge University Press, 1995), 28–32, 53–59, 98–115, 236–238.

16. Cited in Friedrich A. Hayek, *The Constitution of Liberty* (Chicago: University of Chicago Press, 1960), 424; also see 16–19.

17. Elizabeth Cady Stanton, "Home Life," in *The Elizabeth Cady Stanton–Susan B. Anthony Reader*, ed. Ellen Carol DuBois (Boston: Northeastern University Press, 1981, 1992), 132. Also see Cott, *Public Vows*, 67; Amy Dru Stanley, *From Bondage to Contract: Wage Labor, Marriage, and the Market in the Age of Slave Emancipation* (New York: Cambridge University Press, 1998), 177–178.

18. Sometimes the transcript is not so hidden. Point Four of the 1948 platform of Strom Thurmond's States' Rights Democratic Party—the Dixiecrats— weaves together the public and private in a seamless and visible whole: "We stand for the segregation of the races and the racial integrity of each race; the constitutional right to choose one's associates; to accept private employment without governmental interference, and to earn one's living in any lawful way. We oppose the elimination of segregation, the repeal of miscegenation statutes, the control of private employment by Federal bureaucrats called for by the misnamed civil rights program. We favor home-rule, local self-government and a minimum interference with individual rights." *The Rise of Conservatism in America, 1945–2000: A Brief History with Documents*, ed. Ronald Story and Bruce Laurie (Boston: Bedford / St. Martin's, 2008), 39.

19. James Baldwin, "They Can't Turn Back," in *The Price of the Ticket: Collected Nonfiction, 1948–1985* (New York: St. Martin's Press, 1985), 215. I am grateful to Jason Frank for bringing this essay to my attention.

20. Peter Kolchin, *American Slavery 1619–1877* (New York: Hill and Wang, 1993, 2003), 100–102, 105, 111, 115, 117.

21. Thomas Roderick Dew, *Abolition of Negro Slavery,* and William Harper, *Memoir on Slavery,* in *The Ideology of Slavery: Proslavery Thought in the Antebellum South, 1830–1860,* ed. Drew Gilpin Faust (Baton Rouge: Louisiana State University Press, 1981), 65, 100.

22. Neil R. McMillen, *Dark Journey: Black Mississippians in the Age of Jim Crow* (Urbana: University of Illinois Press, 1989), 7.

23. Kolchin, *American Slavery,* 118–120, 123–124, 126; Ira Berlin, *Many Thousands Gone: The First Two Centuries of Slavery in North America* (Cambridge, Mass.: Harvard University Press, 1998), 94–95, 112, 128–132, 149–150, 174–175, 188–189.

24. Calhoun, "Speech on the Reception of Abolition Petitions" (February 6, 1837), in *Union and Liberty,* 473; also see Dew, "Abolition of Negro Slavery," 23–24, 27; Kolchin, *American Slavery,* 170, 181–182, 184, 189.

25. Cited in Kolchin, *American Slavery,* 198.

26. Steven Hahn, *A Nation under Our Feet: Black Political Struggles in the Rural South from Slavery to the Great Migration* (Cambridge, Mass.: Harvard University Press, 2003), 218; McMillen, *Dark Journey,* 125.

27. Patrick Allitt, *The Conservatives: Ideas & Personalities throughout American History* (New Haven, Conn.: Yale University Press, 2009), 19.

28. Edmund Burke, "Speech on the Army Estimates" (February 9, 1790), in *The Portable Edmund Burke,* ed. Isaac Kramnick (New York: Penguin, 1999), 413–414.

29. Edmund Burke, letter to Earl Fitzwilliam (1791), cited in Daniel L. O'Neill, *The Burke-Wollstonecraft Debate: Savagery, Civilization, and Democracy* (University Park: Pennsylvania State University Press, 2007), 211.

30. Cited in Conor Cruise O'Brien, *The Great Melody: A Thematic Biography of Edmund Burke* (Chicago: University of Chicago Press, 1992), 418–419.

31. Edmund Burke, *Letters on a Regicide Peace* (Indianapolis: Liberty Fund, 1999), 127.

32. John Adams, letter to James Sullivan (May 26, 1776), in *The Works of John Adams,* vol. 9, ed. Charles Francis Adams (Boston: Little Brown, 1854), 375.

33. Abigail Adams, letter to John Adams (March 31, 1776), in *The Letters of John and Abigail Adams* (New York: Penguin, 2004), 148–49.

34. John Adams, letter to Abigail Adams (April 14, 1776), in *Letters,* 154.

35. John Adams, letter to James Sullivan (May 26, 1776), in *Works,* 378.

36. John Adams, *A Defense of the Constitutions of Government of the United States of America,* and *Discourses on Davila,* in *The Political Writings of John Adams,* ed. George A. Peck Jr. (Indianapolis: Hackett, [1954] 2003,), 148–149, 190.

37. Cited in Susan Moller Okin, *Justice, Gender, and the Family* (New York: Basic Books, 1989), 18.

38. Keyssar, *Right to Vote,* xxi.

39. Linda K. Kerber, *No Constitutional Right to be Ladies: Women and the Obligations of Citizenship* (New York: Hill and Wang, 1998), 3–46, 124–220; Ira Berlin, Barbara J. Fields, Steven F. Miller, Joseph P. Rediy, and Leslie S. Rowland, *Slaves*

No More: Three Essays on Emancipation and the Civil War (New York: Cambridge University Press, 1992), 5, 15, 20, 48, 54–59.

40. "The ultimate operative unit in our society is the family, not the individual." Milton Friedman, *Capitalism and Freedom* (Chicago: University of Chicago Press, 1962, 1982, 2002), 32; also see 13. "It would be a mistake of major proportions to assume that legal rules are a dominant force in shaping individual character; family, school, and church are much more likely to be powerful influences. The people who run these institutions will use their influence to advance whatever conception of the good they hold, no matter what the state of the law." Richard A. Epstein, "Libertarianism and Character," in *Varieties of Conservatism in America*, ed. Peter Berkowitz (Stanford, Calif.: Hoover Institution Press, 2004), 76. For earlier statements, see William Graham Sumner, "The Family Monopoly," in *On Liberty, Society, and Politics: The Essential Essays of William Graham Sumner*, ed. Robert C. Bannister (Indianapolis, Liberty Fund, 1929), 136; William Graham Sumner, *What the Social Classes Owe to Each Other* (Caldwell, Idaho: Caxton Press, 2003), 63; Ludwig von Mises, *Socialism: An Economic and Sociological Analysis* (Indianapolis: Liberty Fund, 1981), 74–91. More generally, see Okin, *Justice, Gender*, 74–88.

41. Edmund Burke, letter to Earl Fitzwilliam (1791), in O'Neill, *Burke-Wollstonecraft Debate*, 211.

42. James Fitzjames Stephen, *Liberty, Equality, Fraternity*, ed. Stuart D. Warner (Indianapolis: Liberty Fund, 1993), 173.

43. David Farber, *The Rise and Fall of Modern American Conservatism: A Short History* (Princeton, N.J.: Princeton University Press, 2010), 10.

44. Thomas Paine, *Rights of Man, Part I*, in *Political Writings*, ed. Bruce Kuklick (New York: Cambridge University Press, 2000), 130; Lionel Trilling, *The Liberal Imagination* (Garden City, N.Y.: Doubleday Anchor, 1950), 5; Robert O. Paxton, *The Anatomy of Fascism* (New York: Knopf, 2004), 42.

45. Michael Freeden, *Ideologies and Political Theory* (New York: Oxford University Press, 1996), 318.

46. Cited in Russell Kirk, "Introduction," in *The Portable Conservative Reader*, ed. Russell Kirk (New York: Penguin, 1982), xxiii.

47. Mark F. Proudman, "'The Stupid Party': Intellectual Repute as a Category of Ideological Analysis," *Journal of Political Ideologies* 10 (June 2005): 201–202, 206–207.

48. George H. Nash, *The Conservative Intellectual Movement in America since 1945* (Wilmington, Del.: Intercollegiate Studies Institute), xiv; Roger Scruton, *The Meaning of Conservatism* (London: Macmillan, 1980, 1984), 11.

49. "Problem: How did the exhausted come to make the laws about values? Put differently: How did those come to power who are the last?" Friedrich Nietzsche, *The Will to Power*, trans. Walter Kaufmann and R. J. Hollingdale (New York: Vintage, 1968), 34.

50. Kevin Mattson, *Rebels All! A Short History of the Conservative Mind in Postwar America* (Newark, N.J.: Rutgers University Press, 2008), 121–125.

51. Burke, *Reflections*, 243; Russell Kirk, "The Conservative Mind," in *Conservatism in America since 1930*, ed. Gregory L. Schneider (New York: New York University Press, 2003), 107. More recently still, Harvey Mansfield has declared, "But I understand conservatism as a reaction to liberalism. It isn't a position that one takes up from the beginning but only when one is threatened by people who want to take away or harm things that deserve to be conserved." *The Point* (Fall 2010), http://www.thepointmag.com/archive/an-interview-with-harvey-mansfield, accessed April 9, 2011.

52. Burke, *Regicide Peace*, 73.

53. Cited in John Ramsden, *An Appetite for Power: A History of the Conservative Party since 1830* (New York: Harper Collins, 1999), 5.

54. *The Faber Book of Conservatism*, ed. Keith Baker (London: Faber and Faber, 1993), 6; also see Hugh Cecil, *Conservatism* (London: Thornton Butterworth, 1912), 39–44, 241, 244.

55. Robert Peel, speech at Merchant Taylor Hall (May 13, 1838), in *British Conservatism: Conservative Thought from Burke to Thatcher*, ed. Frank O'Gorman (London: Longman, 1986), 125.

56. Nash, *Conservative Intellectual Movement*, xiv.

57. Michael Oakeshott, "Rationalism in Politics" and "On Being Conservative," in *Rationalism in Politics and Other Essays* (Indianapolis: Liberty Press, 1991), 31, 408, 435.

58. At one point in his essay, Oakeshott himself entertains this notion, only to dismiss it: "What would be the appropriateness of this disposition in circumstances other than our own, whether to be conservative in respect of government would have the same relevance in the circumstances of an unadventurous, a slothful or a spiritless people, is a question we need not try to answer: we are concerned with ourselves as we are. I myself think that it would occupy an important place in any set of circumstances." Why that is so he does not say. Oakeshott, "On Being Conservative," 435.

59. Benjamin Disraeli, *The Vindication of the English Constitution*, in *Whigs and Whiggism: Political Writings by Benjamin Disraeli*, ed. William Hutcheon (New York: Macmillan, 1914), 126.

60. Karl Mannheim, "Conservative Thought," in *Essays on Sociology and Social Psychology*, ed. Paul Kesckemeti (London: Routledge & Kegan Paul, 1953), 95, 115; also see Freeden, *Ideologies and Political Theory*, 335ff. Evidence for this argument from the conservative tradition can be found in Frank Meyer, "Freedom, Tradition, Conservatism," in *In Defense of Freedom and Related Essays* (Indianapolis: Liberty Fund, 1996), 17–20; Mark C. Henrie, "Understanding Traditionalist Conservatism," in *Varieties of Conservatism in America*, 11; Nash, *Conservative Intellectual Movement*, 50; Scruton, *Meaning of Conservatism*, 11.

61. Thus, when Irving Kristol claims in his *Reflections of a Neoconservative* that neoconservatism "aims to infuse American bourgeois orthodoxy with a new self-conscious intellectual vigor," he is not departing from conservative norms; he is articulating them. As the conservative sociologist and theologian

Peter Berger writes in *The Sacred Canopy*, "The facticity of the social world or of any part of it suffices for self-legitimation as long as there is no challenge. When a challenge appears, in whatever form, the facticity can no longer be taken for granted. The validity of the social order must then be explicated, both for the sake of the challengers and of those meeting the challenge. . . . The seriousness of the challenge will determine the degree of elaborateness of the answering legitimations." In *Conservatism: An Anthology of Social and Political Thought from David Hume to the Present*, ed. Jerry Muller (Princeton, N.J.: Princeton University Press, 1997), 4, 360.

62. Quintin Hogg, *The Case for Conservatism*, in *British Conservatism*, 76.

63. Boswell, *Life of Johnson*, 1018.

64. Edmund Burke, *An Appeal from the New to the Old Whigs*, in *Further Reflections on the Revolution in France*, ed. Daniel F. Ritchie (Indianapolis: Liberty Fund, 1992), 167.

65. Giuseppe di Lampedusa, *The Leopard* (New York: Pantheon, 2007), 28.

66. Mattson, *Rebels All!* 23, 35–36, 62.

67. Burke, *Regicide Peace*, 142.

68. Kirk, "The Conservative Mind," 109; Oakeshott, "On Being Conservative," 414–415.

69. Cited in Allitt, *Conservatives*, 242; also see Arthur Moeller van den Bruck, *Germany's Third Empire*, in *The Nazi Germany Sourcebook: An Anthology of Texts*, ed. Roderick Stackelberg and Sally A. Winkle (New York: Routledge, 2002), 77–78.

70. Edmund Burke, *Letter to a Noble Lord*, in *On Empire, Liberty, and Reform: Speeches and Letters*, ed. David Bromwich (New Haven, Conn.: Yale University Press, 2000), 479.

71. Cecil is one of the few conservatives to acknowledge how difficult it is to distinguish between reform and revolution (Cecil, *Conservatism*, 221–222). For a useful critique, see Ted Honderich, *Conservatism: Burke, Nozick, Bush, Blair?* (London: Pluto, 2005), 6–31.

72. Peter Kolozi, "Conservatives against Capitalism: The Conservative Critique of Capitalism in American Political Thought," Ph.D. dissertation, CUNY Graduate Center, 2010, 138–172; Clinton Rossiter, *Conservatism in America: The Thankless Persuasion* (New York: Vintage, 1955, 1962), 241–242; Sam Tanenhaus, *Whittaker Chambers: A Biography* (New York: Modern Library, 1997), 165, 466, 488.

73. Nash, *Conservative Intellectual Movement*, xiv.

74. Abraham Lincoln, address at Cooper Institute (February 27, 1860), in *The Portable Abraham Lincoln*, ed. Andrew Delbanco (New York: Penguin 1992), 178–179. The typical conservative vision of reform, notes one scholar, "can be part of other political ideologies on account of—at least on the surface—its sheer reasonableness. It is, by itself, purely relative or 'positional,'" and can thus be applied to or invoked by any ideology." Jan-Werner Müller, "Comprehending Conservatism: A New Framework for Analysis," *Journal of Political Ideologies* 11 (October 2006): 362.

75. Ramsden, *Appetite for Power*, 28.

76. Cited in C. B. Macpherson, *Burke* (New York Hill and Wang, 1980), 22; also see Burke, *Regicide Peace*, 381.

77. Ramsden, *Appetite for Power*, 46, 95. Carnavon's was the minority position on the British right; under the leadership of Derby and Disraeli, the Conservatives presided over the Act's passage. But that should not be taken as evidence of a deep Burkean impulse on the right. Disraeli's North Star throughout the debate was simple opposition to Gladstone. If Gladstone was for it, Disraeli was against it, and vice versa. If there was any vision beyond that, it was partisan and tactical, involving decidedly non-Burkean tactics at that. Explaining his support for a series of measures more radical than anything initially countenanced by the Liberals, Disraeli said to Derby, "The bold line is the safer one." See Ramsden, *Appetite for Power*, 91–99. For a dissenting view, see Gertrude Himmelfarb, "Politics and Ideology: The Reform Act of 1867," in *Victorian Minds* (New York: Knopf, 1968), 333–392.

78. Allitt, *Conservatives*, 48. For other examples, see Allan Bloom, *The Closing of the American Mind* (New York: Simon and Schuster, 1987), 101; Calhoun, "Speech on the Oregon Bill," in *Union and Liberty*, 565; Adams, *Discourses on Davila*, in *Political Writings*, 190–192, 201; *Theodore Roosevelt: An American Mind*, ed. Mario R. DiNunzio (New York: Penguin, 1994), 116, 119; Phillips-Fein, *Invisible Hands*, 82.

79. Michael J. Gerson, *Heroic Conservatism: Why Republicans Need to Embrace America's Ideals (And Why They Deserve to Fail If They Don't)* (New York: Harper Collins, 2007), 261, 264.

80. While Huntington is right to stress the "situational" or "positional" dimensions of conservatism—that it is called into being in response to systemic challenges to the established order—he is wrong to suggest that the conservative defends the established order simply because it is the established order. The conservative defends a particular type of order—the hierarchical institution of personal rule—because he sincerely believes that inequality is a necessary condition of excellence. At times, he is willing to contest the established order, if he believes it is too egalitarian; such was the case with the postwar conservative movement in America. Samuel Huntington, "Conservatism as an Ideology," *American Political Science Review* 51 (June 1957): 454–473.

81. The defense of the free market "became stationary when it was most influential," while it "often progressed when on the defensive" from attacks on the left (Hayek, *Constitution of Liberty*, 7). "It is ironic, although not historically unprecedented, that such a burst of creative energy on the intellectual level [on the right] should occur simultaneously with a continuing spread of the influence of Liberalism in the practical political sphere" (Frank Meyer, "Freedom, Tradition, Conservatism," in *Defense of Freedom*, 15). "In times of crisis," observes Scruton, "conservatism does its best" (Scruton, *Meaning of Conservatism*, 11). On the "dialectical" relationship between left and right in recent American history, see Julian E. Zelizer, "Reflections: Rethinking the

History of American Conservatism," *Reviews in American History* 38 (June 2010): 388–389.

82. Matthew Arnold, *Culture and Anarchy*, in *Culture and Anarchy and Other Writings*, ed. Stefan Collini (New York: Cambridge University Press, 1993), 95.

83. Joseph Schumpeter, "Social Classes in an Ethnically Homogenous Environment," in *Conservatism: An Anthology*, 227.

84. Attaining and maintaining real economic power, Schumpeter adds, requires a continuous "departure from routine." Schumpeter, "Social Classes," 227. "We must make it clear to ourselves that there can be no standing still, no being satisfied for us, but only progress or retrogression, and that it is tantamount to retrogression when we are contented with our present place." Friedrich von Bernhardi, *Germany and the Next War*, trans. Allen Powles (London: Edward Arnold, 1912), 103.

85. Burke, *Reflections*, 207. Also see Justus Möser, "No Promotion According to Merit," in *Conservatism: An Anthology*, 74–77.

86. Burke, *Letter to a Noble Lord*, 484.

87. Fritz Lens, *Psychological Differences between the Leading Races of Mankind*, in *Nazi Germany Sourcebook*, 75.

88. Muller, *Conservatism*, 26–27, 210.

89. Sumner, *What the Social Classes Owe to Each Other*, 59–60, 66–67.

90. Sumner, "Liberty," in *On Liberty, Society, and Politics*, 246.

91. "All ownership derives from occupation and violence. . . . That all rights derive from violence, all ownership from appropriation or robbery, we may freely admit." Mises, *Socialism*, 32.

92. Sumner, "The Absurd Effort to Make the World Over," in *On Liberty, Society, and Politics*, 254.

93. Burke, *Letter to a Noble Lord*, 484.

94. With every passing month, the number of books about American conservatism seems to increase. Among the more notable of the last decade are Rick Perlstein, *Before the Storm: Barry Goldwater and the Unmaking of the American Consensus* (New York: Hill & Wang, 2001); Lisa McGirr, *Suburban Warriors: The Origins of the New American Right* (Princeton, N.J.: Princeton University Press, 2001); Donald Critchlow, *Phyllis Schlafly and Grassroots Conservatism: A Woman's Crusade* (Princeton, N.J.: Princeton University Press, 2005); Kevin Kruse, *White Flight: Atlanta and the Making of Modern Conservatism* (Princeton, N.J.: Princeton University Press, 2005); Jason Sokol, *There Goes My Everything: White Southerners in the Age of Civil Rights, 1945–1975* (New York: Vintage, 2006); Matthew Lassiter, *The Silent Majority: Suburban Politics in the Sunbelt South* (Princeton, N.J.: Princeton University Press, 2006); Joseph Lowndes, *From the New Deal to the New Right: Race and the Southern Origins of Modern Conservatism* (New Haven, Conn.: Yale University Press, 2008); Allan J. Lichtman, *White Protestant Nation: The Rise of the American Conservative Movement* (New York: Grove Press, 2008); Mattson, *Rebels All!*; Steven Teles, *The Rise of the Conservative Legal Movement: The Battle for Control of the Law* (Princeton,

N.J.: Princeton University Press, 2008); Bethany Moreton, *To Serve God and Wal-Mart: The Making of Christian Free Enterprise* (Cambridge, Mass.: Harvard University Press, 2009); Phillips-Fein, *Invisible Hands*. For a recent summary of this literature and possible directions it might take in the future, see Zelizer, "Rethinking the History of American Conservatism," 367–392.

95. T. S. Eliot, "The Literature of Politics," in *To Criticize the Critic and Other Writings* (Lincoln: University of Nebraska Press, 1965), 139.

96. "'Metaphysical pathos' is exemplified in any description of the nature of things, any characterization of the world to which one belongs, in terms which, like the words of a poem, awaken through their associations, and through a sort of empathy which they engender, a congenial mood or tone of feeling on the part of the philosopher or his readers." Arthur O. Lovejoy, *The Great Chain of Being: A Study of the History of an Idea* (New York: Harper & Brothers, 1936), 11. Cited in Joseph F. Femia, *Against the Masses: Varieties of Anti-Democratic Thought since the French Revolution* (New York: Oxford University Press, 2001), 13–14.

97. Cf. Bruce Frohnen, *Virtue and the Promise of Conservatism: The Legacy of Burke and Tocqueville* (Lawrence: University of Kansas Press, 1993); Nash, *Conservative Intellectual Movement*; Allitt, *Conservatives*; Scruton, *Meaning of Conservatism*; Berkowitz, *Varieties of Conservatism*. More useful treatments include Robert Nisbet, *Conservatism: Dream and Reality* (Minneapolis: University of Minnesota Press, 1986); Stephen Holmes, *The Anatomy of Antiliberalism* (Cambridge, Mass.: Harvard University Press, 1993); Albert O. Hirschman, *The Rhetoric of Reaction: Perversity, Futility, Jeopardy* (Cambridge, Mass.: Harvard University Press, 1991); Mannheim, "Conservative Thought"; Muller, *Conservatism*; Femia, *Against the Masses*.

98. Mattson, *Rebels All!*, 3, 11–12, 42, 79. Also see Sam Tanenhaus, *The Death of Conservatism* (New York: Random House, 2009), 16–19, 49–51.

99. Cara Camcastle, *The More Moderate Side of Joseph de Maistre: Views on Political Liberty and Political Economy* (Montreal and Kingston: McGill-Queen's University Press, 2005); Isaiah Berlin, "Joseph de Maistre on the Origins of Modern Fascism," in *The Crooked Timber of Humanity: Chapters in the History of Ideas*, ed. Henry Hardy (New York: Vintage, 1992), 91–174.

100. Nash, *Conservative Intellectual Movement*, 69–70.

101. Published in June 2008, Lichtman's *White Protestant Nation* appeared before the advent of the Tea Party—indeed, before the election of Barack Obama—but its analysis of the continuities between the conservatism that arose in the aftermath of World War I and the conservatism of George W. Bush can be extrapolated to today.

102. Mattson, *Rebels All!*, 7, 15; Farber, *Rise and Fall of Modern American Conservatism*, 78; Donald T. Critchlow, *The Conservative Ascendancy: How the GOP Right Made Political History* (Cambridge, Mass.: Harvard University Press, 2007), 6–13; Tanenhaus, *Death of Conservatism*, 29, 32, 104, 109, 111, 114.

103. "The right's political philosophy, organizing strategy, and grassroots appeal transcend its hostility to liberalism. Modern conservatism has a life, history,

and logic of its own." Lichtman, *White Protestant Nation*, 2. For a different version of the antibacklash argument, see Lowndes, *New Deal to the New Right*, 3–5, 92–93, 160–162.

104. Cf. Zelizer, "Rethinking the History of American Conservatism," 371–374.
105. Cited in Mattson, *Rebels All!*, 112.
106. *Händler und Helden. Patriotische Besinnungen*, in *Nazi Germany Sourcebook*, 36.
107. Noberto Bobbio, *Left & Right: The Significance of a Political Distinction* (Chicago: University of Chicago Press, 1996).
108. Müller, "Comprehending Conservatism," 359; Muller, *Conservatism*, 22–23; J. G. A. Pocock, introduction to Burke, *Reflections on the Revolution in France* (Indianapolis: Hackett, 1987), xlix.
109. Nash, *Conservative Intellectual Movement*, xiv–xv.

Chapter 1

1. Michael Oakeshott, "On Being Conservative," in *Rationalism in Politics and Other Essays* (Indianapolis: Liberty Press, 1991), 408.
2. Russell Kirk, "Introduction," in *The Portable Conservative Reader*, ed. Russell Kirk (New York: Penguin, 1982), xi–xiv; Robert Nisbet, *Conservatism: Dream and Reality* (Minneapolis: University of Minnesota Press, 1986); Peter Viereck, *Conservatism: From John Adams to Churchill* (Princeton, N.J.: D. Van Nostrand, 1956), 10–17.
3. Joseph de Maistre, *Considerations on France*, trans. and ed. Richard A. Lebrun (New York: Cambridge University Press, 1974, 1994), 10. Also see Maistre's criticism of Europe's old regimes in Jean-Louis Darcel, "The Roads of Exile, 1792–1817," and Darcel, "Joseph de Maistre and the House of Savoy: Some Aspects of his Career," in *Joseph de Maistre's Life, Thought, and Influence: Selected Studies*, ed. Richard A. Lebrun (Montreal: McGill-Queen's University Press, 2001), 16, 19–20, 52.
4. Cf. Edmund Burke, *Letter to a Noble Lord*, in *On Empire, Liberty, and Reform: Speeches and Letters*, ed. David Bromwich (New Haven, Conn.: Yale University Press, 2000), 500–501; Burke, *Letters on a Regicide Peace* (Indianapolis: Liberty Fund, 1999), 69–70, 74–76, 106, 108–111, 158–160, 167, 184, 205, 218, 218, 222, 271, 304–305.
5. Edmund Burke, *Reflections on the Revolution in France*, ed. J. C. D. Clark (Stanford, Calif.: Stanford University Press, 2001), 239.
6. Edmund Burke, *A Philosophical Enquiry into the Origins of Our Ideas of the Sublime and the Beautiful*, ed. David Womersley (New York: Penguin, 1998), 177.
7. Burke, *Regicide Peace*, 75.
8. Though sometimes it is the old regime itself. Cf. Burke, *Regicide Peace*, 384–385.
9. Edmund Burke, "Speech on American Taxation" (April 19, 1774), in *Selected Works of Edmund Burke*, vol. 1 (Indianapolis: Liberty Fund, 1999), 186; also see Burke, *Regicide Peace*, 69–70, 154–155, 184–185, 304–306, 384–385. This critique runs counter to Burke's praise for the aristocrat as the man of the long view;

in these texts, Burke claims that the long view blinds men to the problems they face. See Bromwich's brief introduction to Burke's *Letter to a Noble Lord*, in his *On Empire, Liberty, and Reform*, 466.

10. Thomas Roderick Dew, *Abolition of Negro Slavery*, and William Harper, *Memoir on Slavery*, in *The Ideology of Slavery: Proslavery Thought in the Antebellum South, 1830–1860*, ed. Drew Gilpin Faust (Baton Rouge: Louisiana State Press, 1981), 25, 123. Also see John C. Calhoun, "Speech on the Force Bill," "Speech on the Reception of Abolitionist Petitions," and "Speech on the Oregon Bill," in *Union and Liberty: The Political Philosophy of John C. Calhoun*, ed. Ross M. Lence (Indianapolis: Liberty Fund, 1992), 426, 465, 475, 562; Manisha Sinha, *The Counterrevolution of Slavery: Politics and Ideology in Antebellum South Carolina* (Chapel Hill: University of North Carolina Press, 2000), 33–93.

11. Barry Goldwater, *The Conscience of a Conservative* (Princeton, N.J.: Princeton University Press, 1960, 2007), 1.

12. Calhoun, "Speech on the Reception of Abolitionist Petitions," 476.

13. Oakeshott, "On Being Conservative," 407–408.

14. Charles Loyseau, *A Treatise of Orders and Plain Dignities*, ed. Howell A. Lloyd (New York: Cambridge University Press, 1994), 75.

15. Cited in Anne Norton, *Leo Strauss and the Politics of American Empire* (New Haven, Conn.: Yale University Press, 2004), 49.

16. Joseph de Maistre, *St. Petersburg Dialogues or Conversations on the Temporal Government of Providence*, trans. and ed. Richard A. Lebrun (Montreal and Kingston: McGill-Queen's University Press, 1993), 216.

17. Maistre, *Considerations*, 16–17. Also see Jean-Louis Darcel, "The Apprentice Years of a Counter-Revolutionary: Joseph de Maistre in Lausanne, 1793–1797," in *Joseph de Maistre's Life, Thought, and Influence*, 43–44.

18. Burke, *Sublime and the Beautiful*, 86, 96, 121, 165.

19. Burke, *Reflections*, 207, 243, 275. Also see Burke, *Regicide Peace*, 66, 70, 107, 157, 207, 222.

20. Burke, *Regicide Peace*, 184.

21. Darrin M. McMahon, *Enemies of the Enlightenment: The French Counter-Enlightenment and the Making of Modernity* (New York: Oxford University Press, 2001), 27–28.

22. Cited in Robert Perkinson, *Texas Tough: The Rise of America's Prison Empire* (New York: Metropolitan, 2009), 297.

23. Cited in Alexander P. Lamis, "The Two-Party South: From the 1960s to the 1990s," in *Southern Politics in the 1990s*, ed. Alexander P. Lamis (Baton Rouge: Louisiana State University Press, 1990), 8.

24. David Horowitz, "The Campus Blacklist," *FrontPage* (April 18, 2003), http://www.studentsforacademicfreedom.org/essays/blacklist.html,accessed March 24, 2011.

25. Cited in Lamis, "Two-Party South," 8.

26. Phyllis Schlafly, *The Power of the Positive Woman* (New York: Harcourt Brace Jovanovich, 1977), 7–8.

27. "Interview with Phyllis Schlafly," *Washington Star* (January 18, 1976), in *The Rise of Conservatism in America, 1945–2000: A Brief History with Documents*, ed. Ronald Story and Bruce Laurie (Boston: Bedford/St. Martin's, 2008), 104.

28. Susan Faludi, *Backlash: The Undeclared War against American Women* (New York: Doubleday, 1991), 251.

29. Maistre, *Considerations*, 79.

30. "Why the South Must Prevail," *National Review* (August 24, 1957), in *Rise of Conservatism in America*, 53.

31. Gary Wills, *Reagan's America* (New York: Penguin, 1988), 355.

32. Cited in J. C. D. Clark, introduction to Burke, *Reflections*, 104.

33. Alexander Stephens, "The Cornerstone Speech," in *Defending Slavery: Proslavery Thought in the Old South*, ed. Paul Finkelman (Boston: Bedford/St. Martin's, 2003), 91.

34. Goldwater, *Conscience of a Conservative*, 70.

35. Maistre, *Considerations*, 89.

36. Ibid., 69, 74.

37. James Oakes, *The Ruling Race: A History of American Slaveholders* (New York: Vintage, 1982), 37, 42, 141–143, 230–232.

38. Calhoun, "Speech on the Oregon Bill," 564.

39. Cited in Peter Kolchin, *American Slavery 1619–1877* (New York: Hill and Wang, 1993, 2003), 195.

40. Dew, *Abolition of Negro Slavery*, 66–67.

41. Cited in Jacob Heilbrunn, *They Knew They Were Right: The Rise of the Neocons* (New York: Random House, 2008), 6.

42. Burke, *Reflections*, 229; William F. Buckley Jr., "Publisher's Statement on Founding *National Review*," *National Review* (November 19, 1955), in *Rise of Conservatism in America*, 50.

43. Andrew Sullivan, *The Conservative Soul: Fundamentalism, Freedom, and the Future of the Right* (New York: Harper Perennial, 2006), 9.

44. Burke, *Regicide Peace*, 138.

45. Maistre, *Considerations*, 77.

46. Corey Robin, "The Ex-Cons: Right-Wing Thinkers Go Left!" *Lingua Franca* (February 2001), 32. Reprinted in this volume as chapter 5.

Chapter 2

1. Noel Malcolm, *Aspects of Hobbes* (New York: Oxford University Press, 2002), 15–16; Richard Tuck, *Hobbes* (New York: Oxford University Press, 1989), 24; Quentin Skinner, *Visions of Politics*, vol. 3, *Hobbes and Civil Sciences* (New York: Cambridge University Press, 2002), 8–9; A. P. Martinich, *Hobbes* (New York: Cambridge University Press, 1999), 161–162.

2. Skinner, *Visions*, 16.

3. Malcolm, *Aspects of Hobbes*, 20–21; Skinner, *Visions*, 22–23; Martinich, *Hobbes*, 209–210.

4. T. S. Eliot, "John Bramhall," in *Selected Essays 1917–1932* (New York: Harcourt Brace, 1932), 302.

5. Perry Anderson, "The Intransigent Right," in *Spectrum: From Right to Left in the World of Ideas* (New York: Verso, 2005), 3–28.

6. Michael Oakeshott, "On Being Conservative," in *Rationalism in Politics and Other Essays* (Indianapolis: Liberty Press, 1991), 435. Also see the useful remarks of Paul Franco in his foreword to Michael Oakeshott, *Hobbes on Civil Association* (Indianapolis: Liberty Fund, 2000), v–vii; Paul Franco, *Michael Oakeshott: An Introduction* (New Haven, Conn.: Yale University Press, 2004), 10, 103, 106.

7. Friedrich A. Hayek, *The Constitution of Liberty* (Chicago: University of Chicago Press, 1960), 56; Carl Schmitt, *The Leviathan in the State Theory of Thomas Hobbes: Meaning and Failure of a Political Symbol* (Chicago: University of Chicago Press, 2008), 42, 68–69; Leo Strauss, *Natural Right and History* (Chicago: University of Chicago Press, 1953), 165–202; Leo Strauss, "Comments on Carl Schmitt's *Der Begriff des Politischen*," in Carl Schmitt, *The Concept of the Political* (New Brunswick, N.J.: Rutgers University Press, 1967), 89.

8. Hayek, *Constitution of Liberty*, 397–411.

9. Hobbes, *Behemoth*, ed. Ferdinand Tönnies (Chicago: University of Chicago Press, 1990), 204.

10. Benjamin Constant, *The Liberty of the Ancients Compared with That of the Moderns*, in *Political Writings*, ed. Biancamaria Fontana (New York: Cambridge University Press, 1988), 307–328; Karl Marx, *The Eighteenth Brumaire of Louis Bonaparte*, in *The Marx-Engels Reader*, ed. Robert C. Tucker (New York: Norton, 1978), 595.

11. Hobbes, *Behemoth*, 28.

12. Quentin Skinner, *Hobbes and Republican Liberty* (New York: Cambridge University Press, 2008).

13. Skinner, *Hobbes*, xiv.

14. David Wootton, *Divine Right and Democracy* (New York: Penguin, 1986), 28.

15. Ibid., 25–26.

16. Skinner, *Hobbes*, 57ff.

17. Ibid., 27.

18. Hobbes, *Leviathan*, ed. Richard Tuck (New York: Cambridge, 1996), 149.

19. Skinner, *Hobbes*, x–xi, 25–33, 68–72.

20. Ibid., xi, 215.

21. Skinner, *Hobbes*, 211–212.

22. Hobbes, *Leviathan*, 44.

23. Ibid., 145–146.

24. Cited in Skinner, *Hobbes*, 130.

25. Ibid., 116–123, 157, 162, 173.

26. Hobbes, *Leviathan*, 146.

27. Hobbes, *De Cive*, in *Man and Citizen*, ed. Bernard Gert (Indianapolis: Hackett, 1991), 216; Hobbes, *Leviathan*, 148.

28. Greg Grandin, *Empire's Workshop: Latin America, the United States, and the Rise of the New Imperialism* (New York: Metropolitan Books, 2006), 173–174; Naomi

Klein, *The Shock Doctrine: The Rise of Disaster Capitalism* (New York: Metropolitan Books, 2007), 80–82, 84–85.

29. Klein, *Shock Doctrine*, 117.
30. Hobbes, *Leviathan*, 148.
31. Klein, *Shock Doctrine*, 131, 138.

Chapter 3

1. Anne C. Heller, *Ayn Rand and the World She Made* (New York: Knopf, 2009), xii; http://www.randomhouse.com/modernlibrary/100bestnovels.html, accessed April 8, 2011

2. Amy Wallace, "Farrah's Brainy Side," *The Daily Beast* (June 25, 2009), http://www.thedailybeast.com/blogs-and-stories/2009-06-25/farrahs-brainy-side, accessed April 8, 2011; Heller, *Ayn Rand,* 401.

3. Heller, *Ayn Rand,* 167.

4. Ayn Rand, "The Objectivist Ethics," in Rand, *The Virtue of Selfishness* (New York: Penguin, 1961, 1964), 39.

5. Elizabeth Gettelman, "I'm With the Rand," *Mother Jones* (July 20, 2009), http://motherjones.com/media/2009/07/im-rand, accessed April 8, 2011.

6. Ayn Rand, *The Fountainhead* (New York: Signet, 1996), 678.

7. Heller, *Ayn Rand,* 155, 275, 292; Rand, *Fountainhead,* 24–25; http://en.wikipedia.org/wiki/1957_in_literature, accessed April 8, 2011; http://atlasshrugged.com/book/history.html#publication, accessed May 1, 2010.

8. Heller, *Ayn Rand,* 88, 186, 278.

9. Rand, *Fountainhead,* 675; Ayn Rand, *Atlas Shrugged* (New York: Plume, 1957, 1992), 1022.

10. Heller, *Ayn Rand,* 1–3.

11. Ibid., 5.

12. Ibid., 29; Jennifer Burns, *Goddess of the Market: Ayn Rand and the American Right* (New York: Oxford University Press, 2009), 14–15.

13. Cited in Theodor Adorno, *Prisms* (Cambridge: MIT Press, 1967), 109.

14. Heller, *Ayn Rand,* 32, 35, 69, 159, 299, 395–396.

15. Ibid., 38–39, 44, 82–83, 114, 336, 371.

16. Ibid., 9, 11, 15.

17. Burns, *Goddess of the Market,* 3, 229, 285.

18. Ibid., 16–17, 21, 27.

19. Ayn Rand, *For the New Intellectual* (New York: Signet, 1961), 18.

20. Burns, *Goddess of the Market,* 307.

21. Julian Sanchez, "An Interview with Robert Nozick" (July 26, 2001), http://www.trinity.edu/rjensen/NozickInterview.htm, accessed April 8, 2011.

22. Sidney Hook, "Each Man for Himself," *New York Times,* April 9, 1961, BR3.

23. Rand, "The Cult of Moral Grayness," in *The Virtue of Selfishness,* 92.

24. Rand, "Objectivist Ethics," 16.

25. Tara Smith, *Ayn Rand's Normative Ethics: The Virtuous Egoist* (New York: Cambridge University Press, 2006), 28–29; Rand, "Objectivist Ethics," 25.

26. Rand, "Objectivist Ethics," 28.

27. *The Nazi Germany Sourcebook*, ed. Roderick Stackelberg and Sally Winkle (London: Routledge, 2002), 302–303.

28. Ibid., 105.

29. Rand, *Capitalism: The Unknown Ideal* (New York: Signet, 1967), 2, 6, 8, 11, 24.

30. *Nazi Germany Sourcebook*, 131.

31. Ibid., 130.

32. Rand, *Capitalism*, 18.

33. *Nazi Germany Sourcebook*, 105, 131.

34. Rand, *Atlas Shrugged*, 1065.

35. Rand, *Fountainhead*, 681.

36. Burns, *Goddess of the Market*, 16, 22, 25; Heller, *Ayn Rand*, 57.

37. Burns, *Goddess of the Market*, 28, 70.

38. Ibid., 42.

39. Ibid., 177.

40. Ibid., 43.

41. Joseph de Maistre, *St. Petersburg Dialogues*, trans. and ed. Richard Lebrun (Montreal: McGill-Queen's University Press, 1993), 335. Burke also traced the French Revolution back to the Reformation. See Conor Cruise O'Brien, *The Great Melody: A Thematic Biography and Commented Anthology of Edmund Burke* (Chicago: University of Chicago Press, 1992), 452–453.

42. Joseph de Maistre, *Considerations on France*, ed. Richard Lebrun (New York: Cambridge University Press, 1974, 1994), 27.

43. Friedrich Nietzsche, *On the Genealogy of Morals*, trans. Walter Kaufmann (New York: Random House, 1967), 24–56.

44. Friedrich Nietzsche, *The Will to Power*, trans. Walter Kaufmann and R. J. Hollingdale (New York: Random House, 1967), 401. Also see Nietzsche, *Genealogy*, 36, 54; Friedrich Nietzsche, *Beyond Good and Evil* (New York: Vintage, 1989), 116.

45. Burns, *Goddess of the Market*, 2, 4.

46. http://yglesias.thinkprogress.org/archives/2010/03/beck-vs-social-justice.php, accessed April 8, 2011; http://yglesias.thinkprogress.org/archives/2010/03/lds-scholars-confirm-mormon-commitment-to-social-justice.php, accessed April 8, 2011.

47. Rand, *Fountainhead*, 606.

Chapter 4

1. George Will, foreword to Barry Goldwater, *The Conscience of a Conservative* (Princeton, N.J.: Princeton University Press, 2007, 1960), xi.

2. *The Rise of Conservatism in America, 1945–2000: A Brief History with Documents*, ed. Ronald Story and Bruce Laurie (Boston: Bedford/St. Martin's, 2008), 1.

3. William F. Buckley Jr., "Publisher's Statement on Founding *National Review*," *National Review* (November 19, 1955), in *Rise of Conservatism in America*, 51.

4. Joseph de Maistre, *Considerations on France*, trans. and ed. Richard A. Lebrun (New York: Cambridge University Press, 1974, 1994), 69, 74.

5. Judith N. Shklar, "Jean-Jacques Rousseau and Equality," in *Political Thought and Political Thinkers*, ed. Stanley Hoffmann (Chicago: University of Chicago Press, 1998), 290.

6. Edmund Burke, *Reflections on the Revolution in France*, ed. J. C. D. Clark (Stanford, Calif.: Stanford University Press, 2001), 232–233.

7. Hugo Young, *One of Us: A Biography of Margaret Thatcher* (London: Pan Books, 1989, 1991).

8. Goldwater, *Conscience of a Conservative*, 1.

9. Ibid., xxiii.

10. Edmund Burke, *Letters on a Regicide Peace* (Indianapolis: Liberty Fund, 1999), 69.

11. Young, *One of Us*, 406.

12. "Speech at the Meeting of the Citizens of Charleston," in *Union and Liberty: The Political Philosophy of John C. Calhoun*, ed. Ross M. Lence (Indianapolis: Liberty Fund, 1992), 536.

13. Goldwater, *Conscience of a Conservative*, 54.

14. Ibid., 2.

15. Ibid., 3–4.

16. Karl Mannheim, "Conservative Thought," in *Essays on Sociology and Social Psychology*, ed. Paul Kesckemeti (London: Routledge & Kegan Paul, 1953), 106.

17. Goldwater, *Conscience of a Conservative*, 3, 78–79, 119.

18. Mannheim, "Conservative Thought," 107.

19. Goldwater, *Conscience of a Conservative*, 17–18, 25.

20. "Introduction," in *Rightward Bound: Making America Conservative in the 1970s*, ed. Bruce J. Schulman and Julian E. Zelizer (Cambridge, Mass.: Harvard University Press, 2008), 4.

21. Matthew D. Lassiter, "Inventing Family Values," and Joseph Crespino, "Civil Rights and the Religious Right," in *Rightward Bound*, 14, 90–91, 93.

22. Crespino, "Civil Rights," 91, 92–93, 97, 102–103.

23. Marjorie J. Spruill, "Gender and America's Right Turn," in *Rightward Bound*, 77–79.

24. "Interview with Phyllis Schlafly," *Washington Star* (January 18, 1976), in *The Rise of Conservatism in America*, 104–105.

25. Lassiter, "Inventing Family Values," and Paul Boyer, "The Evangelical Resurgence in 1970s American Protestantism," in *Rightward Bound*, 19–20, 34, 37, 40–41.

26. Bethany E. Moreton, "Make Payroll, Not War," in *Rightward Bound*, 53, 55–57, 65, 69.

27. Thomas J. Sugrue and John D. Skrentny, "The White Ethnic Strategy," in *Rightward Bound*, 174–175, 189, 191.

28. Rick Perlstein, *Before the Storm: Barry Goldwater and the Unmaking of the American Consensus* (New York: Hill & Wang, 2001), 17.

Chapter 5

1. Denis Diderot, *Extracts from the* Histoire des Deux Indes, in *Political Writings*, ed. John Hope Mason and Robert Wokler (New York: Cambridge University Press, 1992), 202–203; George Bernard Shaw, *Man and Superman* (New York: Penguin, 2001), 213.
2. Michael Lind, *Up from Conservatism: Why the Right Is Wrong for America* (New York: Free Press, 1997), 235, 257; Arianna Huffington, *How to Overthrow the Government* (New York: Harper Collins, 2001), 8.
3. John Gray, *False Dawn: The Delusions of Global Capitalism* (New York: New Press, 2000), 3, 141.
4. Robert Skidelsky, "What's Wrong with Global Capitalism?" *Times Literary Supplement* (March 27, 1998).
5. Michael Gordon, "Right-of-Center Defense Groups—The Pendulum Has Swung Their Way," *National Journal* (January 24, 1981): 128.
6. Edward N. Luttwak, *Turbo-Capitalism: Winners and Losers in the Global Economy* (New York: Harper Perennial, 2000), 15, 193, 195.
7. Kim Phillips-Fein, "Laissez-Faire No More," *In These Times* (July 11, 1999): 19.
8. Isaiah Berlin, "Joseph de Maistre on the Origins of Modern Fascism," in *The Crooked Timber of Humanity: Chapters in the History of Ideas*, ed. Henry Hardy (New York: Vintage, 1992), 126.
9. John Gray, "After Social Democracy," *Endgames: Questions in Late Modern Political Thought* (Cambridge, U.K. : Polity, 1997), 23–24.
10. Hugo Young, *One of Us: A Biography of Margaret Thatcher* (London: Pan Books, 1989, 1991), 209.
11. John Gray, *Hayek on Liberty* (New York: Routledge, 1984, 1998), 2.
12. John Gray, *Liberalism* (Minneapolis: University of Minnesota Press, 1995), 38.
13. John Gray, "Hayek as a Conservative," in Gray, *Post-Liberalism: Studies in Political Thought* (New York: Routledge, 1996), 33.
14. Gray, *Hayek on Liberty*, 37.
15. Ibid., 14, 37–38.
16. John Gray, "Limited Government: A Positive Agenda," in Gray, *Beyond the New Right: Markets, Government, and the Common Environment* (New York: Routledge, 1995), 15.
17. Gray, *False Dawn*, 2, 111, 119.
18. Ibid., 2.
19. Ibid., 3, 17, 37, 35, 215.
20. Irving Kristol, *Two Cheers for Capitalism* (New York: Signet, 1979), x.
21. Mary Battiata, "Places of Honor," *Washington Post*, November 15, 1980, F1.
22. *Los Angeles Times*, July 20, 1986, 1.

23. Edward Luttwak, *The Pentagon and the Art of War* (New York: Simon and Schuster, 1985), 33–34.

24. Ibid., 134–135.

25. Ibid., 138–139; *Washington Quarterly* (Autumn 1982): 6–7.

26. Luttwak, *Pentagon and the Art of War*, 138, 140, 143–144; *Forbes* (May 26, 1980), 4.

27. Luttwak, *Turbo-Capitalism*, ix.

Chapter 6

1. Joan Biskupic, *American Original: The Life and Constitution of Supreme Court Justice Antonin Scalia* (New York: Farrar, Straus and Giroux, 2009), 340.

2. *Nixon v. Missouri Municipal League*, 541 U.S. 125, 141–142 (2004) (Scalia, concurring).

3. *Hamdi v. Rumsfeld*, 542 U.S. 507, 576 (2004) (Scalia, dissenting).

4. Biskupic, *American Original*, 282.

5. Cited in Mark Tushnet, *A Court Divided* (New York: Norton, 2005), 149.

6. Biskupic, *American Original*, 7, 11, 14, 346.

7. Ibid., 17, 19, 21, 25.

8. Ibid., 23, 40–41, 73.

9. Ibid., 41.

10. Ibid., 66–67.

11. Antonin Scalia, *A Matter of Interpretation: Federal Courts and the Law* (Princeton, N.J.: Princeton University Press, 1997), 23, 145.

12. Ibid., 23.

13. Ibid., 46.

14. Remarks at Catholic University (October 18, 1996), http://www.joink.com/homes/users/ninoville/cua10-18-96.asp, accessed April 8, 2011; Scalia, *A Matter of Interpretation*, 47, 149.

15. Scalia, *A Matter of Interpretation*, 14.

16. Robert H. Bork, *The Tempting of America* (New York: Simon and Schuster, 1990), 133, 188.

17. Biskupic, *American Original*, 25, 209, 211.

18. *PGA TOUR, Inc. v. Casey Martin*, 532 U.S. 661 (2001) (Scalia, dissenting).

19. Alexis de Tocqueville, *Democracy in America* (New York: Harper, 1969), 150.

20. *Lawrence v. Texas*, 539 U.S. 568, 590 (2003) (Scalia, dissenting).

21. Biskupic, *American Original*, 189.

22. *Board of County Commissioners, Wabaunsee County, Kansas v. Umbehr*, 518 U.S. 668, 711 (1996) (Scalia, dissenting).

23. http://www.nytimes.com/2003/06/29/opinion/29DOWD.html?pagewanted=1, accessed April 8, 2011.

24. Biskupic, *American Original*, 362.

25. William J. Brennan, "Speech to the Text and Teaching Symposium," in *Originalism: A Quarter-Century of Debate*, ed. Steven Calabresi (Washington, D.C.: Regnery, 2007), 59, 61.

26. Scalia, *A Matter of Interpretation*, 67.

27. *Citizens United v. Federal Election Commission*, 558 U.S. 201, 209, 212 (2010) (Stevens, dissenting).

28. Biskupic, *American Original*, 9, 134, 196.

29. *Scalia Dissents: Writings of the Supreme Court's Wittiest, Most Outspoken Justice*, ed. Kevin A. Ring (Washington, D.C.: Regnery, 2004), 9.

30. http://www.law.yale.edu/news/5658.htm, accessed April 8, 2011.

31. Biskupic, *American Original*, 8.

32. Jeffrey Toobin, *The Nine: Inside the Secret World of the Supreme Court* (New York: Random House, 2008), 65.

33. Tara Trask and Ryan Malphurs, "'Don't Poke Scalia!' Lessons for Trial Lawyers from the Nation's Highest Court," *Jury Expert* 21 (November 2009): 46.

Chapter 7

1. Daniel Wilkinson, *Silence on the Mountain: Stories of Terror, Betrayal, and Forgetting in Guatemala* (Boston: Houghton Mifflin, 2002), 327–328.

2. Greg Grandin, *The Last Colonial Massacre: Latin America in the Cold War* (Chicago: University of Chicago Press, 2004), 5, 12, 100.

3. Ibid., 16.

4. Ibid., vi.

5. Ibid., 5, 26, 27, 32, 39.

6. Ibid., 5, 9, 47, 59, 90.

7. Wilkinson, *Silence on the Mountain*, 165; Grandin, *Last Colonial Massacre*, 54.

8. Grandin, *Last Colonial Massacre*, 57, 80, 106, 108, 120.

9. Ibid., 80.

10. Ibid., 75, 77, 189–191.

11. Ibid., 1–3, 148.

12. Ibid., 190–191.

Chapter 8

1. Corey Robin, "The Ex-Cons: Right-Wing Thinkers Go Left!" *Lingua Franca* (February 2001): 32–33; Irving Kristol, interview with author (Washington, D.C., August 31, 2000).

2. Ron Suskind, "Faith, Certainty and the Presidency of George W. Bush," *New York Times Magazine*, October 17, 2004.

3. Frank Rich, "The Day before Tuesday," *New York Times*, September 15, 2001, A23; Maureen Dowd, "From Botox to Botulism," *New York Times*, September

26, 2001, A19; David Brooks, "The Age of Conflict: Politics and Culture after September 11," *Weekly Standard,* November 7, 2001.

4. Francis Fukuyama, "Francis Fukuyama Says Tuesday's Attack Marks the End of 'America's Exceptionalism,'" *Financial Times,* September 15, 2001, 1; Nicholas Lemann, "The Next World Order," *New Yorker,* April 1, 2002, 48; David Brooks, "Facing Up to Our Fears," *Newsweek,* October 22, 2001.

5. Andrew Sullivan, "High Impact: The Dumb Idea of September 11," *New York Times Magazine,* December 9, 2001; George Packer, "Recapturing the Flag," *New York Times Magazine,* September 30, 2001, 15–16; Brooks, "Facing Up to Our Fears"; Brooks, "The Age of Conflict."

6. Brooks, "Facing Up to Our Fears."

7. Ibid.

8. On 9/11, trust in government, and the welfare state, see Jacob Weisberg, "Feds Up," *New York Times Magazine,* October 21, 2001, 21–22; Michael Kelly, "The Left's Great Divide," *Washington Post,* November 7, 2001, A29; Robert Putnam, "Bowling Together," *American Prospect* (January 23, 2002); Bernard Weinraub, "The Moods They Are a'Changing in Films," *New York Times,* October 10, 2001, E1; Nina Bernstein, "On Pier 94, a Welfare State That Works, and Possible Models for the Future," *New York Times,* September 6, 2001, B8; Michael Kazin, "The Nation: After the Attacks, Which Side Is the Left On?" *New York Times,* October 7, 2001, section 4, 4; Katrina vanden Heuvel and Joel Rogers, "What's Left? A New Life for Progressivism," *Los Angeles Times,* November 25, 2001, M2; Michael Kelly, "A Renaissance of Liberalism," *Atlantic Monthly* (January 2002): 18–19. On 9/11 and the culture wars, see Richard Posner, "Strong Fiber after All," *Atlantic Monthly* (January 2002): 22–23; Rick Lyman, "At Least for the Moment, a Cooling of the Culture Wars," *New York Times,* November 13, 2001, E1; Maureen Dowd, "Hunks and Brutes," *New York Times,* November 28, 2001, A25; Richard Posner, "Reflections on an America Transformed," *New York Times,* September 8, 2002, Week in Review, 15. On 9/11, bipartisanship, and the new presidency, see "George Bush, G.O.P. Moderate," *New York Times,* September 29, 2001, A18; Maureen Dowd, "Autumn of Fears," *New York Times,* November 23, 2001, Week in Review, 17; Richard L. Berke, "Bush 'Is My Commander,' Gore Declares in Call for Unity," *New York Times,* September 30, 2001, A29; Frank Bruni, "For President, a Mission and a Role in History," *New York Times,* September 21, 2001, A1; "Politics Is Adjourned," *New York Times,* September 20, 2001, A30; Adam Clymer, "Disaster Forges a Spirit of Cooperation in a Usually Contentious Congress," *New York Times,* September 20, 2001, B3. For a general statement of these various themes, see "In for the Long Haul," *New York Times,* September 16, 2001, Week in Review, 10.

9. Judy Keen, "Same President, Different Man in Oval Office," *USA Today,* October 29, 2001, 6A; Christopher Hitchens, "Images in a Rearview Mirror," *The Nation* (December 3, 2001): 9.

10. Lemann, "Next World Order," 44; Joseph S. Nye Jr., *The Paradox of American Power: Why the World's Only Superpower Can't Go It Alone* (New York: Oxford University Press, 2002), 168; Brooks, "The Age of Conflict."

11. George Steiner, *In Bluebeard's Castle: Some Notes toward the Redefinition of Culture* (New Haven, Conn.: Yale University Press, 1971), 11.

12. Cheney cited in Donald Kagan and Frederick W. Kagan, *While America Sleeps: Self-Delusion, Military Weakness, and the Threat to Peace Today* (New York: St. Martin's Press, 2000), 294; Condoleezza Rice, "Promoting the National Interest," *Foreign Affairs* (June 2000): 45; Nye, *Paradox of American Power*, 139.

13. *The Clinton Foreign Policy Reader: Presidential Speeches with Commentary*, ed. Alvin Z. Rubinstein, Albina Shayevich, and Boris Zlotnikov (Armonk, N.Y.: M. E. Sharpe, 2000), 9, 20, 22–23. It should be pointed out that after several years of reduced military spending, Clinton, in his second term, steadily began to increase military appropriations. Between 1998 and 2000, military expenditures went from $259 billion to $301 billion. This increase in spending coincided with a reconsideration of the dangers confronting the United States. In his last years in office, Clinton began to sound the alarm more forcefully against the threat of terrorism and rogue states. See *Clinton Foreign Policy Reader*, 36–42; Paul-Marie de la Gorce, "Offensive New Pentagon Defence Doctrine," *Le Monde Diplomatique,* March 2002.

14. David Halberstam, *War in a Time of Peace* (New York: Scribner, 2001), 22–23, 110–113, 152–153, 160–163, 193, 242.

15. Nye, *Paradox of American Power*, 8–11, 110. On occasion, Clinton even went so far as to suggest that pouring so much money into fighting the Cold War was, if not exactly a waste, then at least an unnecessary strain on the nation's vital resources. "The Cold War," he said at American University in 1993, "was a draining time. We devoted trillions of dollars to it, much more than many of our more visionary leaders thought we should have." *Clinton Foreign Policy Reader,* 9.

16. Brooks, "The Age of Conflict"; Robert D. Kaplan, *The Coming Anarchy: Shattering the Dreams of the Post Cold War* (New York: Vintage, 2000), 23–24, 89. Also see Francis Fukuyama, *The End of History and the Last Man* (New York: Harper Collins, 1992, 2002), 304–305, 311–312.

17. See Robert Putnam, *Bowling Alone: The Collapse and Revival of American Community* (New York: Simon & Schuster, 2000); Dinesh D'Souza, *The Virtue of Prosperity: Finding Values in an Age of Techno-Affluence* (New York: Simon & Schuster, 2000); John B. Judis, *The Paradox of American Democracy: Elites, Special Interests, and the Betrayal of the Public Trust* (New York: Pantheon, 2000); Kagan and Kagan, *While America Sleeps.*

18. Indeed, the Clinton administration's many pronouncements on the issue of multi- and unilateralism sound remarkably similar to those of the administration of George W. Bush. In an address to the United Nations in 1993, Clinton stated, "We will often work in partnership with others and through multilateral institutions such as the United Nations. It is in our national interests to do

so. But we must not hesitate to act unilaterally when there is a threat to our core interests or to those of our allies." That same year, Anthony Lake declared, "We should act multilaterally where doing so advances our interest—and should act unilaterally when that will serve our purpose." In 1994, Clinton affirmed that he sought U.S. "influence over" multilateral decisions and operations. In 1995, he declared, "We will act with others when we can, but alone when we must." Joseph Nye, Clinton's assistant secretary of defense, has since declared, against the counsel and advice of classic balance-of-power realists, that the United States should maintain its monopoly of power as the surest path to peace. As for the debates between realists and humanitarians, internationalists and isolationists, the fact is that many of the neoconservative critics of the Clinton administration are as committed to humanitarian, internationalist intervention as the Clinton administration was. *Clinton Foreign Policy Reader,* 6, 16–17, 26, 28; Nye, *Paradox of American Power,* 15; Robert Kagan and William Kristol, "The Present Danger," *National Interest* (Spring 2000); "Paul Wolfowitz, Velociraptor," *The Economist* (February 9, 2002); Lemann, "Next World Order," 42; Robert Kagan, "Fightin' Democrats," *Washington Post,* March 10, 2002.

19. Kagan and Kagan, *While America Sleeps,* 1–2, 4; Kaplan, *Coming Anarchy,* 157, 172, 176.

20. Brooks, "Age of Conflict"; Steven Mufson, "The Way Bush Sees the World," *Washington Post,* February 17, 2002, B1: "Paul Wolfowitz, Velociraptor."

21. Lemann, "Next World Order," 43, 47–48; Seymour M. Hersh, "The Iraq Hawks," *New Yorker* (December 24 and 31, 2001), 61; Kagan, "Fightin' Democrats"; Kagan and Kagan, *While America Sleeps,* 293, 295.

22. Emily Eakin, "All Roads Lead to D.C.," *New York Times,* March 31, 2002, Week in Review, 4; Lemann, "Next World Order," 44. Also see Alexander Stille, "What Is America's Place in the World Now?" *New York Times,* January 12, 2002, B7; Michael Ignatieff, "The American Empire (Get Used to It)," *New York Times Magazine,* January 5, 2003, 22ff; Bill Keller, "The I-Can't-Believe-I'm-a-Hawk Club," *New York Times* February 8, 2003, A17; Lawrence Kaplan, "Regime Change," *New Republic* (March 3, 2003).

23. Lemann, "Next World Order," 43–44; Hersh, "The Iraq Hawks," 61; George W. Bush, "State of the Union Address," *New York Times,* January 30, 2002, A22: Mufson, "Way Bush Sees the World," B1.

24. Eric Schmitt and Steve Lee Myers, "U.S. Steps Up Air Attack, While Defending Results of Campaign," *New York Times,* October 26, 2001, B1; Susan Sachs, "U.S. Appears to Be Losing Public Relations War So Far," *New York Times,* October 28, 2001, B8: Warren Hoge, "Public Apprehension Felt in Europe over the Goals of Afghanistan Bombings," *New York Times,* November 1, 2001, B2; Dana Canedy, "Vietnam-Era G.I.'s Watch New War Warily," *New York Times,* November 12, 2001, B9.

25. Robin Wright, "Urgent Calls for Peace in Mideast Ring Hollow as Prospects Dwindle," *Los Angeles Times,* March 31, 2002.

26. Ibid.

27. David E. Rosenbaum, "Senate Deletes Higher Mileage Standard in Energy Bill," *New York Times,* March 14, 2002, A28.

28. Diana B. Henriques and David Barstow, "Victim's Fund Likely to Pay Average of $1.6 Million Each," *New York Times,* December 21, 2001, A1. For an excellent critique, see Eve Weinbaum and Max Page, "Compensate All 9/11 Families Equally," *Christian Science Monitor,* January 4, 2002, 11.

29. Tim Jones, "Military Sees No Rush to Enlist," *Chicago Tribune,* March 24, 2002; David W. Chen, "Armed Forces Stress Careers, Not Current War," *New York Times,* October 20, 2001, B10.

30. Andrew Gumbel, "Pentagon Targets Latinos and Mexicans to Man the Front Lines in War on Terror," *The Independent,* September 10, 2003.

31. R. W. Apple Jr., "Nature of Foe Is Obstacle in Appealing for Sacrifice," *New York Times,* October 15, 2001, B2; Frank Rich, "War Is Heck," *New York Times,* November 10, 2001, A23; Alison Mitchell, "After Asking for Volunteers, Government Tries to Determine What They Will Do," *New York Times,* November 10, 2001, B7. Also see Michael Lipsky, "The War at Home: Wartime Used to Entail National Unity and Sacrifice," *American Prospect* (January 28, 2002): 15–16.

32. *The NewsHour,* October 29, 2001, http://www.pbs.org/newshour/bb/white_house/july-dec01/historians_10-29.html, accessed April 8, 2011.

33. Elisabeth Bumiller, "Bush Asks Volunteers to Join Fight on Terrorism," *New York Times,* January 31, 2002, A20; Mitchell, "After Asking for Volunteers," B7. Also see David Brooks, "Love the Service Around Here," *New York Times Magazine,* November 25, 2001, 34.

34. This corporate abdication of government power applies even to those cases—like the first Gulf War or the signing of NAFTA—where many had thought they'd seen the heavy footprints of corporate America. According to the best accounts of the Gulf War and NAFTA, it was political officials, particularly the first President Bush, who pressed these policies, often persuading a reluctant business and military community to follow along. John R. MacArthur, *The Selling of "Free Trade": NAFTA, Washington, and the Subversion of American Democracy* (Berkeley: University of California Press, 2000), 137, 170, 174–175, 194; Halberstam, *Peace in Time of War,* 69–70; Kagan and Kagan, *While America Sleeps,* 244–250.

35. Thomas Friedman, *The Lexus and the Olive Tree: Understanding Globalization* (New York: Farrar, Straus, Giroux, 1999), 373.

Chapter 9

1. Speaking to senior SS officers in Posen on October 4, 1943, Himmler declared, "We had the moral right, we had the duty to our people, to kill this people which wanted to kill us." *The Nazi Germany Sourcebook: An Anthology of Texts,* ed. Roderick Stackelberg and Sally A. Winkle (New York: Routledge, 2002), 370. Also see J. Arch Getty and Oleg V. Naumov, *The Road to Terror: Stalin and the Self-Destruction of the Bolsheviks, 1932–1939* (New Haven, Conn.: Yale Univer-

sity Press, 1999); Christopher R. Browning, *The Origins of the Final Solution: The Evolution of Nazi Jewish Policy, September 1939–March 1942* (Lincoln: University of Nebraska Press/Jerusalem: Yad Vashem, 2004).

2. Seymour M. Hersh, *Chain of Command: The Road from 9/11 to Abu Ghraib* (New York: Harper Collins, 2004), 38–39; Jane Mayer, *The Dark Side: The Inside Story of How the War on Terror Turned into a War on American Ideals* (New York: Doubleday, 2008), 167–168.

3. Joseph S. Nye Jr., *The Paradox of American Power: Why the World's Only Superpower Can't Go It Alone* (New York: Oxford University Press, 2002), 159, 163.

4. Nye, *Paradox of American Power,* 135, 139.

5. Michael Walzer, *Arguing about War* (New Haven, Conn.: Yale University Press, 2004), 33, 43.

6. Cited in Otto Kirchheimer, *Political Justice: The Use of Legal Procedure for Political Ends* (Princeton, N.J.: Princeton University Press, 1961), 29.

7. *United States v. Dennis et al. v. United States,* 183 F.2d 212 (1950).

8. Francis Bacon, *Considerations Touching a War with Spain,* in *The Works of Francis Bacon,* vol. 2 (Philadelphia: A. Hart, 1850), 205.

9. Adolf Hitler, speech on the anniversary of the 1923 Putsch (November 8, 1942), in *Nazi Germany Sourcebook,* 295.

10. Hersh, *Chain of Command,* 231.

11. http://frwebgate.access.gpo.gov/cgi-bin/getdoc.cgi?dbname=2003_presidential_documents&docid=pd03fe03_txt-6, accessed April 8, 2011.

12. http://www.pbs.org/wgbh/pages/frontline/shows/wmd/etc/script.html, accessed April 8, 2011.

13. Edmund Burke, *Reflections on the Revolution in France,* ed. J. C. D. Clark (Stanford, Calif.: Stanford University Press, 2001), 154.

14. Walzer, *Arguing about War,* 88, 155, 160.

15. Ibid., 53.

16. Cited in Avi Shlaim, *The Iron Wall: Israel and the Arab World* (New York: Norton, 2001), 501.

17. Cited in Robert O. Paxton, *The Anatomy of Fascism* (New York: Knopf, 2004), 156.

18. Thomas Carlyle, "Signs of the Times," in *A Carlyle Reader,* ed. G. B. Tennyson (New York: Cambridge University Press, 1984), 34; Chateaubriand cited in Roger Boesche, *The Strange Liberalism of Alexis de Tocqueville* (Ithaca, N.Y.: Cornell University Press, 1987), 84.

19. Hersh, *Chain of Command,* 16, 209, 220, 267; David Brooks, "The Art of Intelligence," *New York Times,* April 2, 2005.

20. Hersh, *Chain of Command,* 13, 17, 62, 265, 271. For additional examples, see Mayer, *Dark Side,* 36, 41–43, 69, 80, 124–125, 132, 161, 241.

21. Hersh, *Chain of Command,* 40; Christian Parenti, *The Freedom: Shadows and Hallucinations in Occupied Iraq* (New York: New Press, 2005), 141.

22. Jean Bethke Elshtain, "Reflections on the Problem of 'Dirty Hands,'" in *Torture,* ed. Sanford Levinson (New York: Oxford University Press, 2004), 79.

23. Elshtain, "Reflections on the Problem," 80, 85–86; Hersh, 22; Mark Danner, *Torture and Truth: America, Abu Ghraib, and the War on Terror* (New York: New York Review Books, 2004), 4, 6, 13, 240, 248, 262, 292, 514, 538.

24. Sanford Levinson, editor of *Torture*, writes that all of the essays gathered in the book, including Elshtain's, were written before the revelations of Abu Ghraib. Though he writes that "no doubt many of the authors would wish to rewrite some of their remarks," none did. He also notes that "the brutal fact is that far less rewriting would be necessary than some might wish." Seven years later, I can find no evidence that Elshtain has rewritten or retracted any of her essay. Levinson, "Acknowledgments," in *Torture*, 20.

25. Levinson, "Contemplating Torture," in *Torture*, 37.

26. Elshtain, "Reflections on the Problem," 83, 86.

27. Michael Walzer, "Political Action: The Problem of Dirty Hands," in *Torture*, 62–63; Walzer, *Arguing about War*, 45.

28. Isaiah Berlin, "The Counter-Enlightenment," in *Against the Current: Essays in the History of Ideas* (Princeton, N.J.: Princeton University Press, 2001), 3.

29. Elshtain, "Reflections on the Problem," 83–84.

30. Isaiah Berlin, "The Apotheosis of the Romantic Will," *The Crooked Timber of Humanity* (New York: Vintage, 1992), 229.

31. Elshtain, "Reflections on the Problem," 87.

32. Levinson, "Contemplating Torture," 23, 38; Henry Shue, "Torture," in *Torture*, 58; Walzer, "Political Action," 72.

33. Machiavelli, letter to Vettori (April 16, 1527), in *The Letters of Machiavelli*, ed. Allan Gilbert (New York: Capricorn, 1961), 249.

Chapter 10

1. David K. Johnson, *The Lavender Scare: The Cold War Persecution of Gays and Lesbians in the Federal Government* (Chicago: University of Chicago Press, 2004), 2, 19, 55, 138.

2. Ibid., 1, 4–5, 102–103, 114.

3. Ibid., 9–10, 108–109.

4. Ibid., 16, 31–37.

5. Aaron Belkin, personal communication, December 10, 2010.

6. Johnson, *Lavender Scare,* 70–72.

7. Ibid., 72.

8. John Stuart Mill, *Utilitarianism* (New York: New American Library, 1974), 310. Also see John Dunn, "Political Obligation," in *The History of Political Theory and Other Essays* (New York: Cambridge University Press, 1996), 66–90; Bernard Williams, *In the Beginning Was the Deed: Realism and Moralism in Political Argument*, ed. Geoffrey Hawthorn (Princeton, N.J.: Princeton University Press, 2005), 3. Mill was referring to the security of persons rather than of nations or states. But his argument about personal security is often extended to nations and states, which are conceived to be persons writ large. See Michael Walzer,

Just and Unjust Wars: A Moral Argument with Historical Illustrations (New York: Basic Books, 1992, 1977), 51–73, though also see 74–108; Barry Buzan, *People, States and Fear: The National Security Problem in International Relations* (Chapel Hill: University of North Carolina Press, 1983), 18–35; Richard Tuck, *The Rights of War and Peace: Political Thought and the International Order from Grotius to Kant* (New York: Oxford University Press, 1999).

9. Arnold Wolfers, "National Security as an Ambiguous Symbol," *Political Science Quarterly* 67 (December 1952): 481.

10. David Cole and James. X. Dempsey, *Terrorism and the Constitution: Sacrificing Civil Liberties in the Name of National Security* (New York: New Press, 2002, 2006), x, 210. Also see Jane Mayer, *The Dark Side: The Inside Story of How the War on Terror Turned into a War on American Ideals* (New York: Doubleday, 2008), 16–17, 34–36.

11. John Solomon, "Bureaucracy Impedes Bomb Detection Work," Associated Press, August 12, 2006.

12. Cole and Dempsey, *Terrorism*, 177–178, 234. Also see Mayer, *Dark Side*, 12–13, 105–106, 116, 119, 156, 166, 177.

13. Nancy V. Baker, *General Ashcroft: Attorney at War* (Lawrence: University Press of Kansas, 2006), 5, 8, 36, 45, 54.

14. Baker, *General Ashcroft*, 67, 82, 106, 108.

15. Mayer, *Dark Side*, 34, 41, 47, 52, 55–67.

16. Johnson, *Lavender Scare*, 56.

17. Ibid., 42–56.

18. Ibid., 55, 90.

19. Baker, *General Ashcroft*, 67.

20. Georg Lukács, *The Historical Novel* (Boston: Beacon, 1962), 22–23.

21. James Risen, *State of War: The Secret History of the CIA and the Bush Administration* (New York: Free Press, 2006), 39, 44.

22. Ibid., 50–52.

23. http://thinkprogress.org/cheney-teleconference, accessed April 8, 2011.

24. http://frwebgate.access.gpo.gov/cgi-bin/getdoc.cgi?dbname=107_cong_public_laws&docid=f:publ056.107.pdf, accessed April 8, 2011.

25. Nancy Chang, *Silencing Political Dissent: How Post–September 11 Anti-Terrorism Measures Threaten Our Civil Liberties* (New York: Seven Stories Press, 2002), 44–45.

26. http://www.leg.state.or.us/03reg/pdf/SB742.pdf, accessed April 8, 2011.

27. Randal C. Archibold, "Protesters Try to Get in Last Word before Curtain Falls," *New York Times*, September 3, 2004.

28. *American Communications Assn. v. Douds*, 339 U.S. 382 (1950).

29. Corey Robin, *Fear: The History of a Political Idea* (New York: Oxford University Press, 2004), 190.

30. Ibid.

31. Ralph S. Brown Jr., *Loyalty and Security: Employment Tests in the United States* (New Haven, Conn.: Yale University Press, 1958), 181; Griffin Fariello, *Red Scare: Memories of the American Inquisition* (New York: Avon, 1995), 43.

32. Gary Younge, "Between a Crisis and a Panic," *Guardian*, March 21, 2005.

33. Eric Boehlert, *Lapdogs: How the Press Rolled Over for Bush* (New York: Free Press, 2006), 17.

34. Ibid., 210–211, 268, 278–279.

35. Cole and Dempsey, *Terrorism*, 221–222.

36. David Cole, *No Equal Justice: Race and Class in the American Criminal Justice System* (New York: New Press, 1999), 7.

37. David Cole, *Enemy Aliens: Double Standards and Constitutional Freedoms in the War on Terrorism* (New York: New Press, 2003), 4–5.

38. Ibid., 6, 18.

39. Ibid., 91–101.

40. John Locke, *A Letter Concerning Toleration*, ed. James H. Tully (Indianapolis: Hackett, 1983), 46; J. S. Mill, *On Liberty*, in *On Liberty and Other Writings*, ed. Stefan Collini (New York: Cambridge University Press, 1989), 13; *Schenck v. United States*, 249 U.S. 47 (1919).

41. Patrick Devlin, *The Enforcement of Morals* (London: Oxford University Press, 1965), 3, 9, 13–14.

42. Nicola Lacey, *A Life of H. L. A. Hart: The Nightmare and the Noble Dream* (New York: Oxford University Press, 2004), 220–221.

43. H. L. A. Hart, "Immorality and Treason," *The Listener* (July 30, 1959).

Chapter 11

1. Jim Sidanius, Michael Mitchell, Hillary Haley, and Carlos David Navarrete, "Support for Harsh Criminal Sanctions and Social Dominance Beliefs," *Social Justice Research* 19 (December 2006): 440; Tom Pyszczynski, Abdolhossein Abdollahi, Sheldon Solomon, Jeff Greenberg, Florette Cohen, and David Weise, "Mortality Salience, Martyrdom, and Military Might: The Great Satan Versus the Axis of Evil," *Personality and Social Psychology Bulletin* 32 (April 2006): 525–537; http://www.gallup.com/poll/101863/Sixtynine-Percent-Americans-Support-Death-Penalty.aspx, accessed April 5, 2011; http://pewforum.org/Politics-and-Elections/The-Torture-Debate-A-Closer-Look.aspx, accessed April 5, 2011; http://www.sourcewatch.org/index.php?title=McCain_Amendment_No._1977, accessed April 5, 2011; Sean Olson, "Senate Approves Abolishment of Death Penalty," *Albuquerque Journal* (March 13, 2009). I am grateful to Shang Ha for providing me with these citations.

2. Andrew Sullivan, *The Conservative Soul: Fundamentalism, Freedom, and the Future of the Right* (New York: Harper Perennial, 2006), 276–277.

3. Francis Fukuyama, *The End of History and the Last Man* (New York: Harper Collins, 1992), xxiii, 147, 150–151, 255–256, 318, 329.

4. This statement comes from MacArthur's 1962 address at West Point, and he attributes it to Plato. No scholar has ever found such a statement in Plato, but it (and the Plato attribution) does appear on a wall in London's Imperial War Museum and in Ridley Scott's 2001 film *Black Hawk Down*. The most likely

source of the statement is George Santayana, in his *Soliloquies in England* (New York: Scribner's, 1924), 102. See Bernard Suzanne's excellent and thorough discussion at http://plato-dialogues.org/faq/faq008.htm#note1, accessed April 8, 2011.

5. *Selections from Treitschke's Lectures on Politics*, trans. Adam L. Gowans (New York: Frederick A. Stokes, 1914), 24–25.

6. Edmund Burke, *A Philosophical Enquiry into the Origin of Our Ideas of the Sublime and the Beautiful*, ed. David Womersley (New York: Penguin, 1998, 2004), 79.

7. Ibid., 82.

8. Ibid., 88.

9. Ibid., 96.

10. Ibid., 164.

11. Ibid., 177–178.

12. Michael Oakeshott, "On Being Conservative," in *Rationalism in Politics and Other Essays* (Indianapolis: Liberty Press, 1962), 408. Also see Walter Bagehot, "Intellectual Conservatism," in *The Portable Conservative Reader*, ed. Russell Kirk (New York: Penguin, 1982), 239–241; Russell Kirk, "What Is Conservatism?" in *The Essential Russell Kirk*, ed. George A. Panichas (Wilmington, Del.: ISI Books, 2007), 7; Roger Scruton, *The Meaning of Conservatism* (London: Macmillan, 1980, 1984), 21–22, 40–43; Robert Nisbet, *Conservatism* (Minneapolis: University of Minnesota Press, 1986), 26–27.

13. Ronald Reagan, First Inaugural Address and address before a Joint Session of the Congress (April 28, 1981), in *Conservatism in America since 1930*, ed. Gregory L. Schneider (New York: New York University Press, 2003), 343, 344, 351, 352.

14. Barry Goldwater, acceptance speech at 1964 Republican National Convention (July 16, 1964), in *Conservatism in America*, 238–239.

15. Hugo Young, *One of Us* (London: Macmillan, 1989, 1991), 224.

16. William Manchester, *The Last Lion: Winston Spencer Churchill: Visions of Glory 1874–1932* (Boston: Little, Brown, 1982), 222–231.

17. Winston Churchill, *My Early Life: 1874–1904* (New York: Scribner, 1996), 77.

18. Burke, *Sublime and the Beautiful*, 177.

19. Ibid., 86.

20. Ibid., 101, 106, 108, 111.

21. Ibid., 96, 123.

22. Ibid., 121.

23. Jean-Jacques Rousseau, *Discourse on the Origin and Foundations of Inequality among Men*, in *Rousseau's Political Writings*, ed. Alan Ritter and Julia Conaway Bondanella (New York: Norton, 1988), 54.

24. John Adams, *Discourses on Davila*, in *The Political Writings of John Adams* (Indianapolis: Hackett, 2003), 176.

25. Ibid., 183–184.

26. Burke, *Sublime and the Beautiful*, 108.

27. Ibid., 109.

28. Ibid.

29. Burke, *Reflections on the Revolution in France*, ed. J. C. D. Clark (Stanford, Calif.: Stanford University Press, 2001), 207–208, 275.

30. Burke, *Letters on a Regicide Peace*, ed. E. J. Payne (Indianapolis: Liberty Fund, 1999), 157.

31. Joseph de Maistre, *Considerations on France*, trans. and ed. Richard A. Lebrun (New York: Cambridge University Press, 1974, 1994), 4, 9–10, 13–14, 16–18, 100.

32. Ibid., 17. For other examples, see Jean-Louis Darcel, "The Roads of Exile, 1792–1817," and Darcel, "Joseph de Maistre and the House of Savoy: Some Aspects of His Career," in *Joseph de Maistre's Life, Thought, and Influence: Selected Studies*, ed. Richard A. Lebrun (Montreal: McGill-Queen's University Press, 2001), 16, 19–20, 52.

33. Cf. David Bromwich, "Introduction," in Edmund Burke, *On Empire, Liberty, and Reform: Speeches and Letters*, ed. David Bromwich (New Haven, Conn.: Yale University Press, 2000), 10; Jan-Werner Müller, "Comprehending Conservatism: A New Framework for Analysis," *Journal of Political Ideologies* 11 (October 2006): 360.

34. Georges Sorel, *Reflections on Violence*, ed. Jeremy Jennings (New York: Cambridge University Press, 1999), 61–63, 72, 75–76.

35. Carl Schmitt, *The Concept of the Political*, trans. George Schwab (New Brunswick, N.J.: Rutgers University Press, 1976), 22, 48, 62–63, 65, 71–72, 74, 78.

36. Schmitt, *Concept of the Political*, 63.

37. Sorel, *Reflections on Violence*, 75.

38. Theodore Roosevelt, address to Naval War College (June, 2, 1897), in *Theodore Roosevelt: An American Mind. Selected Writings*, ed. Mario R. DiNunzio (New York: Penguin, 1994), 175–176, 179.

39. Roosevelt, address to Hamilton Club of Chicago (April 10, 1899), and *An Autobiography*, in *Theodore Roosevelt*, 186, 194.

40. Roosevelt, Naval War College address, 174.

41. John C. Calhoun, "Speech on the Reception of Abolitionist Petitions" (February 6, 1837), in *Union and Liberty: The Political Philosophy of John C. Calhoun*, ed. Ross M. Lence (Indianapolis: Liberty Fund, 1992), 476.

42. Barry Goldwater, *The Conscience of a Conservative* (Princeton, N.J.: Princeton University Press, 1960, 2007), 1.

43. Fukuyama, *End of History*, 315–318, 329; also see chapter 8.

44. John Milton, *Aeropagitica*, in *Complete Poems and Major Prose*, ed. Merritt Y. Hughes (New York: Macmillan, 1957), 728.

45. Burke, *Sublime and the Beautiful*, 145.

46. Maistre, *Considerations on France*, 14, 16, 18–19. Also see Darcel, "The Apprentice Years of a Counter-Revolutionary: Joseph de Maistre in Lausanne, 1793–1797," in *Joseph de Maistre's Life, Thought, and Influence*, 43–44.

47. Maistre, *Considerations on France*, 77.

48. Sorel, *Reflections on Violence*, 63, 160–161.

49. Cited in William Pfaff, *The Bullet's Song: Romantic Violence and Utopia* (New York: Simon and Schuster, 2004), 97.

50. Sorel, *Reflections on Violence*, 76–78, 85.

51. What follows is an abridged account of my discussion in *Fear: The History of a Political Idea* (New York: Oxford University Press, 2004), 88–94. Sources for all quotations cited here can be found there.

52. Fukuyama, *End of History*, 148, 180, 304–305, 312, 314, 328–329.

53. E. M. Forster, *A Passage to India* (New York: Harcourt, 1924), 289.

54. Roosevelt, *The Rough Riders*, in *Theodore Roosevelt*, 30–32, 37. One might also point to Roosevelt's Naval War College address, where several thousand words in praise of manliness and military preparedness come to a climax in a call for the United States to build a modern navy that might well never be used. *Theodore Roosevelt*, 178.

55. Roosevelt, Hamilton Club address, *Theodore Roosevelt*, 185, 188.

56. Roosevelt, Lincoln Club address of February 1899, and Hamilton Club address, ibid., 182, 189.

57. R. J. B. Bosworth, *Mussolini* (New York: Oxford University Press, 2002), 167–169; Robert O. Paxton, *The Anatomy of Fascism* (New York: Knopf, 2004), 87–91.

58. Sam Tanenhaus, *The Death of Conservatism* (New York: Random House, 2009).

59. Seymour Hersh, *Chain of Command: The Road from 9/11 to Abu Ghraib* (New York: Harper Collins, 2004); Jane Mayer, *The Dark Side: The Inside Story of How the War on Terror Turned into a War on American Ideals* (New York: Doubleday, 2008).

60. Mayer, *Dark Side*, 69, 132, 241.

61. Ibid., 55, 120, 150, 167, 231, 301.

62. Ibid., 223.

63. Ibid.

64. Burke, *Sublime and the Beautiful*, 86, 92, 165.

65. Ibid., 104.

66. Ibid., 105.

67. Ibid., 106.

68. Burke, *Reflections*, 232, 239.

Conclusion

1. Frank Meyer, "Freedom, Tradition, Conservatism," in *In Defense of Freedom and Related Essays* (Indianapolis: Liberty Fund, 1996), 15; Roger Scruton, *The Meaning of Conservatism* (London: Macmillan, 1980, 1984), 11; Friedrich A. Hayek, *The Constitution of Liberty* (Chicago: University of Chicago Press, 1960), 7.

2. David Frum, *Comeback: Conservatism That Can Win Again* (New York: Doubleday, 2008); Ross Douthat and Reihan Salam, *Grand New Party: How Republicans Can Win the Working Class and Save the American Dream* (New York: Doubleday, 2008); Mickey Edwards, *Reclaiming Conservatism: How a Great American Political Movement Got Lost—and How It Can Find Its Way Back* (New York: Oxford University Press, 2008); John J. DiIulio Jr., *Godly Republic: A Centrist Blueprint for America's Faith-Based Future* (Berkeley: University of California Press, 2007); Michael J. Gerson, *Heroic Conservatism: Why Republicans Need*

to Embrace America's Ideals (and Why They Deserve to Fail if They Don't) (New York: Harper Collins, 2007); Andrew Sullivan, *The Conservative Soul: Fundamentalism, Freedom, and the Future of the Right* (New York: Harper Perennial, 2006).

3. Sullivan, *Conservative Soul*, 9.

4. George Packer, "The Fall of Conservatism," *The New Yorker* (May 26, 2008).

INDEX

ABC, 212

abolition, 3, 6, 9, 27, 35, 45, 46, 56, 231. *See also*
  emancipation, freedom, race, slavery

Abu Ghraib, 185, 195, 196, 273n24

Adams, Abigail, 14

Adams, John, 14, 15, 33, 34, 225

Addington, David, 242

affirmative action, 107–108

Afghanistan War, 176, 177, 193

agency, 5–16, 53–55, 59, 63–64, 66–69, 72–73,
  81, 95, 105, 156–157, 226–227. *See also*
  democracy, emancipation, freedom,
  power, reform, suffrage

Al Qaeda, 166, 185, 206, 207, 209, 242

Alien Act, 213

Angola, 188

anomie, 49, 169, 171, 193. *See also* bourgeoisie,
  decadence.

Antoinette, Marie, 44, 58, 98–99, 244

American Revolution, 14, 27, 110

Americans with Disabilities Act (ADA), 138–143

Anderson, Perry, 62

anticommunism, 92, 112, 113–114, 121, 125,
  127, 152–154, 157–160, 161, 164, 169,
  201–203, 206–208. *See also* Cold War,
  Communism, CIA, Guatemala, Lavender
  Scare, McCarthyism, national security,
  Soviet Union

Arabs, 185, 212–213, 214

Árbenz, Jacobo, 152, 155, 156, 157, 158

Arendt, Hannah, 33, 78

Arévalo, Juan José, 152, 155

aristocracy, 16, 17, 31, 33, 35, 36, 44, 49, 56, 155,
  228, 229, 248n9. *See also* elites, master
  class, Old Regime, old regime, ruling
  class

Aristotle, 78, 83–88, 93, 94, 225

Argentina, 153, 199. *See also* Dirty War

Arnold, Matthew, 28

Ashcroft, John, 205, 206

Atwater, Lee, 50, 51

authority, *see* hierarchy

Baldwin, James, 10–11

Banfield, Ashleigh, 212

Barry, Norman, 115, 118, 120

battle, *see* struggle

BBC, 216

Beck, Glenn, 94, 96

Bell, Daniel, 176, 184

Bentham, Jeremy, 118, 198

Bernstein, Edward, 26

Bickel, Alexander, 138

Biddle, Nicholas, 27

bin Laden, Osama, 166, 207

Black Hawk Down, 275n4

Bloom, Allan, 57, 173

Blumenthal, Sidney, 43

Boehlert, Eric, 212

Bolshevik Revolution, 35, 42, 81

Bonald, Louis de, 15, 33

bourgeoisie, 164, 171–173, 202, 229–230, 233–234,
  235, 236, 237, 253n61. *See also* anomie,
  decadence

Boykin, Jerry, 241

Brazil, 153. *See also* Dirty War

Brennan, William, 144

Brooks, David, 35, 166, 167, 168, 171, 173, 183, 193

Buckley, William F., 25, 43, 54, 58, 98, 109, 128,
  129, 161, 162, 165

Burke, Edmund, 32, 33, 34, 36, 38, 42, 45, 57,
  109, 113, 133, 202, 229, 230, 243, 247,
  255n77; and the beautiful, 44, 48, 219–220,
  223, 227, 234–235; and change, 25, 27;
  and conservative ideology, 42; and
  counterrevolution, 19, 27, 42, 43–44, 49,
  54; and the French Revolution, 8, 13, 16,
  19, 49, 54, 103, 227; and hierarchy, 8, 31,

Burke, Edmund (*continued*)
44, 219, 225–227; and history, 19, 258n9;
and Old Regime, 44, 49, 98–99, 227; and
order, 8, 13, 24, 45, 58; and power, 16,
44, 48–49, 223–224, 226–228, 230; and
restoration, 54, 59, 98–99; and ruling
class, 31, 100; and the sublime, 29, 48–49,
219–220, 223–224, 227, 232, 233, 234–235,
243–244
Bush, George H.W., 168, 169, 170, 271n34
Bush, George W., 27, 32, 34, 43, 101, 131, 145,
165, 174, 175, 182, 185, 189–190, 193, 197, 205,
208, 209, 240, 243, 257n101, 269n18; and
neoconservatism, 174, 194–195, 240; and
imperialism, 165, 174, 175, 176, 177; and
Iraq War, 41, 185, 189–190, 193; and rights,
207–209, 211, 243; and romanticism, 167,
197; and September 11, 167, 207, 243

Calhoun, John C., 6, 12, 33, 34, 46, 56,
101, 231
capitalism, 16, 30–31, 32, 36, 74–75, 82, 88–89, 94,
106–107, 111–113, 115–120, 121, 124–127, 156,
162, 164–168, 176, 182–183, 229–231, 234,
237, 238, 246, 271n34. *See also* free market,
globalization, neoconservatism
Carnarvon, Lord, 27
Catholicism, 34, 50, 62, 92, 94, 105, 157–158, 234;
and Vatican II, 133. *See also* Christianity,
Protestantism, Scalia
CBS, 211
Chambers, Whittaker, 26, 110
Cheney, Richard, 169, 174, 175, 209
Chile, 74–75, 152, 153, 155, 160. *See also*
democracy, Dirty War
Christianity, 16, 92–94, 143, 186; and Christian
Right, 20, 52, 55, 104, 105–106; and
evangelicals, 104, 105–106; and Intelligent
Design, 18; Nietzsche on, 92–93; Rand
on, 93–94; and Scalia, 133–134, 136; and
school prayer, 137
Churchill, Winston, 20, 34, 110, 187, 218, 222
CIA (Central Intelligence Agency), 153–154,
158, 193, 202, 208, 241, 242
citizenship, 53, 156, 179, 180, 182, 191; and
national interest, 169–170, 172, 186;
noncitizens, 180, 213, 214; and power, 72,
74, 154, 225; and rights, 107, 131, 213–214.
See also agency, rights, rule of law
civil rights movement, 9, 10, 27, 35, 42, 54, 104,
107, 211, 250n18; and desegregation, 104,
205, 250n18. *See also* emancipation, race,
reform, slavery

civil society, 4–5, 8–9, 14, 22, 24, 66–70, 72–73,
75, 101, 117–119, 126, 128, 162, 180, 215–216.
See also Hobbes, Locke, marriage, rule of
law, workplace
Civil War, English, 38, 61, 63, 67
Civil War, United States, 15, 238, *see also*
Confederacy
civil war, 38, 61, 63, 119, 121, 153, 217, 234, 236,
237, 238. *See also* Civil War, struggle, war
Clinton, Bill, 109, 168, 169, 179, 205; as
moderate, 112, 246; and foreign policy,
166, 168, 170–173, 194, 269n13, 269n15,
269–270n18; and 1990s decadence, 165,
171–173, 240; and globalization, 168,
170–173
Cohen, G.A., 9
Cold War, 38, 60, 110, 111, 112, 121, 127, 152,
153, 158, 161, 163, 164, 168, 169–172, 182,
188, 202, 212, 269n15; in Latin America,
152–160. *See also* anticommunism,
Communism, Lavender Scare,
McCarthyism, Soviet Union
Colombia, 125, 155
colonialism, 45, 151–157, 159, 239. *See also* Cold
War, Guatemala, Hawaii, imperialism,
Philippines
common law, 5, 68. *See also* civil society, rule
of law
Communism, 23, 92, 23, 112, 113–114, 119, 120,
121, 125, 127, 129, 152, 154, 158, 161, 164, 169,
176, 201, 202, 207, 210; in Latin America,
152, 153–154, 155–156, 157–158, 159; and
United States Communist Party, 202.
See also anticommunism, Bolshevik
Revolution, Guatemala, Lavender Scare,
McCarthyism, redistribution, Soviet
Union
compromise, *see* moderation
Confederacy, 15, 54, 205
conflict, *see* struggle
Congress, 6, 12, 46, 105, 131, 178, 179, 202, 203,
206, 209, 211, 221
consensus, *see* moderation
conservatism: borrowing from left, 21–22,
24, 35, 43, 49–53, 55, 101, 103, 254n84,
257–258n103; and inequality, 4, 7, 8, 9,
10, 12, 16, 28–30, 43, 46, 47, 53, 56, 57, 58,
89–90, 93, 99, 100, 102–103, 104, 107, 112,
117, 119, 139, 140–143, 153, 172, 212–213, 225,
229–231, 245, 247, 248, 255n80; and organic
change, 21, 24–27, 29–30, 35, 42, 48, 55–57,
59, 64, 74, 99–103, 164, 221–222, 233–234,
254n71, 254n74; and outsiders, 41, 49,

57–8, 79, 98–99, 104, 247; and radicalism, 20–22, 24–27, 33, 52, 90, 92, 104, 105–106, 134–135, 164–165, 171–174, 183, 193–194, 236, 240, 248, 253n58; and traditionalism, 16, 19–23, 29, 32–33, 36, 42–43, 47, 127, 132–134, 221, 246, 255n80; and vitality, 23, 24, 45, 87–88, 113, 141, 146, 166–168, 171–173, 192–194, 206, 218–219, 229, 231–235, 237–241. *See also* counterrevolution, loss, neoconservatism, old regime

conservatism, United States, 32–33, 43, 94, 97, 103–108, 128–129, 161–165, 171–176, 202, 207–208, 246–247, 255n80, 256n94. *See also* conservatism, Republican Party

Conservative (Tory) Party, Britain, 17, 19, 27, 115, 120, 247

Constitution, United States, 10, 13, 20, 22, 27, 130–146, 156, 204, 213, 250n18; and living constitution, 136–137, 205; originalism, 38, 131–133, 135–147. *See also* civil society, rights, rule of law, Scalia, Supreme Court

contract, *see* civil society

Costa Rica, 155

counter-Enlightenment, 113, 117, 154, 160, 192–193, 198, 199. *See also* romanticism

counterrevolution, 4, 8, 14, 16–22, 24–27, 29, 34, 42–44, 49, 52–54, 59, 61–65, 90, 92, 100–103, 105, 140, 220, 228, 233, 236, 253n51, 253–254n61, 255n77; in Guatemala, 151, 153–160. *See also* conservatism

Cuba, 152, 157, 222–223, 238, 239

D'Souza, Dinesh, 25, 57

Dean, John, 43

decadence, 31, 44, 165–169, 171–172, 205–207, 227, 228–233, 238, 240–241, 256n84. *See also* anomie, aristocracy, bourgeoisie, Burke, capitalism, Clinton, neoconservatism

democracy, 3, 14–15, 26, 28, 62, 64, 65, 68, 69, 70, 92, 93, 136, 140, 192; and capitalism, 72, 74–75, 162, 170, 172, 174, 179, 230, 240; and coercion, 215; as direct democracy, 156; and feudalism, 15, 35, 55–57, 99–100, 225; and hierarchy, 13, 18, 52, 56–57, 213; in Latin America, 151, 152, 154, 155–160; and populism, 33; in private sphere, 13–15; promotion of, 41–42, 185, 194; social democracy, 9, 113, 115, 137, 154. *See also* left, populism, reform

Democratic Party, 45, 107, 112, 172, 176, 178, 180, 205, 209, 246, 249n5, 250n18

Department of Commerce, United States, 201–202

Department of Defense, United States, 121, 123, 211

Department of Homeland Security, United States, 204, 211

Department of Justice, United States, 242

Department of State, United States 158, 201

Derby, Earl of, 255n77

Devlin, Patrick, 215–216

Dew, Thomas, 11, 45, 57

Dewey, John, 9, 101

Diderot, Denis, 110

Dirty War, 152

disorder, 7–8, 14, 24, 27, 117–118, 136–138, 151, 153, 155–157, 159–160, 208. *See also* left, hierarchy, natural order, old regime, order, reform, struggle

Disraeli, Benjamin, 22, 32, 57, 255n77

dissent, *see* reform

Dobson, James, 106

Dominican Republic, 155

Donaldson, Sam, 212

Douglas, Paul, 249n5

Dowd, Maureen, 143, 165

Dunlap, Al, 127

Dworkin, Ronald, 144

Eisenhower, Dwight D., 46, 100, 246

El Salvador, 122, 154

Eliot, George, 82, 184

Eliot, T.S., 3, 32, 62

elites, 7, 8, 15, 16, 32, 35–36, 45, 55–57, 90, 92, 98, 118, 123, 126–127, 137, 146, 164, 169–170, 180, 182–183, 204, 288, 229, 231, 237. *See also* aristocracy, hierarchy, master class, old regime, ruling class

Elshtain, Jean Bethke, 195–199, 273n24

emancipation, 9, 16, 27, 28, 35, 42, 57, 73, 106, 107, 115, 154, 225, 241. *See also* abolition, agency, freedom

Engels, Friedrich, 21

Enlightenment, 14, 113, 117, 118, 119, 154. *See also* counter-enlightenment, rationalism

ennui, 114, 169, 171, 193, 220, 221, 222, 238. *See also* anomie, aristocracy, bourgeoisie, decadence, old regime, order, ruling class

Equal Rights Amendment (ERA), 52, 104–105

equality, 3, 8, 9, 10, 52, 54, 56, 57, 74, 89, 93, 102, 104–105, 114, 137, 139–140, 180, 212–214, 225, 248. *See also* Equal Rights Amendment, gender, inequality, left, rights, rule of law

evil, 6, 19, 65–66, 74, 86, 87, 93, 119, 153, 168, 173, 176, 183, 187, 188, 197, 198, 206, 218,

evil (*continued*)
222, 249n5. *See also* national security,
terrorism, war

fascism, 17, 34, 79–80, 87–88, 90, 116, 127,
155, 157, 229, 234. *See also* Fascist Party,
Nietzsche, Rand
Fascist Party, Italy, 23, 193, 239–240
FBI (Federal Bureau of Investigation), 214
fear, 10–11, 19–20, 48, 49, 71, 72–73, 112, 160, 166–
167, 176, 181, 188–190, 207, 211, 223, 232, 234,
236, 243, 247. *See also* counterrevolution,
national security, power, terrorism
federalism, 27, 36, 50–51, 101–102, 103, 250n18.
See also Constitution, Goldwater
feminism, 3, 9, 42, 52, 104–105, 157–158, 206.
See also Equal Rights Amendment,
household, marriage, rape, reproductive
freedom, women's liberation
feudalism, 11, 13, 15, 29, 44, 99, 103, 141, 154,
225; democratic feudalism, 35, 55–57,
99–100; in Guatemala, 154–155. *See also*
aristocracy, hierarchy, inequality, master
class, old regime, ruling class, workplace
force, *see* violence
Force Bill, 6
Frankfurt School, 33
free market, 16, 26, 32, 36, 74, 84, 101, 107,
110–111, 112–117, 118, 119–120, 126–128,
161–165, 168, 170–171, 173–175, 179, 182–183,
246, 247, 255n81. *See also* capitalism,
globalization, labor, libertarianism,
neoconservatism
freedom, 3, 8–9, 15, 22, 30, 56–57, 64, 67–75,
95, 100–103, 105, 116, 163, 168, 199, 205,
229, 248; of religion, 104; and security,
203–204, 208–215, 217; of speech, 104,
145, 147, 211, 215; *See also* emancipation,
national security, reform, rights
French Revolution, 4, 8, 13, 16, 19, 25, 35, 38, 42,
43, 47, 48, 53, 63, 64, 92, 98, 103, 157, 192,
228–229, 233–236, 244; and Jacobins, 13,
48, 49, 59, 63, 100, 227, 232. *See also* Burke,
counterrevolution, Maistre, Old Regime,
Robespierre
Friedman, Milton, 74, 107, 116
Friedman, Thomas, 183
Fukuyama, Francis, 34, 111, 166, 237–238, 243;
and "end of history," 109, 111

gender, 32, 108, 206–207, 278n54; and equality,
10, 52, 104–105, 137; and homosexuality,
201, 202, 207, 215–216; and masculinity,
194, 203, 207, 242; and national security,

194, 201–203, 206–208, 212–213; and role
of women, 5, 8, 10, 15, 52, 104–105, 144,
157–158, 193, 206; and sexuality, 5, 52–53,
137, 143, 202, 206, 216, 249; and traditional
roles, 108, 205, 206–207; and torture, 196.
See also equality, homosexuality, morality,
rights
Geneva Conventions, 241, 242. *See also* rule of
law, terror, torture, war
genocide, 151–153, 159, 190–191
Germany, 36, 87–88, 189
Gerson, Michael, 27–28
Gingrich, Newt, 33, 111
Gladstone, William, 255n77
globalization, 36, 42, 111, 118, 159, 162–164,
169–172, 183, 270n18. *See also* capitalism,
Clinton, free market, imperialism,
Washington Consensus
God, 36, 52, 65–66, 93, 104, 125, 140, 219, 224.
See also Catholicism, Christianity,
morality
Goebbels, Joseph, 87
Gogol, Nikolai, 154
Golden, Harry, 108
Goldwater, Barry, 33, 38, 43, 45–46, 54, 97,
100–103, 108, 222, 231
Graham, Billy, 105–106
Grandin, Greg, 153–145, 156, 159, 160
Gray, John, 109, 111–120, 127, 128
Great Society, 34, 42, 249n5
Great Upheaval, 6
Greenspan, Alan, 127
Guantánamo Bay, 194, 195
Guatemala, 6, 151–160. *See also* Cold War,
counterrevolution, Dirty war, feudalism,
plantation
Gulf War, 170, 271n34

habeas corpus, 131
Hailsham, Lord, 23
Hale, Matthew, 5
Hamilton, Alexander, 57
Harper, William, 11, 45
Hart, H.L.A., 144, 215–216
Hart, Jeffrey, 43
Hayden, Michael, 241
Hayek, Friedrich, 26, 28, 31, 33, 34, 62,
63, 74–75, 115–117, 118–119, 247,
255n81
Hawaii, 239
Hearnshaw, F.J.C., 17
Heidegger, Martin, 78, 113
heroism, 16, 78–79, 83, 85, 88, 89–90, 91, 99.
See also Rand, selfhood

Hersh, Seymour, 193, 241
hierarchy, 4–7, 11–13, 16, 24, 30, 35, 43–44, 45,
    49–50, 53–57, 63–70, 73, 99–100, 102–103,
    154, 210, 212–214, 225–234, 255n80; created
    hierarchy, 53, 227–228; natural hierarchy,
    18, 28–29, 65, 66; and the sublime, 219,
    225–227, 232, 236, 244. *See also* aristocracy,
    Burke, democracy, elites, feudalism,
    monarchy, Old Regime, old regime,
    order, race
Himmler, Heinrich, 271n1
history, 3, 4, 16, 17, 19, 28, 32, 33–34, 42, 47, 54,
    109, 111, 165, 174, 177, 218–219
Hitchens, Christopher, 167
Hitler, Adolph, 88, 89, 185
Hobbes, Thomas, 34, 35, 38, 61–75, 98; and
    absolute monarchy, 62, 64–66, 72, 98; and
    consent, 66–67; and counterrevolution,
    61–70; and fear, 72–73; and freedom,
    64, 67–68, 70–73; and influence on
    conservatism, 73–75; and passion, 67; and
    will, 67–71
homosexuality, 57, 137, 201–202, 206–207, 212,
    215–216; gay rights, 42, 138, 143, 144,
    215–216, 248; and marriage, 203; and the
    military, 203. *See also*, equality, gender,
    Lavender Scare, rights
Honduras, 151, 155
Horowitz, David, 51
household (home), 10, 14, 15, 16, 52, 105, 206,
    252n40
Hume, David, 98, 218
Huntington, Samuel, 28, 255n80

iconoclasm, 135, 146
idealism, 95, 100, 135, 162, 174
ideology, 23, 95, 101, 158, 184, 203; and
    capitalism, 73, 128, 162, 164, 179, 182; and
    conservatism, 7–37, 42, 45, 49, 58, 101, 119,
    133, 154, 164, 193, 218, 254n74
Iklé, Fred, 122
imperialism, 35, 119, 161–165, 168, 170–171,
    173–183, 193, 194, 222, 231, 239–240, 246. *See
    also* Bush, Clinton, colonialism, foreign
    policy, globalization, neoconservatism,
    Roosevelt, war
In These Times, 112
inequality, 4, 7, 43, 53, 89–90, 93, 102–103, 104,
    112, 117, 119, 140–143, 153, 212–213, 245,
    255n80; as competition, 29, 89–90, 102,
    140–141, 142, 225. *See also* feudalism,
    hierarchy, old regime, order, struggle
inheritance, 8, 10, 29, 47, 53, 58, 78, 98, 172.
    See also aristocracy, elites, loss, master

class, old regime, privilege, ruling class,
    traditionalism
Internal Security Act, 214
International Monetary Fund (IMF), 120
Iraq War, 38, 41, 109, 165, 170, 175, 176, 177,
    180–181, 183, 185, 189, 193, 194, 195, 212. *See
    also* Bush, imperialism, neoconservatism,
    September 11, war
Israel, 159, 177
Italy, 121, 133, 239. *See also* Fascist Party

Jackson, Andrew, 27, 57
Jefferson, Thomas, 13, 118
Jim Crow, 42, 53, 103, 104. *See also* abolition,
    civil rights, emancipation,
    racism, slavery
Johnson, Lyndon B., 181, 249n5. *See also* Great
    Society
Johnson, Samuel, 8, 24
journalism, *see* media
Jünger, Ernst, 34, 234

Kant, Immanuel, 81, 85, 198
Keyssar, Alexander, 15
Kirk, Russell, 19, 20, 24, 26, 28
Kirkpatrick, Jeane, 122
Koppel, Ted, 212
Kristol, Irving, 34, 57, 60, 109, 110, 120, 127, 128,
    161, 162, 163, 165, 173, 183, 253–254n61
Kristol, William, 174, 183

labor movement, 3, 5, 211, 229, 231, 246;
    and unions, 6–7, 27, 101, 159, 210–211,
    229, 249n11; and workers' rights, 7,
    9, 101, 112, 210, 246. *See also* equality,
    Great Upheaval, rights, working class,
    workplace
LaHaye, Beverly and Tim, 52–53
Lavender Scare, 201–203, 206–208, 215
left, 17, 26, 31, 37, 42, 43, 58–60, 63, 93, 129,
    205, 214–215, 235, 248; and capitalism,
    8, 9, 114, 117–120, 229–230, 255n81; and
    conservatism, 17, 19–23, 25, 35, 37, 38, 41,
    45–46, 47, 49–52, 58, 100, 101–103, 106, 107,
    109–113, 115, 146–147, 184, 189, 205–206, 218,
    229, 240, 246, 253n51; and Enlightenment,
    154–155, 192; and equality, 7, 9, 95, 105, 205,
    214, 245; in Latin America, 151–161; and
    national security, 165, 189, 205, 208; and
    protest, 82, 97, 101, 210, 248; and rights,
    136–138, 144–146, 205, 212, 241; and welfare
    state, 167. *See also*, conservatism, equality,
    reform, sixties
Lehrer, Jim, 212

Levinson, Sanford, 194, 197, 199, 273n24
Libby, Lewis "Scooter," 166, 174
liberalism, *see* left
libertarianism, 16, 73–74, 83, 84, 90, 101, 111, 118, 127, 246. *See also* freedom, Hobbes, private sphere
liberty, *see* freedom
Lincoln, Abraham, 26
Lindsey, Hal, 106
Lingua Franca, 109, 161
The Listener, 216
Locke, John, 215
London Review of Books, 37–38
London Times, 74
Long, Huey, 99
Los Angeles Times, 123
loss, 8, 21, 23, 28, 47, 58–60, 98–99, 247–248. *See also* Burke, conservatism, inheritance, Maistre, traditionalism
Loyseau, Charles, 47, 53
Luttwak, Edward, 109, 112, 121–128

MacArthur, Douglas, 218, 275–276n4
Macdonald, Dwight, 25
Machiavelli, Niccolò, 68, 119, 120, 200, 242
Maistre, Joseph de, 28, 33, 35, 43, 57, 59, 113, 232–233, 234, 237, 240, 243; and counterrevolution, 48, 53, 55, 228, 232–233; and the French Revolution, 48, 98, 103, 232; and the Old Regime, 44, 55, 92, 228, 229, 233
Mamet, David, 95
Mannheim, Karl, 22, 102–103
Mansfield, Harvey, 253n51
Marat, Jean-Paul, 27
marriage, 4, 5, 8, 11, 14, 15, 35, 52–53, 58, 105, 106, 133, 203, 206–207, 248, 249n2, 249n3. *See also* feudalism, gender, hierarchy, household, private sphere
Martin, Casey, 138–140
Marx, Karl, 21, 64, 116, 125, 128, 144, 155, 157
Marxism, 9, 25, 120, 125, 230, 157, 229, 230, 237. *See also* Cold War, Communism, Guatemala, Soviet Union
mass culture, 31, 32, 80, 166–167, 208. *See also* capitalism, Clinton
masses, 7, 9, 35, 43, 53, 55–57, 78–79, 81, 91, 100, 102, 112, 158, 186–187. *See also* hierarchy, labor movement, reform, workplace
master class, 4, 55, 184; and slavery, 11–14, 45, 55–57, 69; Nietzsche on, 91–93.

See also aristocracy, elites, hierarchy, order, power, ruling class
Mattson, Kevin, 18, 32
Mayer, Jane, 241, 242
McCain, John, 41, 178
McCarthy, Joseph, 133, 202, 211
McCarthyism, 201–203, 206–208, 211, 215. *See also* anticommunism, Communism, Lavender Scare
Mead, Lawrence, 9
media, 32, 50, 152, 211–212
Melville, Herman, 95
Middle East, 42, 164, 165, 177, 183, 185, 194. *See also* Afghanistan War, Iraq War, Israel, Palestine
Mill, John Stuart, 59, 100, 110, 114, 203, 215, 273–274n18
Mises, Ludwig von, 33, 91
moderation, 42, 114, 115, 135, 184, 222, 234–236
modernity, ix, 3, 22, 29, 33, 37, 62, 84, 85, 92, 93, 99, 113, 120, 140–141, 157, 158, 159, 193
monarchy, 22, 44, 53, 55, 59, 61, 98, 99, 100, 208, 228, 233, 234, 236; absolute monarchy, 64, 71–73; despotism, 67–69; divine right, 65–66; and royalism, 61–62, 67–68, 72. *See also* civil society, hierarchy, Hobbes, order
Montt, Efraín Ríos, 151, 152
morality, 14, 29, 44, 45–46, 54, 65, 66, 77, 84–89, 91–93, 98, 113, 119, 126, 134, 136, 137, 138, 146, 153, 163, 164, 166, 172, 173, 178, 183, 188, 192, 195, 198–199, 201–206, 215–216, 221, 244, 252n40, 252n49m, 271n1, 257n96. *See also* Christianity, neoconservatism
Muslims, 185, 212–213, 214

NAFTA (North American Free Trade Agreement), 271n34
Nash, George, 20, 26
The Nation, 37
The National Interest, 110
National Review, 25, 54, 98
National Right to Work Foundation, 210
national security, 184–199, 203–207, 240–244, 273n8; and cultural revanchism, 204–216; and evidence of threat, 188–190, 192–194; and fear, 166, 187–190; and freedom, 203–204, 208–215, 217; and national interest, 162–163, 169–170, 186–187, 203–204; and preemptive action, 175, 188–194, 204; and surveillance, 208–209, 211, 241; and treason, 206, 216. *See also* CIA, foreign

policy, freedom, inequality, Internal
Security Act, neoconservatism, war
National Security Agency (NSA), 208–209
National Socialist (Nazi) Party, 23, 90, 120, 121,
188. *See also* Goebbels, Hitler
nationalism, 31, 35, 48, 98, 103, 161–165, 167, 171,
173–176, 177, 179, 181–183, 186–187, 188,
190–191, 200, 202, 208, 209–211,
232–233, 240. *See also* imperialism,
neoconservatism, war
NBC, 212
neoconservatism, 33, 47, 57, 101, 127, 128, 173,
243–244; and capitalism, 111, 164;
and foreign policy, 41, 172, 174, 185,
193–214, 270n18; and imperialism, 161–165,
168, 173–183, 194, 240–241; and old regime,
35, 37, 92–93; and romanticism, 57–58, 127,
164–165, 173–177, 194–195, 240, 253n61;
and rule of law, 240–243.
See also Buckley, conservatism, Gray,
Kristol, Luttwak
New Deal, 26, 42, 81, 101, 206, 207, 221.
See also welfare state
New Left, 101–102, 114
New Right, 34, 104, 111
New York Times, 78, 84, 179, 181, 208
The New Yorker, 132
The News-Hour, 181
Newsday, 212
Nicaragua, 152, 153, 155, 188
Nietzsche, Friedrich, 31, 34, 41, 62, 90–93, 94,
140, 142, 144, 173, 241. *See also* master class,
morality, Rand
Nisbet, Robert, 26
Nixon, Richard, 34, 46, 50, 96, 100, 104, 106,
107–108, 131, 246
Nock, Albert Jay, 34, 83
Nozick, Robert, 84, 109, 116, 144
Nullification Crisis, 6
Nye, Joseph, 171, 186, 270n18

O'Connor, Sandra Day, 145, 146
Oakeshott, Michael, 21, 34, 42, 47, 62, 109, 218,
253n58
Obama, Barck, 143, 176, 177, 246, 248,
257n101
oil, 164, 178. *See also* Gulf War, Middle East
Old Regime, 44, 99, 227–228, 233, 236. *See also*
Burke, decadence, French Revolution,
Maistre
old regime, 12, 18, 24, 35, 38, 42–49, 53, 63,
64–65, 68, 99–100, 108, 112, 155, 175, 219,
258n8. *See also* aristocracy, conservatism,

elite, hierarchy, inequality, master class,
order, ruling class
Olmsted, Frederick Law, 11
order, 7, 8, 13, 14, 18, 24, 45, 53, 58, 59, 162–164,
168, 173, 194, 210, 216, 253–254n61, 255n80;
and natural order, 8, 13, 18, 28, 65, 102. *See
also* hierarchy, inequality, monarchy, old
regime, traditionalism.
originalism, *see* Scalia

Packer, George, 166
Paine, Thomas, 17, 54
Palestine, 177
Palin, Sarah, 34, 41, 42, 43, 57–58
Palmerston, Lord, 17
Paraguay, 155
Parliament, 10, 13, 61, 64, 67, 68, 120, 235, 236.
See also civil society, English Civil War,
monarchy
Patriot Act, 207, 209
patriotism, *see* nationalism
Paxton, Robert, 17
PBS, 212
peace, 112, 113, 152, 153, 158, 163, 166, 168,
170–173, 187, 190, 191, 214, 216, 218–219,
222, 228, 229, 240, 270n18. *See also*
foreign policy, globalization, left,
neoconservatism, imperialism
Pearl, Daniel, 196
Peel, Sir Robert, 20, 27
Perle, Richard, 174, 175, 190, 193
PGA tour, 138–143
Philippines, 239
Pinochet, Augusto, 74–75
pity, 49, 98–99. *See also* conservatism, loss,
Rousseau
plantation: in Guatemala, 154, 155, 157; under
slavery, 4, 46, 231
Plato, 81, 98, 142, 275–276n4
Podhoretz, Norman, 109, 111, 126
Popular Front, 106, 155
populism, 17, 33, 35, 43, 50, 55–59, 248.
See also democracy, feudalism, loss,
Tea Party
postmodernism, 18, 138, 140, 142, 143
power, 4, 7, 8–9, 17, 18, 19, 28–29, 31, 44, 46–49,
52–59, 61, 63–64, 66–70, 72–74, 78, 81, 89,
92–93, 95, 98, 99, 104, 105, 115, 120, 143,
146, 154, 155, 156, 168, 190, 192, 214, 210,
212–214, 223–224, 226–228, 230, 231–232,
233, 237–238, 240, 247, 249n5; and military
force, 161–164, 168–178, 192, 241; private
life of, 10–16, 23, 72, 153–155, 246, 250n18,

power (*continued*)
    255n80. *See also* feudalism, hierarchy, monarchy, old regime, order, private sphere, violence
presidency, 131–132, 156, 163, 170; and executive power, 131, 135, 205, 241, 242
private sphere, 44, 70, 73, 163; and political life, 13, 10–16, 24, 52, 58, 105, 215–216, 246, 250. *See also* household, workplace, power
privilege, 10, 12, 16, 28–30, 43, 46, 47, 53, 57, 58, 99, 100, 103, 139, 141, 172, 229–231, 247, 248. *See also* aristocracy, elites, inheritance, master class, old regime, ruling class
protest, *see* reform
Protestantism, 92

race, 10–11, 32, 33, 42, 47, 50, 54, 88, 89, 102, 104, 180; and hierarchy, 6, 11–13, 29–30, 50–51, 54, 56, 57, 184; and incarceration, 118; and inequality, 34, 35, 50, 54, 103, 104, 107, 213–214; and segregation, 103, 104, 137, 205, 250n18. *See also* abolition, civil rights movement, emancipation, master class, slavery, violence
Raleigh, Walter, 67
Rand, Ayn, 34, 76–96; and Aristotle, 78, 83–86; and capitalism, 88–89, 94; and individualism, 78, 79, 81–83, 89–90; and fascism, 79, 87–88; and heroism, 83, 85, 88, 89–90, 91; and Hollywood, 76–77, 82–83; and naturalism, 87; and Nietzsche, 90–93, 241; and religion, 92–94
rape, 5, 12, 151–152, 196, 249n2, 249n3. *See also* feminism, gender, hierarchy, violence, women's liberation
Rawls, John, 78, 114, 119, 136, 144
Rather, Dan, 211
rationalism, 22, 45, 67, 69, 79, 85, 88–89, 113, 116–117, 119–120, 158, 160, 188–189, 192–193. *See also* Enlightenment
reaction, *see* conservatism
Reagan, Ronald, 33, 34, 43, 54, 96, 111, 122, 123, 128, 138, 151, 152, 164, 177, 179, 182, 205, 212, 221–222, 246
realism, 42, 172, 175, 195, 235, 270n18. *See also* foreign policy
reason, *see* rationalism
reform, 3, 5, 6, 7, 14, 16, 19, 20–28, 43, 45, 48–50, 52, 53–55, 57–59, 66, 68–70, 71, 80, 82, 92, 95, 97, 99, 101, 109, 110, 113, 115, 140, 152, 155–156, 159, 165, 185, 205, 206–207, 209–211, 235–237, 241, 244, 249n5, 254n71. *See also* left, sixties, Vietnam War, violence

reproductive freedom, 27, 137, 138. *See also* women's liberation
Republican Party, 12, 17, 46, 50, 51, 100, 122, 138, 162, 163, 203, 205, 210, 211, 214, 231, 246, 249n1. *See also* conservatism
revanchism, *see* conservatism
revolution, *see* reform
Rice, Condoleezza, 168, 169, 175
Rich, Frank, 165, 180
rights, 3, 7, 8, 9, 10, 13, 41, 50, 52, 69, 93, 95, 99, 104, 105, 107, 113, 131, 151, 153, 156, 186, 197, 198, 229, 236, 241–242, 246, 249n5; and homosexuality, 42, 138, 144, 215–216; 248; and immigrants, 107, 213; and national security, 201–215; and privacy, 137, 208, 216. *See also* civil rights, equality, homosexuality, labor movement, left, rule of law, women's liberation, sixties
Robespierre, Maximillien, 27, 233
Roman Empire, 68, 121, 122, 175, 202
romanticism, 44, 77, 89, 101, 108, 113–115, 117, 120, 157, 162, 192–199, 235–236, 247–248. *See also* neoconservatism, struggle
Roosevelt, Franklin Delano, 101, 206. *See also* New Deal
Roosevelt, Theodore, 33, 34, 238, 239, 243; and imperialism, 238–239; and Spanish-American War, 230–231, 238; and struggle, 238, 278n54
Rorty, Richard, 142
Rossiter, Clinton, 26
Rousseau, Jean-Jacques, 50, 72, 98, 225
Rumsfeld, Donald, 131, 193–194
rule of law, 7, 14, 20, 65, 67–69, 72–73, 131–132, 134–143, 156, 162, 173, 218, 235, 249n1, 249n2, 252n40; and capital punishment, 217; and international law, 186, 244; in private sphere, 5, 14, 215–216; and torture, 197–199, 241–243; and war on terror, 130–131, 205–207, 241–243. *See also* civil society, equality, inequality, rights, Supreme Court
ruling class, 6, 12, 18, 31, 35, 56, 57, 98–100, 137, 194, 227, 228, 229–231, 233–234, 236–238, 239, 249n1. *See also* aristocracy, elites, hierarchy, master class

Salisbury, Lord, 19, 20
Scalia, Antonin, 34, 57, 130–147; and 24, 130, 132, 147; and Americans with Disabilities

Act (ADA), 139–143; and originalism, 38, 131–133, 135–147; and golf, 138–143; and inequality, 140–142, 146; and liberalism, 146–147; and rule of law, 130–132; and postmodernism, 140, 142–143; and traditionalism, 133–135, 143

Schlafly, Phyllis, 34, 52, 104–105. *See also* Equal Rights Amendment (ERA)

Schmitt, Carl, 34, 62, 229, 243

Schumpeter, Joseph, 28

Scott, Ridley, 275n4

Scruton, Roger, 247

Sedgwick, Theodore, 13

selfhood, 12, 16, 49, 60, 64, 70, 78, 79, 81, 85, 87–91, 100, 102–103, 116, 117, 120, 125, 128, 162, 168, 186, 192, 193, 203, 219–226. *See also* Burke, Rand, struggle

September 11, 38, 109, 131, 163–169, 174–176, 178–179, 181, 204, 206, 207, 209, 214, 240–241, 243, 245. *See also* Afghanistan War, Bush, foreign policy, Iraq War, terrorism, torture, war

sixties, 15, 42, 50, 82, 97, 103, 106, 134, 136, 147, 204, 205, 209, 241, 248, 249n5. *See also* labor movement, reform, university, women's liberation

Skinner, Quentin, 64, 67, 68, 69

slavery, 4, 6, 11–13, 15, 26, 34, 35, 42, 45, 54, 55–57, 68, 69, 92–93, 104. *See also* abolition, Force Bill, Jim Crow, master class, Nullification Crisis, plantation, race, Tarrif of Abominations

Smith, Adam, 84, 98, 116

Social Darwinism, 138, 140, *See also* inequality, struggle

socialism, 3, 23, 26, 37, 93, 95, 107, 112, 114, 129, 155–156, 157, 229, 248; and nationalization, 159; and redistribution, 6, 9, 59, 154

Sombart, Werner, 35

Sorel, Georges, 228–230, 233–234, 237, 243

Soviet Union, 60, 82, 101, 111, 112, 113, 119, 122, 125, 127, 129, 152, 168, 169, 172, 188–189, 201, 202, 203, 207. *See also* Bolshevik Revolution, Cold War, Communism, Joseph Stalin

Spanish-American War, 230–231, 238

Spock, Benjamin, 106

Stalin, Joseph, 185, 202, 237

Stanton, Elizabeth Cady, 10

States' Rights Democratic (Dixiecrat) Party, 250n18

Stephens, Alexander, 54

Strauss, Leo, 33, 62, 173

struggle, 4, 9, 14, 15, 23, 29, 20, 31, 32, 35, 54, 58–59, 60, 75, 79, 87–90, 100, 102, 105, 113, 121, 125, 126, 141, 146, 152, 154, 155, 157, 159, 173, 194, 222, 233, 234, 235–239. *See also* Burke, conservatism, inequality, violence, war

student movement, 24, 47, 82, 106. *See also* university, sixties

suffrage, 15, 35, 59, 135, 137, 170. *See also* citizenship, women's liberation, rights

Sullivan, Andrew, 43, 59, 166, 217, 247

Sullivan, James, 14

Sumner, William Graham, 30, 58

Supreme Court, 5, 7, 15, 130, 131–2, 135–147, 172, 210, 213; and Burger Court, 136; and *Bush v. Gore*, 145, 172; and Warren Court, 5, 136, 137, 241. *See also* Constitution, rule of law, O'Connor, Scalia, Thomas

Taliban, 176. *See also* Afghanistan war

Tanenhaus, Sam, 43, 240

Tariff of Abominations, 6

taxes, 50–51, 101, 116, 118. *See also* Republican Party, welfare state

Tea Party, 33, 55, 101, 248, 257n101

Tenet, George, 241, 242

terrorism, 160, 163, 168, 182, 189, 191–192, 194, 197, 205–206, 207–208, 209, 210, 213; and war on terror, 38, 109, 130–132, 204–205, 209–210, 212–214, 240, 241–243, 245, 269n13. *See also* national security, neoconservatism, rule of law, September 11, torture, war

Thatcher, Margaret, 34, 74–75, 99; and Falklands War, 75; and free market, 115, 120, 128; and ideology, 101, 111, 115, 119, 222–223

Thomas, Clarence, 130, 133, 139, 172, 205

Thurmond, Strom, 250n18

TIPS (Terrorism Information and Prevention System), 214

Tocqueville, Alexis de, 33, 34, 82, 143, 146, 234–237, 243

torture, 130, 185, 187, 193, 194–199, 217, 242–243, 273n24. *See also* Abu Ghraib, Guantánamo Bay, rule of law, terrorism

Total Awareness Program, 214

traditionalism, 16, 19–23, 29, 32–33, 36, 42–43, 47, 127, 132–134, 221, 246, 255n80. *See also* conservatism

Trilling, Lionel, 17, 100

Truman, Harry S., 201

Turner, Henry McNeal, 12

United Nations, 153, 191, 269n18
university, 24, 51, 107, 124, 118, 144. *See also*
    student movement
Uruguay, 153, 155. *See also* Dirty War
utopia, 21, 29, 111, 113, 221. *See also* idealism

Viereck, Peter, 26
Vietnam War, 114, 123, 176, 182, 188
violence, 8, 30, 33, 38, 48, 71, 113, 157–159, 186,
    192, 219, 224, 235; image of, 238–239,
    243–244, 245; as last resort, 191–192; and
    master class, 5, 12; in the private sphere,
    5, 13, 249n2; reality of, 237, 239, 242–244;
    and reform, 7, 45, 48–49, 53, 229, 232–237;
    and vitality, 218–219, 235, 237–241; and
    war, 88, 193. *See also* civil war, national
    security, power, rape, struggle, war

Wall Street Journal, 212
Walzer, Michael, 187, 190–192, 197–198
war, 25, 31, 33, 38, 109, 123, 125, 176, 178, 180,
    187, 188–189, 190–193, 208, 209, 210–211,
    217–219, 220, 224, 233, 237, 241. *See also*
    Afghanistan War, Cold War, imperialism,
    Iraq War, national security, terror
Washington, George, 14
Washington Consensus, 118
Washington Post, 122
Washington Times, 17
welfare state, 9, 10, 42, 45–46, 101, 113, 114–115,
    118, 119, 126, 167, 206, 222, 232. *See also*

democracy, Gray, Great Society,
    New Deal, WPA
Welles, Orson, 106
Wellington, 27
Whitman, Walt, 155
Wilkinson, Daniel, 151
will, 49, 67–72, 85–86, 117, 162–163, 169–170,
    186–187, 203–204, 225, 229, 234.
    See also civil society, rationalism,
    self
Williams, Roger, 108
women's liberation, 14, 35, 42, 52, 104–105, 246,
    248. *See also* Equal Rights Amendment,
    feminism, household, marriage, rape,
    reproductive freedom
Woodward, C. Vann, 12
working class, 112, 115, 184, 233–234. *See also*
    labor movement, masses, workplace
workplace, 3, 4, 5, 8, 10, 16, 112, 154–157, 211.
    See also civil society, feudalism, hierarchy,
    labor movement, working class
Works Progress Administration, 81
World War I, 202, 257n101
World War II, 97, 155, 167, 181, 206

youth, 80, 106, 110, 114, 129, 181, 182, 206,
    222–223. *See also* left, reform, sixties
Yoo, John, 242
Yugoslavia, 119

Zubayda, Abu, 242